THE COMPLETE BOOK OF YEAR-ROUND

Small-Batch
PRESERVING
Over 300 Delicious Recipes

THE COMPLETE BOOK OF YEAR-ROUND

Small-Batch PRESERVING

Over 300 Delicious Recipes

ELLIE TOPP & MARGARET HOWARD

FIREFLY BOOKS

A FIREFLY BOOK

Published by Firefly Books Ltd. 2001

First Printing

U.S. Cataloging-in-Publication Data
  (Library of Congress Standards)

Topp, Ellie
   The complete book of year-round small-batch preserving: over 300
delicious recipes / Ellie Topp ; Margaret Howard. –1st ed.
[350] p. : col. ill. ; cm.
Summary : Recipes for small batches of fruit and vegetable
preserves, fruit butters, pickles, relishes, vinegars and oils.
ISBN 1-55209-575-4
ISBN 1-55209-489-8 (pbk)
1. Fruit - Preservation. 2. Vegetables - Preservation.
3. Canning and preserving. I. Topp, Ellie II. Title.
641.4 21   2001   CIP

Canadian Cataloguing in Publication Data

Topp, Ellie
   The complete book of year-round small-batch preserving : over 300 delicious recipes

Includes index.
ISBN 1-55209-575-4 (bound) 1-55209-489-8 (pbk)
1. Canning and preserving. I. Howard, Margaret   . II. Title.

TX603.65 2001   641.4   C00-932613-8

Published in Canada in 2001 by   Published in the United States in 2001 by
Firefly Books Ltd.   Firefly Books (U.S.) Inc.
3680 Victoria Park Avenue   P.O. Box 1338, Ellicott Station
Willowdale, Ontario, M2H 3K1   Buffalo, New York, 14205

The recipes in *The Complete Book of Year-Round Small-Batch Preserving* were taken from *Put a Lid on It* (first published in Canada in 1997 by Macmillan Canada, an imprint of CDG Books Canada) and *More Put a Lid on It* (first published in Canada in 1999 by Macmillan Canada, an imprint of CDG Books Canada)

Cover design: Interrobang Graphic Design Inc., Interior design by: George Walker
Cover photo: Anne Gardon
Printed and bound in Canada by Friesens, Altona Manitoba

The Publisher acknowledges the financial support of the Government of Canada through the Book Publishing Industry Development Program for our publishing activities.

CONTENTS

Authors' Acknowledgments

We enjoyed working with the talented staff at Firefly Books Ltd. A special thanks to our editor, Jennifer Pinfold. Another special thank you is due Robert Harris of CDG Books Canada, who spent many hours arranging for this edition.

As always, our families provided critique and ongoing support. John Howard supplied many hours of editing expertise for the final manuscript and Clarke Topp was instrumental in evaluating the heating pattern of the flavored oils.

We also wish to acknowledge the significant contributions made by the following: Foodland Ontario who gave us access to their files of fruit and vegetable recipes.

Judi Kingry, Marketing Manager of Bernardin Canada Ltd., who provided photographs and illustrations. Marjorie Hollands RD for the nutrient analysis of our low-sugar spreads.

Dorothy Long, home economist for the Canola Information Service for her support in developing our method for making flavored oils.

Tom Gleeson of the Health Protection Branch, Health Canada, and Dr. Pearl Peterkin, formerly of HPB, for their counsel on aspects of food safety.

Ray Beaulieu, Centre for Food Safety and Applied Nutrition, US Food and Drug Administration, for providing references of recent research on the safety of vegetable-in-oil products.

And to all those many colleagues and friends who so kindly shared their favorite recipes with us.

INTRODUCTION

MULTI-HUED peppers, juicy peaches and nectarines, glowing red and purple grapes—all these delicious fruits beckon to us at the farmer's market or produce counter. We load our shopping baskets with this bounty from all over the world. And then what? We certainly enjoy eating the fresh produce. But deep within most of us lurks a desire to preserve these flavors for future enjoyment.

Many of us remember our grandmothers spending long hours in the summer preserving the produce from their large gardens. While few of us have a desire to return to the era of preserving large quantities of food for the cold months, we are developing a taste for new flavors and want to use them to enhance an otherwise simple meal. A flavorful bit of chutney, a rich salsa, a crisp pickle, a special sauce, or a flavored oil or vinegar adds interest to a meal while fitting a healthy lifestyle. Jams, conserves, marmalades and jellies can be spread on toast, English muffins or tea biscuits with no added butter necessary.

Throughout this book we offer recipes for smaller rather than larger finished amounts. A small yield gives more opportunity to make several different preserves. It also reduces the risk of scorching that is always a danger when cooking larger batches. And it makes large storage areas unnecessary. Most recipes can be made year round and, most important, at your convenience.

Preserving food is great fun and not at all difficult. When you decide to preserve food, there are two important things you must do. The first is to destroy all micro-organisms such as bacteria, molds and yeasts naturally present in food to prevent them from spoiling the preserved product. Having done this, the second thing is to make sure your preserving containers are sealed in such a way that other organisms cannot enter, otherwise they will cause your carefully prepared food to spoil.

Micro-organisms and enzymes naturally present in foods cause many changes to occur. Not all of these changes are bad. Many micro-organisms—bacteria, molds and yeasts—are intentionally used to create new forms of foods. For instance, bacteria added to milk produce creamy yogurt. Enzymes turn milk into curds, and molds introduced into the curds create wonderful cheeses. Wine-makers know the result of yeasts growing in grape juice. However, not all organisms cause changes that are desirable. They can cause food to spoil.

Today's methods of preserving are much easier, thanks to innovations from jar manufacturers. The two-piece closures, are much more foolproof than were the glass-topped sealer jars used in bygone days. And modern jars come in a variety of convenient sizes that let us preserve small amounts quickly without over-whelming our storage areas. The small batches featured in our book let you make a small amount of a tasty preserve in very short order.

We now have access to a wide variety of fruits and vegetables—some of which were unknown to North America until recently. Many of these fruits and veg-etables, such as mangoes, papayas, fresh figs and even strawberries and a variety of peppers are now available year round. Almost all of our recipes can be made throughout the year with this greater availability. However, a few foods are only available for short times of the year. Seville oranges are a good example. They are usually in stores only in January and February. Other fruits and vegetables, although available throughout the year, may be of better quality at certain times. We believe the quality of our own locally grown produce is superior since it arrives fresh in our kitchens without extended storage. At other times, good imported produce is available—just remember, you may be paying more. Preserve when the quality is finest and price is lowest.

FOUR WAYS TO PRESERVE FOOD

Heat, acid, sugar and freezing are the four ways to prevent food from spoiling.

1. Heat

The easiest way to destroy micro-organisms present in food is to heat the food. Processing is the word traditionally used when filled jars of food are heated to specific temperatures for specific lengths of time. The times and temperatures required depend on the density of the food and the size of the jar.

All molds, yeasts and most bacteria are destroyed at the temperature of boiling water. However, some bacteria, such as *Clostridium botulinum*, can form spores that withstand very high temperatures. Therefore, although this bacteria is destroyed by boiling-water temperatures, its spores may survive. These spores develop into bacteria that are able to grow in an airtight environment (such as a canning jar) and produce a poisonous toxin causing botulism. Fortunately these bacteria cannot grow in the presence of acids such as vinegar or lemon juice.

2. Acid

For preserving purposes, food can be divided into two categories:

High-Acid Foods are sufficiently acidic to prevent the growth of any spores that survive boiling-water processing. Most fruits, some vegetables and some tomatoes are high-acid foods. They can be processed at the lower temperatures reached with a boiling-water canner.

Low-Acid Foods are not sufficiently acidic to inhibit the growth of bacteria spores that can survive boiling-water temperatures. The food must be preserved by processing in a pressure canner which reaches much higher temperatures than can be achieved with boiling-water methods. Pressure canning is used to process the canned foods we buy. In this book, we don't deal with pressure canning since few people have the equipment.

Fortunately, there are some low-acid foods that can be safely preserved at boiling-water temperatures by adding acid. This is the secret of pickling. If the acid in a food is strong enough, most micro-organisms cannot grow. Familiar acids used in this process are many types of vinegars and lemon juice. Thus, it is essential to measure the ingredients accurately and not alter either the amount of acid or the amount of vegetable.

A few micro-organisms are able to grow at high acid concentration. Therefore, it is now recommended that all pickled foods be processed in a boiling-water canner for short periods of time.

3. Sugar

Sugar present in high concentrations traps water in food, creating an environment where micro-organisms cannot grow. Jams and jellies are preserved in this way. Molds and some yeasts can grow on the surface of such foods, but only in the presence of air. An airtight seal achieved from heat processing prevents the growth of such molds and yeasts.

4. Freezing

Freezing stores food at such low temperatures that no micro-organism growth can occur. However, some enzyme activity can still go on in frozen vegetables, giving off-flavors. To prevent this, vegetables are generally blanched briefly before freezing. Fruits may be frozen in their raw state. Several of our jams, spreads and curds are frozen to extend their storage.

EASY STEP-BY-STEP PRESERVING

1. Food Selection and Preparation

The best preserves result from using the best ingredients. Use produce that is as fresh as possible and at the peak of quality. Most vegetables should be used as soon as possible, but some fruits may require further ripening. Many tender fruits are picked before they are fully ripe, so wait a day or so until their full flavor has developed. However, most fruits are best for preserving when they are slightly underripe.

Wash the food thoroughly to remove surface dirt and any traces of chemicals. Discard any bruised or moldy fruit since micro-organisms may have started to grow. Fruit with other surface blemishes or imperfections is fine to use. Next read through the recipe and set out the ingredients. Remember to measure accurately.

2. Equipment Preparation

Partially fill a boiling-water canner with approximately the amount of hot water needed to cover the jars during processing. If food is to be processed less than 10 minutes, the jars need to be sterilized. Do this by boiling the jars for 10 minutes in the covered canner. Never put jars in the oven to sterilize. This exposes them to variations in temperature and may cause breakage. Jars do not need to be sterilized when processing times are longer than 10 minutes, but they should be kept hot until they are filled. It is helpful to have an extra kettle of boiling water at hand in case the water level needs to be topped up after the filled jars are placed in the canner. If you live in an area with hard water, add a bit of vinegar to the water to prevent a film forming on the jars.

Place the lids in boiling water for five minutes immediately before using. This sanitizes the lids and softens the sealing compound so an airtight seal is formed.

3. Filling Canning Jars

The processing time given in our recipes is based on the food being hot when it is put into the jars. It is important that the jars be processed immediately following the cooking stage.

A clean metal funnel is helpful to avoid spills when filling jars. Food may be ladled into the jar or poured using a small pitcher or measuring cup.

Leave a head space to allow for expansion of food during processing. For most foods, a head space of ½ inch (1 cm) is needed, although the head space may be as little as ¼ inch (5 mm) for sweet spreads. If the jars are too full, the food may boil out and interfere with the formation of the seal. Too much head space may result in the jar not sealing since the processing time is too short to drive out the extra air. We find it easiest to get in the habit of allowing ½ inch (1 cm) for all foods being processed.

Before placing a lid on the jar, be sure to remove any air trapped between pieces of food. Release any air bubbles by sliding a clean small wooden or plastic spatula between the food and the jar and gently move the food. Top up the liquid level if necessary after releasing the trapped air. Then wipe the rim of the jar with a clean cloth to remove any stickiness that could interfere with the formation of the seal.

Remove a lid from the boiling water and center it on the jar rim. Buy a magnetic lid lifter or glue a small magnet to the end of a wooden dowel rod to lift lids from the boiling water. Then apply the screw band just until it is fingertip tight. Use only your fingertips! During processing, the air in the jar expands and is vented under the lid. When the jar cools, the air contracts and the lid "snaps" down, creating an air-tight vacuum seal. If the lid is too tight, air cannot escape from the jar, possibly resulting in a failed seal.

4. Processing Canning Jars

Heating filled jars of food in boiling water for a specified time is called processing. Place the jars of filled food on the rack of a canner containing boiling water. Adjust the water level to cover the jars by approximately 1 inch (2.5 cm). Cover the canner and return to a boil. Start counting the processing time called for in the recipe when the water has returned to a steady boil. A kitchen timer is helpful for this. The processing time for each food is based on the size of the jar and the density and composition of the food, so follow times exactly. Under-processing can result in spoiled or off-flavored food and over-processing may overcook the food.

If you live at altitudes higher than 1,000 feet (306 meters), longer processing times are needed. At higher altitudes water boils at a lower temperature. So it is necessary to increase processing time if you live at higher elevations. Adjust the time as follows:

- Elevations between 1,000 and 3,000 feet (306 and 915 meters): add 5 minutes to the processing time given in the recipe.

- Elevations between 3,000 and 6,000 feet (916 and 1830 meters): add 10 minutes to the processing time given in the recipe.

- Elevations between 6,000 and 8,000 feet (1,830 and 2,440 meters): add 15 minutes to the processing time given in the recipe.

- Elevations between 8,000 and 10,000 feet (2,440 and 3,050 meters): add 20 minutes to the processing time given in the recipe.

5. Storing Preserved Food

When the processing is finished, turn off the heat and remove the jars from the canner. Use a jar lifter or lift the rack from the water by its handles. Transfer jars to a wooden cutting board or a surface covered with several layers of towels or newspapers. Do not place jars on a cold hard surface or they may break.

Do not tighten the seal; let the jars cool, undisturbed, for 12 to 24 hours. Then check the seal. It is easy to tell if the jars are sealed as the metal lids curve downwards. (You can refrigerate any jars that are not sealed and use the contents for up to three weeks). Remove the screw bands, dry them and store separately. If you prefer, replace them loosely on the jar. The bands are not necessary for storage, as the firm seal achieved by the canning process is strong enough to keep the jar airtight.

When the jars are cool and you have checked the seals, attach labels with contents and date. Preserved foods are best kept in a dark, cool place. Light may cause food to darken and a heat source, such as hot pipes, a furnace or stove, may hasten the loss of quality. A dark closet or a storage area in the basement is ideal.

If our recipes and canning procedures are followed carefully, there should be no problem with spoilage. However, before you open a jar of preserved food, it is a good idea to look closely for any sign of spoilage like a bulging lid or any leakage. The lid should be tight and give resistance when opened. If the lid is loose, or if the food has any off-flavors or mold on the surface, the food must be discarded. Don't take any chances. Plan to use preserved foods within a year. As long as the seal is secure, there is no risk of spoilage for a much longer time, but the quality of the food will deteriorate with extended storage.

EQUIPMENT FOR SAFE BOILING-WATER CANNING

1. Boiling-Water Canner

A boiling-water canner is a large covered container generally made from steel-covered enamel or stainless steel. A rack fits inside to hold the jars, keeping them from touching one another and elevating them from the bottom of the canner to allow water to circulate freely around them. The canner must be deep enough to allow at least 1 inch (2.5 cm) of briskly boiling water to cover the filled jars and the diameter should be no more than 4 inches (10 cm) wider than the burner on the stove.

Space for brisk boiling

Space for 1 inch (2.5 cm) of water above jars

Boiling -Water Canner

courtesy of Bernardin

Any large cooking pot can be used for a canner as long as it has a tight-fitting lid and is large enough to hold the jars. A rack is essential for adequate circulation of water around the jars. A round cake rack can serve this purpose. If the rack does not have handles, you will need a jar lifter for removing the jars from the hot water.

2. Canning Jars and Lids

Before you start a recipe, be sure you have enough clean canning jars that are free from cracks or nicks. Canning jars, sometimes called mason jars, are designed to withstand the temperatures of boiling-water canning. They are available in a variety of shapes and sizes from small half-cup (125 mL) to large two-quart (2 L) jars. Our recipes are designed for small batches, so we generally use the half-pint (250 mL) and pint (500 mL) sizes.

Jars come in two sizes, standard and wide mouth. The standard size is most commonly used, but wide-mouthed jars are useful for packing foods in larger pieces, such as dill pickles. Lids are made in two pieces, a lid and a screw band to keep the lid in place. The lid has a sealing compound that allows it to form a seal with the jar. Each lid is used one time only to ensure a proper jar seal. The screw band can be reused.

POSSIBLE CAUSES FOR SEAL FAILURE OR SPOILED FOOD

- Food was not processed in the canner for the correct time. It is important to start counting processing time just after the water in the canner returns to a boil.

- Processing time was not adjusted for altitude (see page 12).

- New sealing lids were not used or were not softened in boiling water.

- Screw bands were put on too tight or were re-tightened after processing.

- Too much or insufficient head space was left in the jar.

- The jar was cracked before, during or after processing. Cracking during processing could result from adding cold water to a canner of filled jars, placing hot jars on a cold surface or using jars not designed to withstand boiling-water temperatures.

- The quantity of ingredients called for in the recipe were not measured accurately.

- The vinegar was not of the standard 5% acetic acid. Always use vinegars of known acidity for canning purposes. For more about vinegars, see page 131.

SWEET SPREADS

Sweet Spreads

USING THE many different fruits available throughout the year, the variety and marvelous flavors of your homemade sweet spreads will greatly exceed those of even the best commercial jams and spreads. The following pages contain a selection of spreads that feature exciting fruit combinations not even considered by commercial jam makers. Try them to liven up your breakfast table. And a gift jar of a homemade jam or other sweet spread is always appreciated. Remember to include the recipe with it.

Name That Spread!

Jams, preserves, jellies, marmalades, conserves and fruit butters all share the same characteristic consistency, thanks to a gel formed by pectin. What makes them different from one another is the size or absence of fruit pieces, the method of cooking and the addition of other ingredients. Fruit curds are unique because they are the only spread in this category thickened by eggs.

Jam is a mixture of fruit and sugar made either from fruits that are high in pectin content or with added pectin. The fruit is usually chopped very finely or mashed.

A **preserve** is the same as a jam but the fruit is in larger pieces.

Jelly is the same as jam except that the cooked fruit has been strained to give a clear spread. Jellies are usually made from fruits high in pectin or with added pectin.

Marmalade is a jam made from citrus fruit. Marmalades generally do not have pectin added since citrus rinds and seeds contain enough pectin to form a soft gel.

A **conserve** is a jam with the addition of nuts, dried fruits and often spices.

Fruit butter is a sweet spread made by cooking fruit pulp with sugar until it has a thick, smooth consistency with no liquid remaining. Spices are often added.

Fruit curd is a sweet spread made from citrus fruit, sugar, butter and eggs cooked gently until thickened.

FOUR ESSENTIAL SWEET SPREAD INGREDIENTS

Four ingredients are essential for making sweet spreads: fruit, sugar, pectin and acid. But it isn't enough that these four substances are present—the proportion between them is critical to forming a gel. Following tested recipes, such as the ones found in this book or those supplied by pectin manufacturers, gives the best chance of success. To add flavor we like to suggest such extras as small amounts of liqueurs, nuts, spices and citrus zest. Generally, these are added at the last minute just before bottling.

1. Fruit

Fruit for all sweet spreads should be firm and ripe and always of good quality. Never use overripe fruit, since pectin disappears as fruit ripens, resulting in a jam that may not form a gel. Slightly underripe fresh fruit contains the most pectin, especially important for making spreads with no added pectin. Irregular-shaped fruit or fruit that is scarred is perfectly good, but discard any that is spoiled or moldy. Always wash or rinse fruit before use to remove any traces of dust, dirt or chemicals.

Fruit frozen without sugar, or with just a small amount of sugar, is great for making jam and other sweet spreads. Plan to freeze such fruits as rhubarb, berries and cherries when they are plentiful to make into jam later at your convenience. Choose clean, slightly underripe fruits at the peak of the growing season. Place the fruit in single layers on shallow cookie trays in the quantities required for each recipe you plan to use. Freeze the trays of fruit and then package in airtight labeled containers. The natural flavor is better preserved by adding a small amount of sugar (note the amount for the quantity of fruit so you can subtract it later from the sugar called for in the recipe). When you use the frozen fruit to make a sweet spread, there is no need to defrost it first. Just use it in the recipe as you would fresh fruit.

2. Sugar

Sugar is a vital ingredient in all sweet spreads. It links with the pectin to form a gel and high concentrations prevent the growth of micro-organisms. Sugar enhances the natural flavor of the fruit, so for that reason, a combination of a little sugar with an artificial sweetener is often used for our Light 'n' Low-Sugar Spreads (page 117).

Timing the addition of sugar affects the texture of the fruit used in sweet spreads. If fruit and sugar are simply cooked together, the fruit quickly breaks down. However, when sugar is combined with fruit for several hours before cooking, the fruit shrinks as part of its juice is drawn out. This partially dehydrated fruit keeps its shape in the finished spread. Our Elegant Oven Strawberry Jam (page 25) is a perfect example of this process.

3. Pectin

Pectin is a naturally occurring gum-like substance found in many fruits and vegetables. Fruits contain pectin in varying amounts depending on ripeness, variety and growing conditions. Pectin concentration is greatest in the cores, seeds and skins of the fruit and decreases considerably as the fruit ripens. Pectin molecules link with sugar and acid to form the gel that gives sweet spreads their smooth, semi-solid consistency. Some fruits may have enough pectin to make spreads that set well, while others require added pectin.

Adding pectin to the fruit often produces a spread with a fresher taste, and it allows fully ripe fruit to be used. It also shortens cooking time since there is no need to concentrate the natural pectin before a gel can form. The set cooking time of added-pectin recipes means there is no question as to when the spread is done. Since more sugar is required when pectin is added to a recipe, the yield from a given amount of fruit increases. Three sources of pectin are available for making sweet spreads:

Commercial pectin: Commercial pectin is a concentrated extract from high-pectin fruits such as apples and citrus fruits. It is available in liquid and dry form, which are not interchangeable. We have used both in testing our recipes. Be sure to check the "best before" date on the package.

Homemade apple pectin: Make your own pectin extract from apples (page 45). This interesting source allows you to make a very small amount of jam with just a few pieces of fruit.

High-pectin/low-pectin fruits: Combine high-pectin fruits with low pectin-ones to provide the required level of pectin. Adding apple (high pectin) to rhubarb (low pectin) or red currants (high pectin) to raspberries (low pectin) are good examples.

GUIDE TO PECTIN CONTENT OF FRUITS

High-Pectin Fruits	Low-Pectin Fruits
apples (sour* and sweet)	apricots*
cherries (sour* and sweet)	blueberries
crabapples*	elderberries
cranberries*	figs
currants (red* and black*)	nectarines
gooseberries*	peaches
grapefruit*	pears
grapes*	pineapple
kiwifruit*	raspberries*
lemons,* limes*	rhubarb*
oranges*	strawberries*
plums (some kinds)*	
quinces	

Fruits marked with an asterisk (*) are high in the acid
needed to combine with pectin for gel formation.

4. Acid

As well as having adequate pectin, fruit must contain the correct amount of acid to form a gel. Too much acid will form a gel that sets too quickly and too firmly, making the sweet spread "weep" as moisture is squeezed out. Marmalades often have too much acid so baking soda is added to reduce their acidity. Too little acid prevents a gel from forming so lemon juice is added to low-acid fruits to increase their acidity.

TWO TESTS FOR DETERMINING GEL FORMATION

The balance between fruit, sugar, pectin and acid is critical for gel formation. This balance is a delicate one, so it is essential to measure all ingredients accurately. Do not change the prescribed amounts, especially the amounts of sugar and acid. Always use tested recipes. Even then, a gel is not guaranteed, because the amounts of natural sugar, pectin and acid in the fruit vary due to weather and storage conditions. Some types of gels, especially in marmalades, may require several hours or even days for the pectin to set. Others form quickly, even before complete cooling. In general, marmalades and conserves form a lighter gel than jams and jellies. Do not make double recipes of sweet spreads as the longer cooking time required for a larger amount may cause the pectin to break down, preventing a gel from forming. There are two tests to determine when a sweet spread will form a gel.

1. Freezer Test

Place two or three small plates in the freezer ahead of time. Test for gel formation by putting a spoonful of hot fruit mixture on one chilled plate. Immediately return it to the freezer and wait for 2 minutes. Meanwhile, remove the saucepan from the heat source to prevent overcooking. If the mixture is sufficiently cooked, it will form a gel that moves slowly as the plate is tilted. If it runs off the plate, cook for another 2 minutes and repeat until freezer test indicates a gel is formed.

2. Sheet or Spoon Test

Begin cooking. Test for gel formation by periodically dipping a cool metal spoon into the hot fruit mixture and immediately lifting the spoon so the mixture runs off. At first the drops will be light and syrupy. As the mixture continues to cook, the drops from the spoon will become heavier. When the mixture "sheets" from the spoon (the drops become very thick and two drops run together before dropping off), it will form a gel on cooling and no further cooking is required.

Spoon Test

PROCESSING SWEET SPREADS

Sweet spreads are processed by freezing or by processing in a boiling-water canner for 5 minutes. Detailed instructions for boiling-water processing are found on page 21. Note that sterilized canning jars with two-piece closures must be used to get an airtight seal when using the boiling-water procedure. Processing sweet spreads often allows the fruit to rise to the top. Stir before serving to break the gel and distribute the fruit. If not processed or frozen, sweet spreads may be stored in the refrigerator for up to 3 weeks.

For many years paraffin wax was used to seal jam jars, but it is no longer recommended. A layer of paraffin on top of a sweet spread does not give the necessary airtight seal. Molds may grow in the small cracks and pinholes that occur as the wax cools. We used to think that simply removing any mold appearing on the sweet spread was sufficient to make it safe. However, research has since found that mold growth may produce harmful substances that can penetrate unseen throughout the jar. So invest in some of the attractive small canning jars that may be processed in a boiling-water bath. They are safe as well as pretty!

ESSENTIAL SWEET SPREAD EQUIPMENT

A large saucepan is essential to allow the fruit mixture to come to a full rolling boil. It should be heavy to allow even distribution of heat and made of stainless steel or enamel to prevent reaction with the acid in the mixture. In our recipes, a "large saucepan" means one that holds approximately 4 quarts (4 L). A few of the larger recipes call for a "very large saucepan," meaning one that holds at least 6 quarts (6 L). Sweet spreads should be preserved in canning jars closed with a screw band and a new metal lid. It is best to use the smaller half-cup (125 mL) or half-pint (250 mL) canning jars because a breakdown of the gel may occur with the longer cooling time required for larger quantities. This results in a more liquid product.

You will also need a boiling-water canner with a rack for processing the fruit mixture, a ladle or pitcher for putting the fruit mixture into jars, and tongs or lifters for lifting the jars from the boiling water (unless the canner rack has handles).

PROCEDURE FOR SHORTER TIME PROCESSING

Below is the step-by-step procedure for processing foods that require less than 10 minutes processing time. Use this procedure for all sweet spreads as directed in the recipes.

If the recipe requires a preparation and cooking time longer than 20 minutes, begin preparation of the ingredients first. Then sterilize the jars, while the prepared food is cooking. If the ingredients require a shorter preparation and cooking time, begin heating the canner before you start your recipe.

20 Minutes Before Processing

Partially fill a boiling-water canner with hot water. Place the number of clean canning jars needed to hold the quantity of finished food prepared in the recipe into the canner. Have a kettle with boiling water handy to top up the water level in the canner after you have put in the jars. Cover and bring the water to a boil over high heat. Boil for at least 10 minutes to sterilize jars. This step generally requires 20 to 30 minutes, depending on the size of your canner.

5 Minutes Before Processing

Approximately 5 minutes before you are ready to fill the jars, place lids in hot or boiling water according to manufacturer's directions.

Filling Jars

Remove jars from canner and pour or ladle the foods into hot jars to within ½ inch (1 cm) of top rim (head space). If the food is in large pieces, remove trapped air bubbles by sliding a clean small wooden or plastic spatula between glass and food; readjust the head space to ½ inch (1 cm). Wipe jar rim to remove any stickiness. Center lid on jar; apply screw band just until fingertip tight.

courtesy of Bernardin

Remove air bubbles

Processing Jars

Place jars in canner and adjust water level to cover jars by 1 to 2 inches (2.5 to 5 cm). Cover canner and return water to boil. Begin timing when water returns to a boil. Process for 5 minutes.

Remove jars from canner to a surface covered with newspapers or with several layers of paper towels and cool for 24 hours. Check jar seals (sealed lids turn downward). Label jars with contents and date and store in a cool, dark place.

Leave proper
'head space'

courtesy of Bernardin

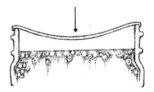

Cool jars 24 hours;
check for vacuum seal.
Sealed lids curve downward

JAMS FOR ALL SEASONS

G RACE YOUR breakfast table with spreads few commercial jam-makers even think of. When you make your own, even the common ones are more concentrated and flavorful. You'll find nothing in a store to match our Peach Lavender Jam (page 41).

The wide variety of fruits available year-round make "in season" and "out of season" distinctions less important to home jam-makers. Even so, fresh, locally grown fruits at the peak of their growing season are still the most flavorful. But frequently we are simply too busy when local fruit is most plentiful to preserve all that we would like. So, use your freezer to store fruit until you are ready to use it. Measure, bag and label fruits by recipe, then freeze. Make your frozen treasures into fresh-tasting jams during the long winter months. For example, tuck blueberries in your freezer to make Mango Blueberry Freezer Jam (page 58) when mangoes are plentiful and inexpensive. And there is no problem with using previously frozen fruit in a freezer jam that will again be frozen for longer storage.

We have discovered that adding warmed sugar to our uncooked freezer jams helps the sugar to dissolve in the fruit. This process is also useful in Old-Fashioned Raspberry Jam (page 37), as raspberries are low in pectin. Warmed sugar dissolves faster in the simmering fruit, thereby protecting the pectin from breaking down.

Homemade Apple Pectin (page 45), made when apples are plentiful, can be used with any quantity of fruit. This allows you to make as little as one jar of jam. Thus, small quantities of leftover fruit can be readily converted into interesting jam. One day we had a couple of pears approaching ripeness. Adding a few frozen blueberries along with apple pectin, sugar and lemon juice made one jar of a great-tasting jam. With apple pectin handy on the shelf, preparing the jam took less than 20 minutes.

Some fruits you may want to use for jam do not contain enough pectin to form a gel in a reasonable cooking time. To get a nice gel in a short cooking time, add commercial pectin, our Homemade Apple Pectin (page 45) or fruits with a higher pectin content.

SERVING SUGGESTIONS:

Add jam to some plain yogurt to make personalized fruit-flavored yogurts. Or mix yogurt, jam and a ripe banana in a blender to make a refreshing smoothie. Jams can be used to make a quick trifle. Spread ladyfingers with jam and top with a custard sauce. Spoonfuls of jam are a perfect topping for a plain cheesecake or a filling for a jelly roll cake. And, of course, breakfast toast would be nothing without jam.

 TIP *A small amount of sugar added to fruit that is being frozen results in better flavor retention. But remember to reduce the sugar in your recipe by the amount added to the frozen fruit.*

LIST OF RECIPES

ELEGANT OVEN STRAWBERRY JAM

An early version of this "amazingly successful" recipe appeared in *The Laura Secord Canadian Cookbook* under the name of Sunshine Strawberry Jam. The briefly cooked berries were set in the sun for 2 to 3 days to allow evaporation. Modern convection ovens greatly speed up this process and avoid the problem of "crawlies" getting to the jam before it is finished.

8 cups	**halved or quartered strawberries**	**2 L**
4 cups	**granulated sugar**	**1 L**
¼ cup	**balsamic vinegar or lemon juice**	**50 mL**

1. Combine berries and sugar in a very large stainless steel or enamel saucepan. Let stand for 2 hours, stirring several times.

2. Add vinegar and bring to a boil over high heat; reduce heat and boil gently, uncovered, for 10 minutes.

3. Pour into two 13 x 9-inch (3.5 L) glass baking dishes and place in a convection or standard oven at 150°F (65°C). Bake until mixture is thickened and will form a gel*, about 3 hours for convection and 10 hours for standard, stirring occasionally.

4. Ladle into sterilized jars and process as directed on page 21 (Shorter Time Processing Procedure).

Makes 4 cups (1 L).

VARIATION:

Herb Strawberry Jam
Insert a sprig of fresh mint or basil in each jar before filling with jam.

* To determine when mixture will form a gel, see page 19.

FAVORITE STRAWBERRY JAM

Generations have made strawberry jam to preserve this favorite summer fruit. Traditionally, low-pectin strawberries are cooked for long periods to achieve a gel. Our method uses standing periods alternating with much shorter cooking times. It makes a jam that retains its lovely red color and fresh flavor.

4 cups	**halved or quartered firm strawberries, (depending on size)**	**1 L**
2 cups	**granulated sugar**	**500 mL**
¼ cup	**lemon juice**	**50 mL**

1. Mix berries and sugar and let stand for 8 hours, stirring occasionally.

2. Place berry mixture in a medium stainless steel or enamel saucepan. Bring to a boil over medium heat. Add lemon juice, return to a boil and boil rapidly for 5 minutes. Remove from heat, cover and let stand for 24 hours.

3. Bring berries to a full boil over high heat and boil rapidly for 5 minutes, stirring constantly. Remove from heat.

4. Ladle into sterilized jars and process as directed on page 21 (Shorter Time Processing Procedure).

Makes 2½ cups (625 mL).

VARIATION:

Strawberry Rhubarb Jam
Add 1 cup (250 mL) finely chopped rhubarb to strawberries in step 1.
Makes 3 cups (750 mL).

SHERRIED STRAWBERRY PRESERVE

Whole strawberries with a hint of sherry are suspended in this delightful preserve. A perfect accompaniment to fresh biscuits. Stir before serving to break gel and distribute fruit.

5 cups	whole small firm strawberries	1.25 L
	(about 2½ pints)	
4 cups	granulated sugar	1 L
3 tbsp	lemon juice	45 mL
1	pouch liquid fruit pectin	1
½ cup	medium-dry sherry	125 mL

1. Stir together berries, sugar and lemon juice in a large bowl. Cover and let stand for 4 hours, stirring occasionally.

2. Place berries in a very large stainless steel or enamel saucepan. Bring to a boil over high heat and boil rapidly for 2 minutes, stirring constantly. Remove from heat; stir in pectin and sherry.

3. Ladle into sterilized jars and process as directed on page 21 (Shorter Time Processing Procedure).

Makes 5½ cups (1.4 L).

VARIATION:

Strawberry Preserves with White Wine
Use white wine in place of the sherry for a more delicate flavor.

FRESH FIG AND STRAWBERRY JAM

This jam is so good it disappears from the shelf. The fresh figs lend an amazing texture and taste to the strawberries. Be sure to make as much of it as jar and cupboard space allows whenever you can get your hands on fresh figs. Otherwise you may be like Margaret—she raved about it and then gave away so many jars she didn't have any left for herself!

1 lb	fresh green figs, stemmed and cut into small pieces	500 g
2 cups	quartered strawberries	500 mL
2 cups	granulated sugar	500 mL
3 tbsp	lemon juice	45 mL

1. Place figs, strawberries, sugar and lemon juice in a medium stainless steel or enamel saucepan. Cover and let stand for 1 hour, stirring occasionally.

2. Bring to a boil over high heat, reduce heat to medium and boil rapidly, uncovered, until mixture will form a gel*, about 15 minutes, stirring frequently. Remove from heat.

3. Ladle into sterilized jars and process as directed on page 21 (Shorter Time Processing Procedure).

Makes about 4 cups (1 L).

TIP *Fresh figs have a longer season than we realized. California figs are ready in May and are available from Greece and Italy in late summer and fall. If you missed them, occasionally you can find figs from South America in the late fall and early winter. Remember that fresh figs are extremely perishable and should be used as soon as possible after purchase. They may be stored in a refrigerator for up to 3 days.*

* To determine when mixture will form a gel, see page 19.

FESTIVE CRANSTRAWBERRY JAM

This jam's ruby-rich appearance is just right with festive Christmas food. It adds great color to your breakfast table and wonderful taste to toast and muffins all year round.

1	pkg (15 oz/425 g) frozen sliced strawberries in light syrup, thawed	1
2 cups	fresh or frozen cranberries	500 mL
1	large unpeeled orange, cut into large pieces	1
3 cups	granulated sugar	750 mL
1	pouch liquid fruit pectin	1
2 tbsp	orange liqueur or frozen orange juice concentrate	25 mL

1. Place strawberries in a very large stainless steel or enamel saucepan.

2. Coarsely chop cranberries and orange in a food processor. Remove and add to saucepan. Stir in sugar. Bring to a full boil over high heat and boil hard for 2 minutes, stirring constantly. Remove from heat and stir in pectin and liqueur.

3. Ladle into sterilized jars and process as directed on page 21 (Shorter Time Processing Procedure).

Makes 6 cups (1.5 L).

SERVING SUGGESTION:

Cinnamon Tortilla Roll-ups
An interesting use for this jam as well as many others.
Warm a small flour tortilla in either the microwave oven or in a non-stick skillet. Mix 1 tbsp (15 mL) each of plain low-fat yogurt, low-fat ricotta cheese and 1 tsp (5 mL) Festive Cranstrawberry Jam. Spread mixture evenly over tortilla, add a dash of ground cinnamon or nutmeg, roll up and enjoy!

FOUR FRUIT RED JAM

Use fresh or frozen fruit, but remember to measure frozen fruit before thawing and thaw before crushing.

2 cups	raspberries or loganberries, crushed	500 mL
2 cups	red currants, crushed	500 mL
2 cups	sliced strawberries, crushed	500 mL
1½ cups	chopped sour cherries	375 mL
4 cups	granulated sugar	1 L
¼ cup	lemon juice	50 mL

1. Place raspberries, currants, strawberries, cherries, sugar and lemon juice in a large stainless steel or enamel saucepan. Cover and let stand for 10 minutes.

2. Bring to a boil over high heat, stirring constantly. Boil rapidly, uncovered, until mixture will form a gel*, about 15 minutes, stirring frequently. Remove from heat.

3. Ladle into sterilized jars and process as directed on page 21 (Shorter Time Processing Procedure).

Makes about 5 cups (1.25 L).

SERVING SUGGESTION:

Red Fruit Sauce
This one is excellent for pancakes, French toast or waffles.
Melt ½ cup (125 mL) Four Fruit Red Jam in a small saucepan over low heat. Stir 1 tsp (5 mL) cornstarch into ½ cup (125 mL) cherry juice and ¼ cup (50 mL) water. Whisk into melted jam, boil gently, uncovered, over low heat until slightly thickened. Stir in ½ tsp (2 mL) ground cinnamon, a small amount of grated lemon rind and ½ cup (125 mL) sour cherries.
Makes about 1¾ cups (425 mL).

* To determine when mixture will form a gel, see page 19.

RED AND BLACK CURRANT CASSIS JAM

The strong, rich taste of two kinds of currants reinforced by a currant-based liqueur makes this a jam for the true currant lover. Currants are very high in pectin, so don't over cook them. They thicken up considerably after cooking.

2½ cups	black currants, washed and stemmed	625 mL
2½ cups	red currants, washed and stemmed	625 mL
1 cup	water	250 mL
3 cups	granulated sugar	750 mL
2 tbsp	lemon juice	25 mL
3 tbsp	Cassis	45 mL

1. Place fruit and water in a large stainless steel or enamel saucepan. Bring to a boil over high heat, cover, reduce heat and boil gently for 10 minutes, stirring occasionally.

2. Add sugar, lemon juice and liqueur. Bring to a full boil over high heat, stirring constantly. Boil rapidly uncovered until mixture will form a gel*, about 10 minutes. Remove from heat.

3. Ladle into sterilized jars and process as directed on page 21 (Shorter Time Processing Procedure).

Makes 5 cups (1.25 L).

* To determine when mixture will form a gel, see page 19.

SOUR CHERRY GOOSEBERRY JAM

Tart sour cherries wonderfully complement the sweet gooseberries in this simple recipe.

2 cups	chopped pitted sour cherries (about 4 cups/1 L whole fruit)	500 mL
2 cups	chopped gooseberries (about 2½ cups/625 mL whole fruit)	500 mL
1 cup	water	250 mL
4 cups	granulated sugar	1 L

1. Combine cherries, gooseberries and water in a large stainless steel or enamel saucepan. Bring to a boil, reduce heat, cover and boil gently for 15 minutes.

2. Add sugar, return to a full boil and boil rapidly, uncovered, until mixture will form a gel*, about 15 minutes, stirring frequently. Remove from heat.

3. Ladle into sterilized jars and process as directed on page 21 (Shorter Time Processing Procedure).

Makes 4 cups (1 L).

VARIATION:

Ginger Sour Cherry Gooseberry Jam
Add 2 tbsp (25 mL) chopped Candied Ginger (page 301) or crystallized ginger in Step 2.

SERVING SUGGESTION:

Fruit Fool
Summer fruits shine in jams and so why not allow them to come forth and shine again in a fruit fool. Most fools are silky-smooth yet oh-so-simple to make.
Beat 1 cup (250 mL) whipping cream in a medium bowl with an electric mixer until firm, but not stiff peaks. Gently fold in ½ cup (125 mL) your choice of jam, 2 tbsp (25 mL) Cranberry Orange Liqueur (page 304) or other fruit liqueur, and 1 tsp (5 mL) grated lemon zest. Serve immediately or refrigerate for a few hours.
Makes 4 to 6 servings.

* To determine when mixture will form a gel, see page 19.

Sherried Strawberry Preserve (page 27)

Spiced Wine Pear Jam (page 42)

GOOSEBERRY RHUBARB JAM

This combination of two tart, old-fashioned country garden fruits gives us a jam with a wonderful flavor and glorious color. If you are making this jam with frozen fruit, chop and measure while fruit is still frozen.

2 cups	finely chopped rhubarb	500 mL
½ cup	water	125 mL
2 cups	gooseberries, stems removed and coarsely chopped	500 mL
2 tbsp	lemon juice	25 mL
5½ cups	granulated sugar	1.375 L
1	pouch liquid fruit pectin	1

1. Place rhubarb and water in a very large stainless steel or enamel saucepan. Bring to a boil over high heat, reduce heat, cover and boil gently for 3 minutes.

2. Stir gooseberries, lemon juice and sugar into rhubarb. Return to a full boil over high heat and boil hard for 1 minute, stirring constantly. Remove from heat and stir in pectin.

3. Ladle into sterilized jars and process as directed on page 21 (Shorter Time Processing Procedure).

Makes 5 cups (1.25 L).

VARIATION:

Gingered Gooseberry Rhubarb Jam
Add ⅓ cup (75 mL) finely chopped Candied Ginger (page 301) or crystallized ginger in Step 2.

GINGERED RHUBARB JAM WITH HONEY

In England it's traditional to combine ginger with rhubarb. In this jam, ginger adds a pungent spiciness while honey offsets rhubarb's strong tartness.

1	lemon	1
2 cups	chopped fresh or frozen rhubarb	500 mL
1	large tart apple, peeled, cored and finely chopped	1
½ cup	water	125 mL
1½ cups	granulated sugar	375 mL
1 cup	liquid honey	250 mL
1½ tbsp	finely chopped Candied Ginger (page 301) or crystallized ginger	20 mL

1. Remove thin outer rind from lemon with vegetable peeler and cut into fine strips with scissors or sharp knife; or use a zester. Place lemon rind in a medium stainless steel or enamel saucepan. Squeeze juice from lemon and reserve 1 tbsp (15 mL).

2. Add rhubarb, apple and water to saucepan. Bring to a boil over high heat, cover, reduce heat and boil gently for 15 minutes or until fruit is tender.

3. Add sugar, honey, ginger and reserved lemon juice. Return to a boil and boil rapidly, uncovered, until mixture will form a gel*, about 8 minutes, stirring frequently. Remove from heat.

4. Ladle into sterilized jars and process as directed on page 21 (Shorter Time Processing Procedure).

Makes 3¼ cups (800 mL).

 TIP *Freeze fresh rhubarb to use when it is not in season.*

* To determine when mixture will form a gel, see page 19.

BLUEBARB JAM

Only by using frozen fruit can we make this wonderful jam from fruits having different growing seasons.

3½ cups	chopped fresh or frozen rhubarb	875 mL
½ cup	water	125 mL
2¼ cups	coarsely chopped fresh or frozen blueberries	550 mL
1 tbsp	lemon juice	15 mL
1	box dry fruit pectin	1
5½ cups	granulated sugar	1.375 L

1. Place rhubarb and water in a very large stainless steel or enamel saucepan. Bring to a boil over high heat, cover, reduce heat, and simmer for 5 minutes, stirring often.

2. Add blueberries, lemon juice and pectin; mix well. Bring to a boil over high heat, stirring constantly. Add sugar, return to a full boil and boil hard for 1 minute, stirring constantly. Remove from heat. Ladle into sterilized jars and process as directed on page 21 (Shorter Time Processing Procedure).

Makes 6 cups (1.5 L).

SPICED BLUEBERRY HONEY JAM

Honey adds its own delicate nuance to the more defined blueberry and nutmeg flavors in this delightful jam. It can be made any time with frozen blueberries.

2½ cups	fresh or frozen coarsely chopped blueberries	625 mL
2½ cups	granulated sugar	625 mL
1 cup	liquid honey	250 mL
1 tbsp	lemon juice	15 mL
½ tsp	ground nutmeg	2 mL
1	pouch liquid fruit pectin	1

Place blueberries, sugar, honey, lemon juice and nutmeg in a large stainless steel or enamel saucepan. Bring to a full boil over high heat and boil hard for 2 minutes, stirring constantly. Remove from heat and stir in pectin. Ladle into sterilized jars and process as directed on page 21 (Shorter Time Processing Procedure).

Makes 4 cups (1 L).

TIP   *Use a small grater to grate the seed of a nutmeg for freshest flavor.*

RASPBERRY AND BLUEBERRY JAM

The flavors of the two berries and the citrus fruit combine beautifully in this interesting jam. Make this jam year round from either fresh or frozen berries.

3 cups	fresh or frozen unsweetened raspberries	750 mL
2 cups	fresh or frozen unsweetened blueberries	500 mL
1	large orange	1
6½ cups	granulated sugar	1.625 L
2 tbsp	lemon juice	25 mL
1	pouch liquid fruit pectin	1

1. Mash raspberries and blueberries in a very large stainless steel or enamel saucepan.

2. Remove thin outer rind from orange with vegetable peeler and cut into fine strips with scissors or sharp knife; or use a zester. Add to saucepan. Remove and discard remaining white rind. Finely chop orange in food processor with on/off motion to measure ½ cup (125 mL). Add orange pulp, sugar and lemon juice to saucepan.

3. Bring fruit to a full boil over high heat and boil hard for 1 minute, stirring constantly. Remove from heat and stir in pectin.

4. Ladle into sterilized jars and process as directed on page 21 (Shorter Time Processing Procedure).

Makes 7 cups (1.75 L).

VARIATIONS:

Raspberry Cranberry Jam
Replace blueberries with 2 cups (500 mL) fresh or frozen cranberries, finely chopped.

Raspberry Plum Jam
Replace blueberries with 2 cups (500 mL) finely chopped plums. A small amount of finely chopped fresh mint makes a nice addition.

OLD-FASHIONED RASPBERRY JAM

The intense raspberry flavor of this jam makes it a long-time favorite. Warming the sugar beforehand keeps the jam boiling evenly and ensures success.

| 4 cups | granulated sugar | 1 L |
| 4 cups | raspberries | 1 L |

1. Place sugar in an ovenproof shallow pan and warm in a 250°F (120°C) oven for 15 minutes. (Warm sugar dissolves better).

2. Place berries in a large stainless steel or enamel saucepan. Bring to a full boil over high heat, mashing berries with a potato masher as they heat. Boil hard for 1 minute, stirring constantly.

3. Add warm sugar, return to a boil and boil until mixture will form a gel*, about 5 minutes.

4. Ladle into sterilized jars and process as directed on page 21 (Shorter Time Processing Procedure).

Makes 4 cups (1 L).

TIP   *To make a small boiling-water canner, tie several screw bands together with string or use a small round cake rack in the bottom of a large covered Dutch oven. Be sure the pan is high enough for 2 inches (5 cm) of water to cover the jars when they are sitting on the rack.*

* To determine when mixture will form a gel, see page 19.

RASPBERRY JAM WITH CHAMBORD

This elegant jam is an ideal gift for a special friend. The unparalleled flavor of fresh raspberries is wonderfully complemented by raspberry liqueur.

3¾ cups	crushed raspberries	925 mL
	(about 5 cups/1.25 L whole berries)	
4 cups	granulated sugar	1 L
3 tbsp	lemon juice	45 mL
1	pouch liquid fruit pectin	1
⅓ cup	Chambord, Framboise or	75 mL
	Raspberry Liqueur (page 305)	

1. Combine berries, sugar and lemon juice in a very large stainless steel or enamel saucepan. Let stand for 10 minutes.

2. Place pan over high heat, bring to a full boil and boil hard for 2 minutes, stirring constantly. Remove from heat; stir in pectin and liqueur. Ladle into sterilized jars and process as directed on page 21 (Shorter Time Processing Procedure).

Makes 6 cups (1.5 L).

PEAR RASPBERRY JAM

Make this jam at just about any time of the year. Good pears are available almost all year round and the raspberries in this recipe are frozen. Pear Raspberry Jam can give a fresh addition to your jam shelf.

6	medium pears, peeled, cored and chopped	6
1	pkg (15 oz/425 g) frozen raspberries in light syrup, thawed	1
6 cups	granulated sugar	1.5 L
2 tsp	grated lemon rind	10 mL
2 tbsp	lemon juice	25 mL
1	pouch liquid fruit pectin	1

Place pears, raspberries, sugar, lemon rind and juice in a very large stainless steel or enamel saucepan. Bring to a full boil over high heat and boil hard for 2 minutes, stirring constantly. Remove from heat and stir in pectin. Ladle into sterilized jars and process as directed on page 21 (Shorter Time Processing Procedure).

Makes 6 cups (1.5 L).

CRANBERRY PEAR LEMON JAM

Combine these three distinctly flavored fruits for a delicious breakfast jam. Its tart tangy flavor also marries well with roasted poultry and pork.

4	large Bartlett pears, peeled, cored and diced (about 4 cups/1 L)	4
3 cups	coarsely chopped fresh or frozen cranberries	750 mL
½ cup	water	125 mL
2 tsp	grated lemon rind	10 mL
2 tbsp	lemon juice	25 mL
1¾ cups	granulated sugar	425 mL

1. Combine pears, cranberries, water and lemon rind in a large stainless steel or enamel saucepan. Bring to a boil over high heat, cover, reduce heat and cook for 5 minutes, stirring frequently.

2. Gradually add lemon juice and sugar, stirring until sugar is dissolved. Boil rapidly, uncovered, until mixture will form a gel*, about 15 minutes, stirring frequently. Remove from heat.

3. Ladle into sterilized jars and process as directed on page 21 (Shorter Time Processing Procedure).

Makes 5 cups (1.25 L).

* To determine when mixture will form a gel, see page 19.

PEACH PEAR JAM WITH LIME

Two fall fruits combine to make one of our favorite jams. This started off as Ellie's peach recipe. One day, with not enough peaches to make the jam, she added some pears. Since these fruits are best in season for making this jam, this is a larger recipe than many others.

	Rind of 1 lime	
2 cups	finely chopped peeled peaches	500 mL
2 cups	finely chopped peeled pears	500 mL
1	box dry fruit pectin	1
5 cups	granulated sugar	1.25 L

1. Remove thin outer rind from lime with vegetable peeler and cut into fine strips with scissors or sharp knife; or use a zester. Place lime rind in a small microwavable container with ¼ cup (50 mL) water. Microwave on High (100%) for 1 minute. Drain and discard liquid; reserve rind.

2. Place peaches, pears, lime rind and pectin in a very large stainless steel or enamel saucepan. Bring to a boil over high heat, stirring constantly. Add sugar, return to a full boil and boil hard for 1 minute, stirring constantly. Remove from heat.

3. Ladle into sterilized jars and process as directed on page 21 (Shorter Time Processing Procedure).

Makes 7 cups (1.75 L).

PEACH LAVENDER JAM

Many people do not think of cooking with lavender, an edible herb that subtly accents the flavor of fresh fruits such as peaches, strawberries, raspberries, orange and lemon, but it adds a wonderful flavor to this jam.

2 tbsp	dried lavender flowers *	25 mL
½ cup	boiling water	125 mL
4 cups	finely chopped peaches (about 5-6 medium peaches)	1 L
2 tbsp	lemon juice	25 mL
6 cups	granulated sugar	1.5 L
1	pouch liquid fruit pectin	1

1. Place lavender flowers in a small bowl. Pour boiling water over flowers and steep for 20 minutes. Strain and discard flowers.

2. Combine lavender liquid, peaches, lemon juice and sugar in a very large stainless steel or enamel saucepan. Bring to a full boil over high heat and boil hard for 2 minutes, stirring constantly. Remove from heat and stir in pectin.

3. Ladle into sterilized jars and process as directed on page 21 (Shorter Time Processing Procedure).

Makes 6 cups (1.5 L).

TIP   *Look for organically grown lavender at herb fairs and herb specialty growers. For an added touch, place a small sprig on top of jam before sealing.

Spiced Wine Peach Jam

Spices and wine do interesting flavorful things to ordinary peaches in this sophisticated jam.

½ cup	golden raisins	125 mL
⅓ cup	dry red wine or juice *	75 mL
4 cups	finely chopped peaches	1 L
	(about 5 to 6 medium peaches)	
3 tbsp	lemon juice	45 mL
1	box dry fruit pectin	1
5 cups	granulated sugar	1.25 L
1 tsp	ground cinnamon	5 mL
½ tsp	ground allspice	2 mL

1. Bring raisins and wine to a boil in a small saucepan, remove from heat, drain and discard liquid.

2. Combine raisins, peaches, lemon juice and pectin in a very large stainless steel or enamel saucepan. Bring to a boil over high heat, stirring constantly. Add sugar, return to a full boil and boil hard for 1 minute, stirring constantly. Remove from heat and stir in cinnamon and allspice.

3. Ladle into sterilized jars and process as directed on page 21 (Shorter Time Processing Procedure).

Makes about 6 cups (1.5 L).

Variation:

Spiced Wine Pear Jam
Replace peaches with 4 cups (1 L) finely chopped pears. Ground nutmeg is an excellent substitution for the cinnamon.

 TIP   *Wine can be replaced with pineapple or orange juice.*

FRESH APRICOT JAM

This very easy-to-make recipe produces a lovely fresh-tasting jam. It may be all that is needed to spur a neophyte's interest in jam-making.

3 cups	coarsely chopped unpeeled fresh apricots (about 2 lb/1 kg, or 14 to 20 apricots)	750 mL
3½ cups	granulated sugar	875 mL
¼ cup	lemon juice	50 mL

1. Stir together apricots, sugar and lemon juice in a large bowl. Cover and let stand at room temperature for 12 hours, stirring occasionally.

2. Place apricot mixture in a medium stainless steel or enamel saucepan. Bring to a boil over high heat, stirring frequently. Reduce heat to medium and boil rapidly, uncovered, until mixture will form a gel*, about 25 minutes, stirring frequently. Remove from heat.

3. Ladle into sterilized jars and process as directed on page 21 (Shorter Time Processing Procedure).

Makes about 3½ cups (875 mL).

SERVING SUGGESTION:

Crunchy Apricot Breakfast Yogurt
In a small bowl, combine 1 cup (250 mL) plain or vanilla low-fat yogurt. Stir in ½ cup (125 mL) Fresh Apricot Jam and 1 cup (250 mL) granola-type cereal just before serving. Makes about 2 cups (500 mL).

* To determine when mixture will form a gel, see page 19.

AUTUMN FRUIT JAM

Plums, apples and pears are all in season at the same time. Together they make a jam that reflects the luscious essence of early fall fruits. The high pectin content of plums and apples compensates for the low pectin in pears to produce a well-set jam.

5	plums, sliced	5
2	medium apples, peeled, cored and chopped	2
2	medium pears, peeled, cored and chopped	2
1 cup	water	250 mL
2 tsp	grated lemon rind	10 mL
2 tbsp	lemon juice	25 mL
3 cups	granulated sugar	750 mL
½ tsp	each: ground cinnamon and ginger	2 mL

1. Combine plums, apples, pears, water, lemon rind and lemon juice in a large stainless steel or enamel saucepan. Bring to a boil over high heat, cover, reduce heat and cook for 10 minutes or until fruit is softened.

2. Add sugar to fruit and return to a boil, stirring constantly until sugar is dissolved. Boil rapidly, uncovered, until mixture will form a gel*, about 30 minutes, stirring occasionally. Stir in cinnamon and ginger.

3. Ladle into sterilized jars and process as directed on page 21 (Shorter Time Processing Procedure).

Makes 4 cups (1 L).

VARIATIONS:

Replace cinnamon and ginger with 1 tbsp (15 mL) vanilla extract added to cooked jam just before bottling.

Nectarine Plum Apple Jam
Use 4 nectarines, peeled and chopped, instead of pears.

* To determine when mixture will form a gel, see page 19.

HOMEMADE APPLE PECTIN

The pectin content of apples decreases during storage, so remember to make this pectin in the fall when apples are at their freshest. The straining process is made easier if the apple mixture is first pressed through a coarse sieve to remove most of the solids and then strained through several layers of cheesecloth or a jelly bag for extra clarity.

7	tart apples (about 2 lb/1 kg)	7
4 cups	water	1 L
2 tbsp	lemon juice	25 mL

1. Cut apples into quarters (do not peel or core). Combine with water and lemon juice in a large stainless steel or enamel saucepan. Bring to a boil over high heat, cover, reduce heat and simmer for 40 minutes, stirring occasionally.

2. Strain through a coarse sieve and discard solids. Then pour liquid through a jelly bag or several layers of cheesecloth.

3. Ladle into sterilized jars and process as directed on page 21 (Shorter Time Processing Procedure).

Makes 4 cups (1 L).

 TIP   *Use your imagination to combine your favorite fruits with an equal amount of Homemade Apple Pectin for your own signature breakfast spread.*

Suggested Fruit Combinations for Making Jam Using Homemade Apple Pectin:

- ½ cup (125 mL) chopped kiwifruit and ½ cup (125 mL) chopped mango.
- ½ cup (125 mL) chopped pears and ½ cup (125 mL) chopped blueberries.
- ½ cup (125 mL) chopped fresh pineapple and ½ cup (125 mL) chopped papaya.
- ½ cup (125 mL) chopped blueberries and ½ cup (125 mL) chopped plums.
- 1 cup (250 mL) frozen raspberries, thawed and mashed, with 1 tsp (5 mL) chopped fresh mint stirred in after cooking.
- 1 cup (250 mL) chopped sweet cherries, with ½ tsp (2 mL) lemon juice.

1. For each 1 cup (250 mL) finely chopped fruit, add 1 cup (250 mL) Homemade Apple Pectin and ¾ cup (175 mL) granulated sugar.

2. Combine fruit, pectin and sugar in a stainless steel or enamel saucepan. Add 1 tsp (5 mL) lemon juice if fruit is low acid (see chart on page 19). Bring to a boil over high heat and boil rapidly, uncovered, until mixture will form a gel*, about 10 to 15 minutes, stirring frequently.

3. Ladle into jars, cover and store in refrigerator for up to 3 weeks. If desired, process as directed on page 21 (Shorter Time Processing Procedure).

Each recipe makes about 1¼ cups (300 mL) jam.

* To determine when mixture will form a gel, see page 19.

PLUM AND CRABAPPLE JAM

Crabapples are more commonly used in jellies than jams. Combined with plums they impart a sweet-tart flavor and a gorgeous color to this quite different jam. Do not overcook it. Since plums and crabapples are naturally high in pectin, this jam thickens considerably after it's cooked.

3 cups	quartered unpeeled crabapples	750 mL
	(about 4 cups/1 L whole fruit)	
1½ cups	water	375 mL
1	cinnamon stick about 4 inches(10 cm) long	1
4 cups	sliced blue or purple plums	1 L
	(about 8 large or 16 small plums)	
5 cups	granulated sugar	1.25 L
¾ cup	dry red or white wine or grape juice	175 mL

1. Place crabapples, water and cinnamon stick in a very large stainless steel or enamel saucepan. Bring to a boil over high heat, cover, reduce heat and boil gently for 10 minutes or until fruit is soft. Remove from heat and discard cinnamon stick. Press crabapples through a sieve; discard solids.

2. Return crabapple pulp to saucepan. Add plums, sugar and wine. Bring to a full boil and boil rapidly, uncovered, until mixture will form a gel*, about 20 minutes, stirring frequently. Remove from heat.

3. Ladle into sterilized jars and process as directed on page 21 (Shorter Time Processing Procedure).

Makes 6 cups (1.5 L).

* To determine when mixture will form a gel, see page 19.

PLUM AMARETTO JAM

The almond flavor of the liqueur nicely complements the tartness of the plums in this rich purple jam. Plums are seldom used for jam, but after tasting this one you'll want to take a plum to breakfast more often.

3 cups	chopped tart red or purple plums (about 8 to 10 plums)	750 mL
3 cups	granulated sugar	750 mL
¼ cup	water	50 mL
3 tbsp	lemon juice	45 mL
¼ cup	Amaretto liqueur	50 mL

1. Combine plums, sugar, water and lemon juice in a large stainless steel or enamel saucepan.

2. Bring to a boil over high heat, reduce heat to medium and boil rapidly until mixture will form a gel*, about 20 minutes, stirring frequently. Remove from heat and stir in liqueur.

3. Ladle into sterilized jars and process as directed on page 21 (Shorter Time Processing Procedure).

Makes 4 cups (1 L).

* To determine when mixture will form a gel, see page 19.

MANGO PLUM JAM

A great small-batch jam to make any time you find nice ripe mangoes. Plums give an interesting flavor twist to the exotic sweet-tart flavor of mangoes.

1 cup	finely chopped plums (about 3 to 4 plums)	250 mL
½ cup	water	125 mL
1	mango, peeled and diced	1
½	box dry fruit pectin*	½
1 tbsp	lemon juice	15 mL
3 cups	granulated sugar	750 mL

1. Place plums and water in a large stainless steel or enamel saucepan. Bring to a boil over high heat, cover, reduce heat and simmer for 10 minutes, stirring frequently.

2. Stir mango, pectin and lemon juice into plums; mix well. Return to a boil over high heat, uncovered, stirring constantly. Add sugar, return to a full boil and boil hard for 1 minute, stirring constantly. Remove from heat.

3. Ladle into sterilized jars and process as directed on page 21 (Shorter Time Processing Procedure).

Makes 4 cups (1 L).

TIP *The remaining pectin can be used to make Microwave Winter Pear Amaretto Jam (page 55).*

FESTIVE KIWIFRUIT DAIQUIRI JAM

This is a favorite of people who like jams that are less sweet.

1½ cups	finely chopped kiwifruit (about 5 kiwifruit)	375 mL
⅓ cup	lime juice (about 2 limes)	75 mL
¼ cup	water	50 mL
2 tbsp	dried cranberries or cherries, coarsely chopped	25 mL
3 cups	granulated sugar	750 mL
1	pouch liquid fruit pectin	1
¼ cup	dark rum	50 mL

Place kiwifruit, lime juice, water, cranberries and sugar in a large stainless steel or enamel saucepan. Bring to a full boil over high heat and boil hard for 2 minutes, stirring constantly. Remove from heat; stir in pectin and rum. Ladle into sterilized jars and process as directed on page 21 (Shorter Time Processing Procedure).

Makes 4 cups (1 L).

WINTER PEAR AND APRICOT JAM

Bosc and Anjou pears keep for long periods, making them available for most of the winter. The tartness of dried apricots combines with the sweetness of pears to make a great winter jam.

½ cup	finely chopped dried apricots	125 mL
1¼ cups	water	425 mL
2 cups	finely chopped cored, peeled winter pears (Bosc or Anjou)	500 mL
2 tsp	lemon juice	10 mL
1	box dry fruit pectin	1
4½ cups	granulated sugar	1.125 L

1. Soak apricots in water for 4 hours or overnight.

2. Pour apricots into a very large stainless steel or enamel saucepan. Add pears, lemon juice and pectin. Bring to a full boil over high heat, stirring constantly. Add sugar, return to a full boil and boil hard for 1 minute, stirring constantly. Remove from heat. Ladle into sterilized jars and process as directed on page 21 (Shorter Time Processing Procedure). Note that this jam is slow to set.

Makes 6 cups (1.5 L).

AUSTRALIAN SPICED DRIED FIG JAM

Fig lovers will enjoy this succulent spread that Ellie discovered while in Australia. It is delicious as a cake and cookie filling and be sure to try it in Spiced Fig Jam Bars (page 338).

8 oz	dried figs*	250 g
2¼ cups	water	550 mL
4½ cups	granulated sugar	1.125 L
¼ tsp	ground cinnamon	1 mL
¼ tsp	ground nutmeg	1 mL
1	box dry fruit pectin	1
1 tsp	grated lemon rind	5 mL
¼ cup	lemon juice	50 mL

1. Combine figs and water in a medium bowl. Let stand for 8 hours or overnight.

2. Drain figs, reserving liquid. Remove and discard stems and chop fruit finely. Place chopped fruit in a 4-cup (1 L) liquid measure and add reserved liquid and enough water to bring level to 3 cups (750 mL).

3. Combine sugar, cinnamon and nutmeg in a bowl. Set aside.

4. Place fig mixture, pectin, lemon rind and juice in a large stainless steel or enamel saucepan. Bring to a boil over high heat, stirring constantly. Add sugar-spice mixture, return to a full boil and boil hard for 1 minute, stirring constantly. Remove from heat.

5. Ladle into sterilized jars and process as directed on page 21 (Shorter Time Processing Procedure).

Makes 5 cups (1.25 L).

TIP

Since figs come in a variety of package sizes it is important to check the weight.

MICROWAVE STRAWBERRY LIME JAM

You'll want to make a jar of this easy small-batch recipe when imported berries are available and you long for the taste of fresh strawberry jam. The same goes for peaches . . . see the variation below.

1½ cups	granulated sugar	375 mL
2 cups	sliced, hulled strawberries	500 mL
2 tbsp	lime juice	25 mL

1. Place sugar and strawberries in two alternating layers in a deep 12-cup (3 L) microwavable bowl. Pour lime juice over top. Do not stir.

2. Microwave, uncovered, on High (100%) for 5 minutes, stirring twice. Microwave, uncovered, on High for 10 minutes or until mixture will form a gel*, stirring every 4 minutes.

3. Ladle into sterilized jars and process as directed on page 21 (Shorter Time Processing Procedure).

Makes 1½ cups (375 mL).

VARIATIONS:

Strawberry Lemon Jam: Replace lime juice with lemon juice.
Spiced Strawberry Jam: Tie 1 cinnamon stick, 2 whole cloves and 2 allspice berries loosely in cheesecloth and add to fruit during last 10 minutes of cooking. Remove and discard spice bag before bottling.
Peach Lime Jam: Prepare with same amount of peaches, sugar and 1 tbsp (15 mL) lime juice.
Extras to stir into any of the above variations before bottling: 1 tbsp (15 mL) finely chopped Candied Ginger (page 301) or crystallized ginger; or 1 tbsp (15 mL) Amaretto; or ½ tsp (2 mL) ground nutmeg or cinnamon.

* To determine when mixture will form a gel, see page 19.

MICROWAVE GINGER PLUM JAM

Microwave purple plums anytime they are available for this small-batch, ginger-spiked jam. It takes about half an hour to prepare. Make a wonderful plum glaze for oven-roasted salmon by melting some of the jam and brushing it on the salmon while it is roasting.

3 cups	chopped purple plums (about 10 to 12 plums)	750 mL
2 cups	granulated sugar	500 mL
4 tsp	lemon juice	20 mL
¼ cup	finely chopped Candied Ginger (page 301) or crystallized ginger	50 mL

1. Place plums and sugar in a deep 8-cup (2 L) microwavable container. Stir in lemon juice.

2. Microwave, uncovered, on High (100%) for 7 minutes, stirring twice. Add ginger; microwave, uncovered, on High for 15 to 18 minutes or until mixture will form a gel*, stirring every 4 minutes.

3. Ladle into sterilized jars and process as directed on page 21 (Shorter Time Processing Procedure).

Makes 2½ cups (625 mL).

TIP   *Each summer, plums arrive in our markets in great variety—bright yellow and green (best known as greengage), iridescent red and dark purple. One fresh plum contains about 35 calories, which compares with 81 calories in a fresh apple and 100 in a fresh pear or banana. Plums are a very good low-calorie snack.*

* To determine when mixture will form a gel, see page 19.

Microwave Peach Jam with Orange Liqueur

Intense peach flavor is highlighted by orange in this elegant and attractive jam.

3 cups	chopped fresh or frozen peaches	750 mL
2 cups	granulated sugar	500 mL
2 tbsp	lemon juice	25 mL
2 tbsp	orange liqueur or frozen orange juice concentrate, thawed	25 mL

1. Place peaches and sugar in a deep 8-cup (2 L) microwavable container. Stir in lemon juice.

2. Microwave, uncovered, on High (100%) for 7 minutes, stirring twice. Microwave, uncovered, on High for 12 to 15 minutes or until mixture will form a gel*, stirring every 4 minutes. Stir in liqueur.

3. Ladle into sterilized jars and process as directed on page 21 (Shorter Time Processing Procedure).

Makes 2 cups (500 mL).

 If peaches are still frozen, you may need to add 2 to 3 minutes to the total cooking time.

Serving Suggestion:

Peach Shake
A marvelous shake is easily made using this jam.
Place 1 cup (250 mL) vanilla frozen yogurt, ½ cup (125 mL) orange juice and ¼ cup (50 mL) Microwave Peach Jam with Orange Liqueur in a blender container. Process until smooth. Add milk or plain yogurt if you prefer a less thick shake.

* To determine when mixture will form a gel, see page 19.

MICROWAVE WINTER PEAR AMARETTO JAM

The pear varieties found in winter, such as Bosc and Anjou, need the moist heat of microwave cooking to transform the relatively dry pears into a delicious jam. The almond of the liqueur highlights the taste of pears.

1½ cups	diced peeled winter pears (Bosc, Anjou)	375 mL
½ cup	chopped peeled tart apple	125 mL
2 tbsp	apple juice, cider or water	25 mL
½	box dry fruit pectin*	½
2 cups	granulated sugar	500 mL
1 tbsp	Amaretto liqueur	15 mL

1. Combine pears, apple, apple juice and pectin in a 3-quart (3 L) microwavable container. Microwave, uncovered, on High (100%) for 6 minutes or until mixture comes to a boil, stirring twice.

2. Add sugar. Microwave, uncovered, on High for 4 minutes or until mixture returns to a full boil and boil hard for 1 minute. Stir in liqueur.

3. Ladle into sterilized jars and process as directed on page 21 (Shorter Time Processing Procedure).

Makes 3 cups (750 mL).

TIP   *The remaining half box of dry fruit pectin can be used to make Mango Plum Jam (page 49).*

BLUEBERRY FREEZER JAM WITH COINTREAU

Orange highlights the intense blueberry taste of this freezer jam. Freezing the jam eliminates cooking and retains the fresh flavor of the fruit.

2½ cups	granulated sugar	625 mL
1½ cups	crushed blueberries	375 mL
	(about 2 cups/500 mL whole fruit)	
1	orange, peeled and finely chopped	1
1 tbsp	Cointreau or other orange liqueur	15 mL
1	pouch liquid fruit pectin	1

1. Place sugar in an ovenproof shallow pan and warm in a 250°F (120°C) oven for 15 minutes. (Warm sugar dissolves better).

2. Combine blueberries, orange and sugar in a large bowl and let stand for 10 minutes, stirring occasionally.

3. Stir in liqueur and pectin, stirring constantly for 3 minutes.

4. Ladle jam into clean jars or plastic containers to within ½ inch (1 cm) of rim. Cover with tight-fitting lids. Label jars and let stand at room temperature until set, up to 24 hours.

5. Refrigerate for up to 3 weeks or freeze for longer storage.

Makes 3 cups (750 mL).

KIWIFRUIT RASPBERRY FREEZER JAM

This colorful combination produces a handsome jam. Fresh mint adds a refreshing note.

3½ cups	granulated sugar	875 mL
1 cup	crushed fresh or frozen raspberries	250 mL
1 cup	finely chopped kiwifruit	175 mL
1	pouch liquid fruit pectin	1
2 tbsp	finely chopped fresh mint (optional)	25 mL
1 tbsp	lemon juice	15 mL

1. Place sugar in an ovenproof shallow pan and warm in a 250°F (120°C) oven for 15 minutes. (Warm sugar dissolves better).

2. Place raspberries and kiwifruit in a large bowl. Stir in sugar and let stand for 10 minutes, stirring occasionally.

3. Add pectin, mint and lemon juice, stirring constantly for 3 minutes.

4. Ladle jam into clean jars or plastic containers to within ½ inch (1 cm) of rim. Cover with tight-fitting lids. Label jars and let stand at room temperature until set, up to 24 hours.

5. Refrigerate for up to 3 weeks or freeze for longer storage.

Makes 4 cups (1 L).

VARIATION:

Kiwifruit Loganberry Freezer Jam
Replace raspberries with same amount of loganberries.

 TIP   *Use a potato masher to crush fruit. Using a food processor will over-process it.*

MANGO BLUEBERRY FREEZER JAM

Capture the fragrant, exotic, sweet-tart flavor of mangoes and combine it with the rich blue color of blueberries in this ambrosial jam. Folded into plain yogurt or spooned over a pudding, it makes a super simple dessert.

2¾ cups	granulated sugar	675 mL
1 cup	finely chopped mangoes	250 mL
	(about 2 mangoes)	
¾ cup	chopped blueberries, fresh or frozen	175 mL
1 tsp	finely grated orange rind	5 mL
1	pouch liquid fruit pectin	1
1½ tbsp	lemon juice	20 mL

1. Place sugar in an ovenproof shallow pan and warm in a 250°F (120°C) oven for 15 minutes. (Warm sugar dissolves better).

2. Combine mangoes, blueberries, orange rind and sugar in a large bowl and let stand for 10 minutes, stirring occasionally.

3. Add pectin and lemon juice, stirring constantly for 3 minutes.

4. Ladle jam into clean jars or plastic containers to within ½ inch (1 cm) of rim. Cover with tight-fitting lids. Label jars and let stand at room temperature until set, up to 24 hours.

5. Refrigerate for up to 3 weeks or freeze for longer storage.

Makes 3½ cups (875 mL).

TIP *To cut a mango, set it upright on a cutting board with the narrow side facing you. Slice off one side, just clearing the long flat seed. Repeat on the opposite side. Using a paring knife, carefully cut the flesh from the skin in a single piece, keeping as close to the skin as possible. Peel skin from the fruit left on the seed, then cut off the flesh.*

MINTED RASPBERRY PEACH FREEZER JAM

The freshness of mint enhances this uncooked classic fruit combination.

3½ cups	granulated sugar	875 mL
1 cup	mashed fresh or frozen unsweetened raspberries	250 mL
⅔ cup	finely chopped peeled peaches (1 large peach)	150 mL
2 tbsp	finely chopped fresh mint	25 mL
2 tbsp	lemon juice	25 mL
1	pouch liquid fruit pectin	1

1. Place sugar in an ovenproof shallow pan and warm in a 250°F (120°C) oven for 15 minutes. (Warm sugar dissolves better).

2. Combine raspberries, peaches, mint and warm sugar in a large bowl and let stand for 10 minutes, stirring occasionally.

3. Add lemon juice and pectin, stirring constantly for 3 minutes.

4. Ladle jam into clean jars or plastic containers to within ½ inch (1 cm) of rim. Cover with tight-fitting lids. Label jars and let stand at room temperature until set, up to 24 hours.

5. Refrigerate for up to 3 weeks or freeze for longer storage.

Makes 4 cups (1 L).

PAPAYA AND PINEAPPLE FREEZER JAM

Uncooked, the fresh flavors of papaya, pineapple and lime bring the taste of the tropics to this pale golden succulent jam. We have used this jam as a dessert topping or folded into plain yogurt as a simple dessert.

3½ cups	granulated sugar	875 mL
1	lime	1
1	papaya, peeled, seeded and finely chopped	1
¾ cup	finely chopped fresh pineapple, peeled and cored	175 mL
1	pouch liquid fruit pectin	1

1. Place sugar in an ovenproof shallow pan and warm in a 250°F (120°C) oven for 15 minutes. (Warm sugar dissolves better).

2. Remove thin outer rind from lime with vegetable peeler and cut into fine strips with scissors or sharp knife; or use a zester. Place lime rind in a small microwavable container with ¼ cup (50 mL) water. Microwave on High (100%) for 1 minute. Drain and discard liquid; reserve rind. Squeeze lime and reserve juice.

3. Place papaya in a 2-cup (500 mL) measuring cup and add enough chopped pineapple to make 1¾ cups (425 mL) fruit. Transfer to a large bowl. Stir in lime rind and warmed sugar and let stand for 10 minutes, stirring occasionally.

4. Stir in 2 tbsp (25 mL) lime juice and pectin, stirring constantly for 3 minutes.

5. Ladle jam into clean jars or plastic containers to within ½ inch (1 cm) of rim. Cover with tight-fitting lids. Label jars and let stand at room temperature until set, up to 24 hours.

6. Refrigerate for up to 3 weeks or freeze for longer storage.

Makes 4 cups (1 L).

Pineapple Orange Rosemary Freezer Jam

The flavor of fresh pineapple combines wonderfully with orange and rosemary to make a delightful golden spread. Fold into plain yogurt for a quick and simple dessert.

3½ cups	granulated sugar	875 mL
1	sweet orange	1
1¼ cups	finely chopped fresh pineapple	300 mL
1	pouch liquid fruit pectin	1
4	sprigs fresh rosemary	4

1. Place sugar in an ovenproof shallow pan and warm in a 250°F (120°C) oven for 15 minutes. (Warm sugar dissolves better).

2. Remove thin outer rind from orange with vegetable peeler and cut into fine strips with scissors or sharp knife; or use a zester. Squeeze juice from orange. Place orange rind and juice in a large bowl. Stir in pineapple and sugar and let stand for 10 minutes, stirring occasionally.

3. Stir in pectin, stirring constantly for 3 minutes.

4. Insert a sprig of rosemary into each jar or plastic container. Ladle jam into jars or plastic containers to within ½ inch (1 cm) of rim. Cover with tight-fitting lids. Label jars and let stand at room temperature until set, up to 24 hours.

5. Refrigerate for up to 3 weeks or freeze for longer storage.

Makes 4 cups (1 L).

CHAPTER TWO

JELLIES MADE EASY

ONE OF the best things about making jellies is their easy preparation—no peeling or coring, just wash, chop and use the lot. Jellies can be made from a variety of fruits and vegetables—berries, pears, apples, crabapples, plums, citrus fruits and sweet and hot peppers. Some of the very tastiest are made with wine and herbs.

Traditionally, jellies are made with the juice from cooked fruit strained through a clean jelly bag. A jelly bag is made of fabric with a sufficiently close weave to remove enough fruit pulp to ensure a clear jelly. You can buy one or you can line a colander or strainer with several layers of cheesecloth or an unused all-purpose cloth. Set the colander over a large bowl, pour in the fruit mixture and allow it to stand until the juice has drained through. This process can require up to several hours, but if you first press the fruit pulp through a coarse sieve to remove the larger solids, the resulting liquid will flow through the cloth much more quickly. The secret to a clear jelly is to let the juice drain through the cloth on its own. Avoid the temptation to squeeze out that last little bit of juice! Add sugar to the strained juice and cook until a gel stage is reached (see page 19). A properly set jelly retains its shape and quiver when removed from the jar.

Many of our recipes make jelly making even easier. They use prepared juices so there is no need for washing, chopping or straining. Peach Amaretto Jelly with Almonds (page 74) uses frozen peach nectar. Apple Cider Cinnamon Jelly (page 68) starts with fresh apple cider. Some herb and wine jellies fall into this "super-simple, quick and easy" category. A few jellies have some suspended fruit or vegetable pieces left in for eye-appeal and flavor. Commercial pectin, or our Homemade Apple Pectin (page 45), must be added to jellies made from juices that have not been cooked with their skins or seeds and to jellies made from fruits containing very little pectin.

Many flavorings can be added to jellies. Scented geranium leaves as well as herbs like lemon, thyme, mint and angelica give exciting interest to herb jellies. Examples of this treatment are our Sherried Rosemary Grape Juice Jelly (page 65) and Basic Herb Wine Jelly (page 67). Rose petals and even fruit leaves such as peach and plum impart an almond flavor. Try adding whole herbs of your choice to wine jellies.

SERVING SUGGESTIONS:

Jellies have so many uses. We love the pepper jellies as appetizers with cream cheese and crackers. Our Cranberry Hot Pepper Jelly (page 70) and our wine jellies go superbly with chicken, turkey and duck. Roasted or broiled meats whether hot or cold, are greatly enhanced by Spiced Apple Jelly (page 69) and Apple Cranberry Wine Jelly (page 65). Of course, sweet jellies such as Tangerine Lemon (page 76), Grapefruit Raspberry Honey (page 71), and Red Currant and Raspberry Jelly (pages 75) go wonderfully on rolls, hot biscuits and muffins. We are sure you will find your own favorite uses.

 TIP   *Give a jar of sparkling jelly as a hostess gift. Wrap it in a square of cellophane tied just above the lid and include the recipe.*

LIST OF RECIPES

Wine Jellies

Wine jelly adds a wonderful flavor note to many meals. This basic recipe can be used with sherry, port, claret or Bordeaux. For a more delicate jelly, use white wine.

Basic Wine Jelly

2 cups	wine	500 mL
¼ cup	strained lemon juice	50 mL
3½ cups	granulated sugar	875 mL
1	pouch liquid fruit pectin	1

1. Place wine, lemon juice and sugar in a large stainless steel or enamel saucepan. Bring to a boil over high heat and boil hard for 1 minute, stirring constantly. Remove from heat and stir in pectin.

2. Ladle into sterilized jars and process as directed on page 21 (Shorter Time Processing Procedure).

Makes 4½ cups (1.125 L).

Cranberry Port Wine Jelly

Be sure to use pure cranberry juice. Beverages labeled "Beverage," "Drink" or "Cocktail" have been diluted and have a less-intense flavor.

1 cup	port or claret	250 mL
1 cup	pure cranberry juice	250 mL
3½ cups	granulated sugar	875 mL
1	pouch liquid fruit pectin	1

Proceed as for Basic Wine Jelly, substituting the cranberry juice for half of the wine.

Makes 4½ cups (1.125 L).

Sour Cherry Hazelnut Conserve (page 104)

Flavored Oils (Chapter 11), Jams (Chapter 1) and Marmalades (Chapter 3)

SHERRIED ROSEMARY GRAPE JUICE JELLY

This delicate jelly has an affinity with poultry. The rosemary flavor also lends itself to pork or a leg of lamb.

1 cup	dry sherry	250 mL
1 cup	white grape juice	250 mL
3½ cups	granulated sugar	875 mL
1	pouch liquid fruit pectin	1
1	stem fresh rosemary, thyme or other fresh herb	1

1. Proceed as for Basic Wine Jelly, substituting grape juice for half of the wine. Add herb to jar before processing.

Makes 4½ cups (1.125 L).

APPLE CRANBERRY WINE JELLY

This special variation of traditional cranberry jelly is quickly prepared.

2½ cups	fresh or frozen cranberries	625 mL
4	large cooking apples, peeled, cored and chopped	4
1 cup	dry white wine	250 mL
1½ cups	granulated sugar	375 mL

1. Combine cranberries, apples and wine in a large stainless steel or enamel saucepan. Bring to a boil over high heat, cover, reduce heat and cook gently for 15 minutes or until fruit is soft. Strain through a sieve, discard pulp and return sieved liquid to saucepan.

2. Add sugar and return to a boil. Boil uncovered, until mixture forms a gel*, approximately 10 minutes, stirring frequently. Remove from heat.

3. Ladle into sterilized jars and process as directed on page 21 (Shorter Time Processing Procedure).

Makes 3 cups (750 mL).

* To determine when mixture will form a gel, see page 19.

JELLIES À L'HERBE

Herbs give unique twists to jellies that make wonderful gifts. Making them is much like making tea: the herbs are steeped in boiling water or wine.

BASIC HERB JELLY

Beautifully simple and sparkling jelly—serve with poultry, cheese and crackers, a cold meat salad plate or sliced meat sandwiches.

1¼ cups	water	300 mL
2 tbsp	fresh herb leaves or 2 tsp (10 mL) dried	25 mL
3½ cups	granulated sugar	875 mL
1 cup	juice	250 mL
2 tbsp	vinegar or lemon juice	25 mL
1	pouch liquid fruit pectin	1

1. Combine water and herb leaves in a small saucepan. Bring mixture to a boil; remove from heat. Cover and allow to steep for 5 minutes. Strain through a lined sieve; discard leaves.

2. Place 1 cup (250 mL) of the liquid in a large stainless steel or enamel saucepan; add sugar, juice and vinegar or lemon juice. Bring to a full boil over high heat and boil hard for 1 minute, stirring constantly. Remove from heat and stir in pectin.

3. Ladle into sterilized jars and process as directed on page 21 (Shorter Time Processing Procedure).

Makes about 4½ cups (1.125 L).

VARIATIONS:

Many juices may be used in making herb jellies. Match the herb and the vinegar to the juice and proceed as above. Some examples are:
Grape juice, thyme and lemon juice
Tomato juice, basil and red wine vinegar
Orange juice, basil and rice vinegar
White grape juice, sage and cider vinegar
Apple juice, mint, thyme, savory, marjoram or oregano and cider vinegar

BASIC HERB WINE JELLY

Use white wine if the jelly is to accompany poultry or pork, or red wine if it is to accompany red meats. Either way, it's a sparkling clear jelly enhanced with the flavor of your favorite herb. Some herbs to try are sage, basil, mint, savory, thyme, marjoram and oregano. The amount used may be increased or decreased according to individual taste preferences.

1¾ cups	dry white or red wine	425 mL
¼ cup	white or red wine vinegar	50 mL
3 tbsp	fresh herb leaves or 1 tbsp (15 mL) dried	45 mL
3½ cups	granulated sugar	875 mL
1	pouch liquid fruit pectin	1

1. Combine wine, vinegar and herb leaves in a large stainless steel or enamel saucepan. Bring mixture to a boil; remove from heat. Cover and allow to steep for 30 minutes to extract flavors.

2. Strain mixture through a lined sieve; discard leaves. Return liquid to saucepan and stir in sugar. Bring to a boil over high heat and boil rapidly for 1 minute, stirring constantly. Remove from heat and stir in pectin.

3. Ladle into sterilized jars and process as directed on page 21 (Shorter Time Processing Procedure).

Makes 4 cups (1 L).

TIP   *Add several garlic cloves to Basic Herb Wine Jelly made with white wine and rosemary for a perfect jelly to serve with a crown roast of lamb or lamb chops.*

APPLE CIDER CINNAMON JELLY

The full-bodied taste of fresh apple cider spiced with cinnamon is marvelous on toast and hot biscuits. Try heating the jelly and serve over pancakes or French toast. Reserve the cinnamon stick and add a small piece to each jar for an attractive garnish and more intense cinnamon flavor.

2½ cups	fresh-pressed apple cider	625 mL
1	stick cinnamon, 4 inches (10 cm), broken into 4 pieces	1
3½ cups	·granulated sugar	875 mL
1	pouch liquid fruit pectin	1

1. Combine cider and cinnamon pieces in a large stainless steel or enamel saucepan. Cover and bring to a boil over high heat, reduce heat and boil gently for 5 minutes. Strain cider through several layers of cheesecloth, reserving cinnamon pieces to add to jars. Rinse saucepan.

2. Measure 2 cups (500 mL) cider and return to saucepan; add sugar. Bring to a full boil over high heat, stirring constantly. Stir in pectin, return to a full boil and boil hard for 1 minute, stirring constantly. Remove from heat.

3. Ladle into sterilized jars, add one piece of cinnamon to each jar and process as directed on page 21 (Shorter Time Processing Procedure).

Makes 4 cups (1 L).

SPICED APPLE JELLY

We adapted this recipe from one Margaret's neighbor makes every fall using her own apples. Don't peel, core or remove the seeds and stems before cooking; they add pectin as well as color and flavor to the jelly. The crabapple variation is wonderful with poultry.

2 lb	apples, cut into large pieces (about 8 cups/2 L)	2 L
6 cups	water	1.5 L
¼ cup	cider vinegar	50 mL
½ tsp	whole cloves	2 mL
2	cinnamon sticks, 3 inches (7.5 cm) long	2
1½ cups	granulated sugar	375 mL

1. Combine apples, water, vinegar, cloves and cinnamon sticks in a large stainless steel or enamel saucepan. Cover and bring to a boil over high heat, reduce heat and boil gently for 30 minutes. Strain mixture through a coarse sieve; discard solids. Pour liquid through a jelly bag.

2. Return strained liquid to pan and add sugar. Bring to a boil and boil rapidly, uncovered, until mixture will form a gel,* about 15 minutes, stirring occasionally. Remove from heat.

3. Ladle into sterilized jars and process as directed on page 21 (Shorter Time Processing Procedure).

Makes 2 cups (500 mL).

VARIATION:

Spiced Crabapple Jelly
Replace apples with the same weight of crabapples.

* To determine when mixture will form a gel, see page 19.

CRANBERRY HOT PEPPER JELLY

The color is as intense as the flavor of this sparkling red jelly. Adding cranberry to popular pepper jelly makes it perfect for the festive season. Keep it on hand for an easy appetizer with cream cheese on crackers, or to accompany any roast meat, especially game such as venison. Our version has medium heat, but you may easily change it by adding or omitting a jalapeño pepper.

1	large sweet red pepper	1
2	jalapeño peppers, seeded, or other hot pepper	2
¼ cup	water	50 mL
¾ cup	cider vinegar	175 mL
¾ cup	frozen cranberry cocktail concentrate, thawed	175 mL
3 cups	granulated sugar	750 mL
1	pouch liquid fruit pectin	1

1. Finely chop sweet and jalapeño peppers in food processor. Place in a small saucepan with water and vinegar. Bring mixture to a boil, cover, reduce heat and boil gently for 10 minutes. Strain mixture through a coarse sieve, pressing with back of a spoon to extract as much liquid as possible; discard solids. Pour liquid through a jelly bag.

2. Place strained liquid, cranberry concentrate and sugar in a medium stainless steel or enamel saucepan. Bring to a full boil over high heat, stirring constantly. Stir in pectin, return to a full boil and boil hard for 1 minute, stirring constantly. Remove from heat.

3. Ladle into sterilized jars and process as directed on page 21 (Shorter Time Processing Procedure).

Makes 3 cups (750 mL).

VARIATION:

Cranberry Hot Pepper Jelly with Balsamic Vinegar
Replace ¼ cup (50 mL) cider vinegar with balsamic vinegar.

GRAPEFRUIT RASPBERRY HONEY JELLY

With the bright color of raspberry and hint of honey, this jelly will become an instant favorite.

2	grapefruit, coarsely chopped	2
3 cups	water	750 mL
3 cups	fresh or frozen unsweetened raspberries	750 mL
3 cups	granulated sugar	750 mL
1 cup	liquid honey	250 mL

1. Place grapefruit and water in a medium stainless steel or enamel saucepan. Bring to a boil over high heat, cover, reduce heat and boil gently for 20 minutes. Add raspberries, return to a boil and boil gently for 5 minutes.

2. Pour fruit through a coarse strainer, pressing pulp to extract juice. Discard solids. Pour liquid through a jelly bag.

3. Return strained liquid to pan and add sugar and honey. Bring to a boil and boil rapidly, uncovered, until mixture will form a gel*, about 15 minutes, stirring occasionally. Remove from heat.

4. Ladle into sterilized jars and process as directed on page 21 (Shorter Time Processing Procedure).

Makes 2 cups (500 mL).

* To determine when mixture will form a gel, see page 19.

JALAPEÑO MINT JELLY

Jalapeño peppers and a double hit of mint liven up traditional mint jelly. Try it with crackers and cheese and with lamb or chicken.

1¼ cups	finely chopped fresh mint, divided	425 mL
1½ cups	water	375 mL
3½ cups	granulated sugar	875 mL
¾ cup	cider vinegar	175 mL
2 tbsp	strained fresh lemon juice	25 mL
2	jalapeño peppers, finely chopped	2
1	pouch liquid fruit pectin	1

1. Bring 1½ cups (375 mL) mint and water to a boil in a small saucepan. Remove from heat, cover and let stand for 30 minutes to steep. Strain through a lined sieve pressing with the back of a spoon to extract as much liquid as possible; discard mint.

2. Combine mint liquid, sugar, vinegar, lemon juice and peppers in a large stainless steel or enamel saucepan. Bring to a full boil over high heat and boil hard for 2 minutes, stirring constantly. Remove from heat; stir in pectin and remaining mint.

3. Ladle into sterilized jars and process as directed on page 21 (Shorter Time Processing Procedure).

Makes 4 cups (1 L).

VARIATION:

Lemon Balm Jelly
Use lemon balm leaves in place of the mint and omit the jalapeño peppers.

SPARKLING SWEET PEPPER JELLY

Pieces of red, yellow and orange pepper sparkle like jewels in this exotic jelly. Our favorite way to serve it is with cream cheese spread on melba toast rounds. We also like it with a sliver of Cheddar cheese on a cracker. If you like your pepper jelly hot, see the variation below.

½ cup	each: evenly diced sweet red, orange and yellow pepper	125 mL
¾ cup	white wine vinegar	175 mL
3 cups	granulated sugar	750 mL
1	pouch liquid fruit pectin	1

1. Combine peppers, vinegar and sugar in a medium stainless steel or enamel saucepan. Bring to a full boil over high heat and boil hard for 1 minute, stirring constantly. Add pectin; return to a boil and boil rapidly for 1 minute. Remove from heat.

2. Ladle into sterilized jars and process as directed on page 21 (Shorter Time Processing Procedure).

Makes 3½ cups (875 mL).

VARIATIONS:

Sparkling Hot Pepper Jelly
Use 2 jalapeño peppers, seeded and diced, to replace the yellow or orange pepper.

Sparkling Apricot Hot Pepper Jelly
Use 2 jalapeño peppers, seeded and diced, to replace the yellow pepper and use ¼ cup (50 mL) chopped dried apricots, soaked in water for 4 to 6 hours, to replace the orange pepper.

PEACH AMARETTO JELLY WITH ALMONDS

While in Arizona, Margaret found a beautiful sparkling peach jelly with floating slices of almonds. This is her version.

2 cups	strained peach nectar	500 mL
¼ cup	strained lemon juice	50 mL
3½ cups	granulated sugar	875 mL
1	pouch liquid fruit pectin	1
2 tbsp	amaretto liqueur	25 mL
¼ cup	sliced almonds	50 mL

1. Combine nectar, lemon juice and sugar in a large stainless steel or enamel saucepan. Bring to a full boil over high heat and boil hard for 1 minute, stirring constantly. Remove from heat and stir in pectin and liqueur.

2. Ladle into sterilized jars. Divide almonds between jars and stir into jelly. Process as directed on page 21 (Shorter Time Processing Procedure).

Makes 4 cups (1 L).

During processing, you will find that the almonds have floated to the top of the jelly. Stir them into the jelly to redistribute them after opening.

Frozen concentrated peach cocktail, which comes in 12-oz/341 mL cans, may be prepared using 2 parts water rather than 3. Use it to replace peach nectar, reducing sugar to 3 cups (750 mL) because the peach cocktail already contains sugar.

Red Currant and Raspberry Jelly

The high pectin content of red currants makes them a perfect partner for raspberries, which have much less pectin. The resulting intense red jelly has an exquisite flavor for serving on hot biscuits or muffins. When melted, it makes a wonderful red-hued glaze for a simple fresh fruit tart. This recipe was inspired by a jelly recipe from Fred Yule, one of Margaret's neighbors.

4 cups	red currants, stemmed	1 L
¾ cup	water	175 mL
4 cups	raspberries	1 L
7 cups	granulated sugar	1.75 L
1	pouch liquid fruit pectin	1

1. Using a potato masher, crush currants in a very large stainless steel or enamel saucepan. Add water and bring to a boil over high heat, reduce heat, cover and boil gently for 10 minutes. Add raspberries, return to a boil and boil gently for 3 minutes.

2. Strain mixture through a coarse sieve, pressing pulp to extract juice; discard solids. Pour juice through a jelly bag. You should have a total of 4 cups (1 L) juice.

3. Combine strained juice and sugar in a very large stainless steel or enamel saucepan. Bring to a boil over high heat and boil hard for 1 minute, stirring constantly. Remove from heat and stir in pectin.

4. Ladle into sterilized jars and process as directed on page 21 (Shorter Time Processing Procedure).

Makes 8 cups (2 L).

Tangerine Lemon Jelly

We love this jewel-like jelly on hot biscuits or with cream cheese and bagels. For a special gift, add a sprig of fresh rosemary to the jelly before processing.

3	lemons	3
9-10	tangerines	9-10
1	box dry fruit pectin	1
4½ cups	granulated sugar	1.125 L

1. Squeeze lemons and tangerines to give 4 cups (1 L) juice. Bring juice to a boil over high heat in a large stainless steel or enamel saucepan, cover, reduce heat and simmer for 10 minutes, stirring occasionally. Remove from heat.

2. Strain juice through a jelly bag. Return strained liquid to saucepan and stir in pectin. Bring to a full boil over high heat, reduce heat and boil gently for 1 minute, stirring constantly. Add sugar, return to a full boil and boil hard for 1 minute, stirring constantly. Remove from heat.

3. Ladle into sterilized jars and process as directed on page 21 (Shorter Time Processing Procedure).

Makes 5½ cups (1.375 L).

TIP *To obtain a very clear jelly without a jelly bag, strain the liquid through a lined sieve. We have found disposable cloth works really well for this.*

TROPICAL FRUIT JELLY

It's our great fortune to have access to the wonderful exotic flavors of tropical fruits. Passion fruit, mango and papaya combine to give this jelly a truly tropical flavor. Passion fruit juice is worth the effort to find. Look in specialty shops selling Indian and Pacific Rim foods. Be sure to buy the one with no added water.

1½ cups	passion fruit juice	375 mL
½	mango, peeled and cubed	½
½	papaya, peeled, seeded and cubed	½
½ cup	water	125 mL
¼ cup	lime juice	50 mL
1 tsp	grated lime rind	5 mL
3½ cups	granulated sugar	875 mL
1	pouch liquid fruit pectin	1

1. Combine passion fruit juice, mango, papaya and water in a large stainless steel or enamel saucepan. Bring to a boil over high heat, reduce heat, cover and boil gently for 15 minutes. Add lime juice and rind. Remove from heat.

2. Strain juice through a coarse sieve, pressing pulp to extract as much liquid as possible; discard solids. Pour juice through a jelly bag (there should be 2 cups/500 mL—if not, top up with extra passion fruit juice).

3. Combine strained liquid and sugar in saucepan. Bring to a full boil over high heat, stirring constantly. Stir in pectin, return to a full boil and boil hard for 1 minute, stirring constantly. Remove from heat.

4. Ladle into sterilized jars and process as directed on page 21 (Shorter Time Processing Procedure).

Makes 4 cups (1 L).

CHAPTER THREE

MARVELOUS MARMALADES

MARMALADES, although similar to jams, always include the pulp of one or more citrus fruits—oranges, lemons, grapefruits, limes and tangerines. The citrus rind is suspended in the mixture to intensify the citrus flavor and to add color and texture. Other fruits are sometimes added to create mouth-watering combinations—for example, try our Blueberry Orange Marmalade or our Pear Apple Ginger Marmalade (pages 81 and 91).

Since citrus fruits are high in pectin, most cooked marmalades require no added pectin to set. The white portion of the rind and the seeds, which are used in many marmalade recipes, is where most of the pectin is found. The rind and seeds are discarded after cooking if their bitter flavor is not wanted in the finished marmalade. Commercial pectin, however, is needed for our Citrus Freezer Marmalade (page 95). Since only the thin outer rind of the citrus fruit is used, it does not contain sufficient pectin to make the gel.

The very best time to make marmalade is during the winter when citrus fruits are at their best quality and lowest price. The bitter Seville-type oranges are available only for a short time during late January and early February. However, you can prolong this short season by freezing the oranges whole and then making our superb Traditional English Seville Marmalade (page 80) when time permits.

Marmalades do take a bit of time, but are well worth the effort. Citrus zesters, vegetable peelers, juice extractors and food processors take much of the labor out of their preparation.

Not all marmalades are bittersweet, as many people think. They range from a sweet Microwave Gingered Peach Marmalade (page 94) to an Old-Fashioned Tomato Marmalade (page 93) that even grandma would be proud of. To make a marmalade that is a bit more upbeat, try Mango (page 90) or Lemon Ginger Zucchini (page 89).

SERVING SUGGESTIONS:

Use marmalades in sweet bread recipes such as Marmalade Fruit Muffins (page 314) for flavor and moistness. Enjoy Marmalade Sauce (page 311) on waffles or pancakes. Serve Blueberry Orange Marmalade (page 81) to people who are not fond of the more bitter pure citrus ones. And, of course, most of us adore marmalade on our breakfast toast.

LIST OF RECIPES

TRADITIONAL ENGLISH SEVILLE MARMALADE

Don't be put off by the taste of fresh Seville-type oranges. Because of its high acid content, the Seville is not an eating orange. Yet its bitterness is magically transformed into a traditional English-style marmalade. Seville-type oranges are generally available in January and February, so mark your calendar to make a batch or two to enjoy throughout the year.

4	Seville-type oranges	4
2	lemons, very thinly sliced	2
4 cups	water	1 L
¼ tsp	baking soda	1 mL
4 cups	granulated sugar	1 L

1. Remove thin outer rind from oranges with vegetable peeler and cut into fine strips with scissors or sharp knife; or use a zester. Place rind, lemons and water in a very large stainless steel or enamel saucepan. Bring to a boil over high heat, cover, reduce heat and boil gently for 25 minutes, stirring occasionally.

2. Remove and discard remaining white rind from oranges. Cut oranges in half. Working over a bowl to catch juices, remove seeds with a sharp knife or fork. Place orange halves and juice in a food processor or blender and process until finely chopped.

3. Add chopped pulp and baking soda to lemon mixture in saucepan. Bring to a boil over high heat, reduce heat, cover and boil gently for 20 minutes, stirring frequently.

4. Add sugar to fruit mixture. Return to a boil and boil rapidly, uncovered, until mixture will form a gel*, about 20 minutes, stirring frequently. Remove from heat.

5. Ladle into sterilized jars and process as directed on page 21 (Shorter Time Processing Procedure).

Makes about 6½ cups (1.625 L).

 TIP *If you are using frozen Seville-type oranges, remove the rind from the orange while it is still frozen.*

* To determine when mixture will form a gel, see page 19.

BLUEBERRY ORANGE MARMALADE

Blueberries and citrus enhanced with a hint of cinnamon make this marmalade quite unusual. The recipe is adapted from one developed by the Wild Blueberry Producers Association of Nova Scotia.

1	small orange	1
1	lemon	1
2 cups	water	500 mL
1	cinnamon stick, about 3 inches (7.5 cm) long	1
2 cups	fresh or frozen wild blueberries	500 mL
2 cups	granulated sugar	500 mL

1. Squeeze juice from orange and lemon, including any pulp. Discard seeds and set juice aside. Slice rinds into very thin slices. Place rinds, water and cinnamon in a large stainless steel or enamel saucepan. Bring to a boil over high heat, reduce heat, cover and boil gently for 25 minutes or until rinds are very tender. Remove and discard cinnamon stick.

2. Add blueberries and reserved juice; return to a boil, cover and boil gently for 10 minutes.

3. Add sugar; bring to a boil and boil rapidly, uncovered, until mixture will form a gel*, about 15 minutes, stirring frequently. Remove from heat.

4. Ladle into sterilized jars and process as directed on page 21 (Shorter Time Processing Procedure).

Makes 3 cups (750 mL).

* To determine when mixture will form a gel, see page 19.

BLOOD ORANGE PORT MARMALADE

The intense colors of blood oranges and port wine combine to give this unique marmalade a beautiful deep ruby color. Use this marmalade as a baste for chicken or fish or invite it to the breakfast table.

2	blood oranges	2
1	lemon	1
1 cup	water	250 mL
½ cup	port wine	125 mL
1¼ cups	granulated sugar	300 mL

1. Remove thin outer rind from oranges with a vegetable peeler and cut into fine strips with scissors or sharp knife; or use a zester. Place in a large stainless steel or enamel saucepan. Squeeze juice from oranges, discarding rind and seeds. Add juice and any pulp to saucepan.

2. Squeeze juice from lemon and slice rind into thin slices. Add lemon juice, rind, water and wine to saucepan. Bring to a boil over high heat, reduce heat, cover and boil gently for 30 minutes.

3. Add sugar, bring to a boil and boil rapidly, uncovered, until mixture will form a gel*, about 15 minutes, stirring frequently. Remove from heat.

4. Ladle into sterilized jars and process as directed on page 21 (Shorter Time Processing Procedure).

Makes 2 cups (500 mL).

SERVING SUGGESTION:

Marmalade Cream
Any marmalade may be used to make this accompaniment for fresh fruit, although Blood Orange Port Marmalade is especially tasty.
Process 1 cup (250 mL) cottage cheese or low-fat ricotta in a blender or food processor until smooth. Remove and stir in ⅓ cup (75 mL) marmalade, 1 tbsp (15 mL) orange liqueur or concentrated orange juice, and 1 square semisweet chocolate, grated. Cover and refrigerate. Serve as a dip or spoon over fresh strawberries, melon, peaches or a fruit of your choice.
Makes about 1¼ cups (300 mL).

* To determine when mixture will form a gel, see page 19.

CRANBERRY ORANGE MARMALADE

The shiny scarlet cranberry lends a tartness to complement the orange of this marmalade. Make this marmalade when cranberries are at their peak between Thanksgiving and Christmas. But since cranberries freeze well, you can also make this marmalade year round.

2	medium oranges	2
1	lemon	1
3 cups	water	750 mL
2 cups	fresh or frozen cranberries	500 mL
4 cups	granulated sugar	1 L

1. Remove thin outer rind from oranges and lemon with vegetable peeler and cut into very fine strips with scissors or sharp knife; or use a zester. Place rind and water in a large stainless steel or enamel saucepan. Bring to a boil over high heat, cover, reduce heat and boil gently for 20 minutes.

2. Remove and discard remaining white rind and seeds from oranges and lemon. Finely chop pulp and cranberries in a food processor or blender and add to saucepan. Bring to a boil over high heat; reduce heat, cover and boil gently for 10 minutes, stirring occasionally.

3. Add sugar to fruit mixture. Return to a boil over high heat and boil rapidly, uncovered, until mixture will form a gel*, about 20 minutes, stirring frequently. Remove from heat.

4. Ladle into sterilized jars and process as directed on page 21 (Shorter Time Processing Procedure).

Makes about 5 cups (1.25 L).

* To determine when mixture will form a gel, see page 19.

FRESH MANDARIN ORANGE MARMALADE

This delicate, fresh-tasting orange marmalade appeals to those who dislike the intense flavor of traditional marmalades. Clementines, close cousins to the mandarin orange, are often less expensive and just as flavorful. The Fresh Mandarin Orange Cranberry Marmalade (below) makes a festive holiday spread and an attractive gift.

3	mandarin or clementine oranges	3
1	lemon	1
1 cup	water	250 mL
1¼ cups	granulated sugar	425 mL

1. Remove peel from oranges and slice thinly. Place in a small stainless steel or enamel saucepan. Remove thin outer rind from lemon with a vegetable peeler and cut into fine strips with scissors or sharp knife; or use a zester. Add rind and water to saucepan. Bring to a boil over high heat, reduce heat, cover and boil gently for 20 minutes.

2. Remove and discard white rind and seeds from lemon. Chop orange and lemon pulp finely in a food processor or with a sharp knife. Add to saucepan, return to a boil, cover and boil gently for 20 minutes.

3. Add sugar, return to a boil and boil rapidly, uncovered, until mixture will form a gel*, about 10 minutes, stirring frequently. Remove from heat.

4. Ladle into sterilized jars and process as directed on page 21 (Shorter Time Processing Procedure).

Makes 2 cups (500 mL).

VARIATION:

Fresh Mandarin Orange Cranberry Marmalade
Add ¼ cup (50 mL) chopped Dried Cranberries (page 302) to marmalade a few minutes before it reaches the gel stage.

* To determine when mixture will form a gel, see page 19.

BRANDIED PROCESSOR GRAPEFRUIT MARMALADE

Imagine making a marmalade with no chopping or slicing! Just place all the fruit in a food processor and process. A splash of brandy and you have a gourmet spread that is an ideal gift.

2	small grapefruit (about ½ lb/250 g each)	2
1	lemon	1
2½ cups	water	625 mL
3¾ cups	granulated sugar	925 mL
2 tbsp	brandy	25 mL

1. Cut grapefruit and lemon into large pieces. Remove seeds and place in a tea ball or tie in a square of cheesecloth; set aside. Place fruit in a food processor and pulse until very finely chopped. You should have 2½ cups (625 mL) chopped fruit.

2. Place fruit and seeds in a large stainless steel or enamel saucepan. Add water, bring to a boil over high heat, reduce heat, cover and boil gently for 25 minutes. Remove and discard seeds.

3. Add sugar and bring to a full boil and boil rapidly, uncovered, until mixture will form a gel*, about 20 minutes, stirring frequently. Remove from heat and stir in brandy.

4. Ladle into sterilized jars and process as directed on page 21 (Shorter Time Processing Procedure).

Makes 4 cups (1 L)

* To determine when mixture will form a gel, see page 19.

RUBY-RED GRAPEFRUIT MARMALADE

Eat your grapefruit on your toast? You certainly can with this grapefruit marmalade.
The ruby-red fruit makes a delicious and attractive delicate pink marmalade.

3	pink grapefruit	3
2	lemons	2
3 cups	water	750 mL
3½ cups	granulated sugar	875 mL

1. Remove thin outer rind from grapefruit and lemons with vegetable peeler and cut
   into fine strips with scissors or sharp knife; or use a zester. Place rind and water in a
   large stainless steel or enamel saucepan. Bring to a boil over high heat; cover,
   reduce heat and boil gently for 20 minutes.

2. Remove and discard remaining white rind and seeds from fruit. Finely chop pulp in
   a food processor or blender and add to saucepan. Bring to a boil over high heat,
   reduce heat, cover and boil gently for 10 minutes, stirring frequently.

3. Add sugar to fruit. Return to a boil over high heat and boil rapidly, uncovered, until
   mixture will form a gel*, about 30 minutes, stirring frequently. Remove from heat.

4. Ladle into sterilized jars and process as directed on page 21 (Shorter Time
   Processing Procedure).

Makes 4½ cups (1.125 L).

VARIATION:

Spirited Marmalades
*Liqueurs, rum, brandy, whiskey or nuts turn marmalade into an elegant and luscious
breakfast preserve.*
When the mixture will form a gel, add 2 tbsp (25 mL) of the chosen spirit or nuts and
cook 5 minutes longer before bottling.

* To determine when mixture will form a gel, see page 19.

TANGERINE GRAPEFRUIT MARMALADE

Tangerines, grapefruit and lemons give this tangy marmalade its unique flavor. As with many marmalades, this one may require several days to set.

2	tangerines	2
2	lemons	2
1	small grapefruit	1
3 cups	water	750 mL
2½ cups	granulated sugar	625 mL

1. Peel tangerines and slice rind thinly. Place rind in a large stainless steel or enamel saucepan. Remove thin outer rind from lemons and grapefruit with a vegetable peeler and cut into fine strips with scissors or sharp knife; or use a zester. Add to saucepan. Remove and discard thick white rind from grapefruit and lemons.

2. Cut all fruit pulp into large pieces and remove all seeds, being careful to catch all juice. Finely chop all fruit pulp in a food processor or blender and reserve. Place seeds in a tea ball or tie in a square of cheesecloth and add to saucepan. Add water, bring to a boil over high heat, reduce heat, cover and boil gently for 20 minutes.

3. Add reserved fruit pulp to saucepan and return to a boil. Cover and boil gently for 20 minutes. Remove and discard seeds.

4. Add sugar to saucepan and return to a boil; boil rapidly, uncovered, until mixture will form a gel*, about 15 minutes, stirring frequently. Remove from heat.

5. Ladle into sterilized jars and process as directed on page 21 (Shorter Time Processing Procedure).

Makes 3½ cups (875 mL).

* To determine when mixture will form a gel, see page 19.

FIVE FRUIT MARMALADE

In early winter when honey tangerines, grapefruit, lemons, limes and sweet oranges are at their best, make this tangy variation of a traditional marmalade. Don't just eat it at breakfast. Try it as a glaze on chicken breasts, baked ham and roasted pork.

2	lemons	2
2	limes	2
2–3	medium oranges	2–3
1	grapefruit	1
2	tangerines, peeled	2
4 cups	water	1 L
¼ tsp	baking soda	1 mL
5½ cups	sugar	1.375 L

1. Remove thin outer rind from lemons, limes, 2 oranges and grapefruit with vegetable peeler and cut into fine strips with scissors or sharp knife; or use a zester. Place in a very large stainless steel or enamel saucepan. Remove the white rind in large pieces from lemons, oranges and grapefruit and place in saucepan. Add water; bring to a boil over high heat, cover, reduce heat and boil gently for 25 minutes.

2. Remove and discard remaining white rind from limes. Finely chop all fruit pulp in a food processor or blender; it should measure 4 cups (1 L). (Add the chopped pulp of the remaining orange if needed). Add fruit and baking soda to saucepan. Bring to a boil over high heat, cover, reduce heat and boil gently for 20 minutes, stirring frequently. Using tongs, remove and discard the large pieces of rind.

3. Add sugar to saucepan and return to a boil, stirring constantly. Boil rapidly, uncovered, until mixture will form a gel*, about 30 minutes, stirring frequently. Remove from heat.

4. Ladle into sterilized jars and process as directed on page 21 (Shorter Time Processing Procedure).

Makes about 6 cups (1.5 L).

 TIP *Use Five-Fruit Marmalade to make Marmalade Squares (page 339).*

* To determine when mixture will form a gel, see page 19.

LEMON GINGER ZUCCHINI MARMALADE

Fresh ginger combines with lemon to give a magnificent zing to this marmalade. It's a nice change from the sweeter types. Chop the ginger finely for a stronger flavor.

3	lemons	3
1	medium orange	1
2½ cups	water	625 mL
½ cup	chopped fresh peeled gingerroot	125 mL
1 cup	shredded zucchini	250 mL
4½ cups	granulated sugar	1.125 L

1. Remove thin outer rind from lemons and orange with vegetable peeler and cut into fine strips with scissors or sharp knife; or use a zester. Place in a large stainless steel or enamel saucepan. Remove the remaining white rind in large pieces and add to saucepan. Stir in water and gingerroot. Bring to a boil over high heat, cover, reduce heat and boil gently for 25 minutes. Using tongs, remove and discard white rind.

2. Finely chop fruit pulp in a food processor or blender. Add pulp and zucchini to saucepan. Bring to a boil over high heat, reduce heat, cover and boil gently for 20 minutes, stirring occasionally.

3. Add sugar to fruit mixture. Return to a boil and boil rapidly, uncovered, until mixture will form a gel*, about 30 minutes, stirring frequently.

4. Ladle into sterilized jars and process as directed on page 21 (Shorter Time Processing Procedure).

Makes about 4½ cups (1.125 L)

* To determine when mixture will form a gel, see page 19.

MANGO MARMALADE

The exotic sweet-tart flavor of mango permeates this tropical marmalade.

2	lemons, very thinly sliced	2
2 cups	water	500 mL
2	mangoes, peeled and thinly sliced	2
2 cups	granulated sugar	500 mL

1. Combine lemons and water in a medium stainless steel or enamel saucepan. Bring to a boil over high heat, cover, reduce heat and boil gently for 25 minutes, stirring occasionally.

2. Add mangoes to saucepan. Bring to a boil over high heat, stirring constantly; reduce heat, cover and boil gently for 20 minutes, stirring occasionally.

3. Stir in sugar. Return to a boil and boil rapidly, uncovered, until mixture will form a gel*, about 15 minutes, stirring frequently.

4. Ladle into sterilized jars and process as directed on page 21 (Shorter Time Processing Procedure).

Makes about 3 cups (750 mL).

* To determine when mixture will form a gel, see page 19.

PEAR APPLE GINGER MARMALADE

This unusual combination of pears and apples produces a very fresh-tasting marmalade.

2	lemons	2
1½ cups	water	375 mL
4 cups	sliced peeled pears	1 L
4 cups	sliced peeled apples	1 L
¼ tsp	baking soda	1 mL
4 cups	granulated sugar	1 L
3 tbsp	finely chopped Candied Ginger (page 301) or crystallized ginger	45 mL

1. Remove thin outer rind from lemons with a vegetable peeler and cut into fine strips with scissors or a sharp knife; or use a zester. Place in a large stainless steel or enamel saucepan. Remove white rind in large pieces from lemons and place in saucepan. Add water; bring to a boil over high heat, cover, reduce heat and boil gently for 20 minutes.

2. Finely chop lemon pulp in a food processor or with a sharp knife. Add lemon, pears, apples and baking soda to saucepan. Bring to a boil over high heat, cover, reduce heat and boil gently for 20 minutes, stirring frequently. Using tongs, remove and discard the large pieces of rind.

3. Add sugar and ginger to saucepan. Return to a boil over high heat and boil rapidly, uncovered, until mixture will form a gel*, about 20 minutes, stirring frequently. Remove from heat.

4. Ladle into sterilized jars and process as directed on page 21 (Shorter Time Processing Procedure).

Makes about 5½ cups (1.375 L).

* To determine when mixture will form a gel, see page 19.

Fresh Pineapple Marmalade with Lemon

Be sure your pineapple is fully ripe to best enjoy the flavor of this wonderful marmalade. It should be slightly soft to the touch with a strong color and no sign of green.

2	lemons	2
2 cups	chopped fresh pineapple, peeled and cored (about ½ pineapple)	500 mL
2½ cups	water	625 mL
3 cups	granulated sugar	750 mL

1. Remove thin outer rind from lemons with vegetable peeler and cut into fine strips with scissors or sharp knife; or use a zester. Place in a large stainless steel or enamel saucepan. Remove and discard remaining white rind and seeds.

2. Finely chop lemon and pineapple in a food processor or blender. Add fruit and water to saucepan. Bring to a boil over high heat, cover, reduce heat and boil gently for 20 minutes, stirring frequently.

3. Add sugar to saucepan, return to a boil over high heat and boil rapidly, uncovered, until mixture will form a gel*, about 35 minutes, stirring frequently. Remove from heat.

4. Ladle into sterilized jars and process as directed on page 21 (Shorter Time Processing Procedure).

Makes 3½ cups (875 mL).

* To determine when mixture will form a gel, see page 19.

OLD-FASHIONED TOMATO MARMALADE

Tomatoes impart a delicate fresh flavor to this preserve that is unique among marmalades. It's John Howard's family recipe. A variation adds chopped gingerroot during the cooking for a marmalade that is extra-special served with chicken, pork or fish.

5 cups	**coarsely chopped peeled tomatoes**	**1.25 L**
	(about 2½ lb/2 kg)	
2	**large oranges**	2
1	**lemon**	1
4 cups	**granulated sugar**	1 L

1. Place tomatoes in a very large stainless steel or enamel saucepan.

2. Halve and seed oranges and lemon. Finely chop fruit in food processor or blender and add to tomatoes. Bring mixture to a full boil over high heat. Slowly add sugar, stirring until sugar is completely dissolved. Return to a boil and boil rapidly until mixture will form a gel*, about 1 hour, stirring frequently. Remove from heat.

3. Ladle into sterilized jars and process as directed on page 21 (Shorter Time Processing Procedure).

Makes about 6 cups (1.5 L).

VARIATION:

Gingered Tomato Marmalade
Add 3 tbsp (45 mL) finely chopped peeled gingerroot during cooking.

* To determine when mixture will form a gel, see page 19.

MICROWAVE GINGERED PEACH MARMALADE

Ginger adds a peppery pungency to the fresh peach flavor of this delightful marmalade. Freezing peaches in season allows us to make this small-batch microwave marmalade in the winter when oranges and lemons are at their best.

1	medium orange	1
1	lemon	1
½ cup	water or white wine	125 mL
2 cups	finely chopped peeled peaches, fresh or frozen	500 mL
2 cups	granulated sugar	500 mL
2 tbsp	finely chopped Candied Ginger (page 301) or crystallized ginger	25 mL

1. Remove thin outer rind from orange and lemon with a vegetable peeler and cut into fine strips with scissors or sharp knife; or use a zester. Place rinds and water in a deep 8-cup (2L) microwavable container. Microwave, covered, on High (100%), for 5 minutes, stirring once. Microwave on Medium High (70%) for 5 minutes.

2. Meanwhile, remove and discard white rind and seeds from orange and lemon. Chop orange and lemon pulp finely in a food processor or with a sharp knife. Add to rind mixture. Microwave, covered, on High for 5 minutes, stirring once.

3. Add peaches, sugar and ginger. Microwave, uncovered, on High for 6 minutes, stirring every 3 minutes. Microwave on High for 12 to 15 minutes or until mixture will form a gel*, stirring every 4 minutes.

4. Ladle into sterilized jars and process as directed on page 21 (Shorter Time Processing Procedure).

Makes 2½ cups (625 mL).

* To determine when mixture will form a gel, see page 19.

CITRUS FREEZER MARMALADE

Remember this easy recipe anytime you crave the fresh taste of citrus on your breakfast toast.

4 cups	granulated sugar	1 L
¼ cup	very thinly sliced thin outer orange rind*	50 mL
2 tbsp	very thinly sliced thin outer lemon rind*	25 mL
1½ cups	diced orange pieces (about 3 oranges)	375 mL
¼ cup	diced lemon pieces (about 1 lemon)	50 mL
¼ cup	lemon juice	50 mL
1	pouch liquid fruit pectin	1

1. Place sugar in an ovenproof shallow pan and heat in a 250°F (120°C) oven for 15 minutes to warm sugar. (Warm sugar dissolves better).

2. Place orange and lemon rind in a small saucepan, cover with cold water, bring to a boil over high heat, reduce heat, cover and boil gently for 15 minutes or until tender; drain.

3. Combine orange and lemon pieces, rind and sugar in a large bowl. Allow to stand for 10 minutes, stirring occasionally.

4. Add lemon juice and pectin; stir constantly for 3 minutes.

5. Ladle marmalade into clean jars or plastic containers to within ½ inch (1 cm) of top rim. Cover with tight-fitting lids. Wipe jars, label and let stand at room temperature until set, up to 24 hours.

6. Store in refrigerator for up to 3 weeks or freeze for longer storage.

Makes 4½ cups (1.125 L).

TIP

Remove the thin outer rind from lemons and oranges with a vegetable peeler and cut into fine strips with scissors or a sharp knife. A handy tool called a zester makes an easy job of removing the colored outside rind or zest without including the more bitter layer underneath.

CHAPTER FOUR

CONSERVES, BUTTERS AND CURDS

CONSERVES are jams garnished with nuts—walnuts, pecans, and almonds—and sometimes with dried fruits. Often more than one fruit is used to give a rich, flavorful spread. It generally isn't necessary to add commercial pectin, since many fruits in combination often produce enough natural pectin to form a light gel.

Most of the summer fruits, such as cherries and blueberries, as well as fall cranberries, apples, pears and plums, lend themselves well to conserves. In an earlier era, conserves were often eaten as a dessert. Today, they are more commonly enjoyed as either a dessert sauce or a spread. And, in some cases, they are served as a savory accompaniment to meats: Apricot Grand Marnier Conserve (page 98) is a delicious example.

Generally, conserves are made the same way as jams. When dried fruits are called for, it is best to soak them for anywhere from a few hours to overnight. They will swell and soften as they absorb water and give a much better final yield after soaking.

Softer, fully sun-ripened fruits are the best choice for fruit butters and are made by cooking fruit until it is very soft, and then puréeing it in a blender or food processor. Sugar and often some spices are then added and the mixture cooked until very thick.

Fruit butters have that great creamy taste associated with their namesake—butter—but contain no fat. Like butter, they can be used in baking to partially or completely replace the fat. Bran Ginger Muffins and Light Chocolate Brownies (pages 312 and 337) use this increasingly popular lower-fat style of cooking. Served with nippy cheeses, like Cheddar or Stilton, and plain crackers, fruit butters become an easy snack or an elegant dessert. Some make fine accompaniments to savory dishes.

Curds, commonplace in an earlier day, are gaining in popularity as refreshing additions to other foods. The traditional lemon curd has been updated with less fat and a far easier microwave cooking method (page 115). Microwave Orange Curd with Candied Peel (page 116) is a wonderful variation of this traditional treat.

It is best to make fruit curds in small amounts to store in half-pint (250 mL) jars. Curds may be kept refrigerated for 3 weeks, but their fresh taste fades quickly and they are better eaten sooner than later. Freeze them for extended storage, keeping them ready for a fast defrost before using as an easy dessert.

SERVING SUGGESTIONS:

We think conserves are among the very best items for gift giving. They offer a special touch of luxury that makes them a bit more special than other spreads. Conserves can be served with a plain cookie and a piece of Brie or Camembert cheese for afternoon tea.

Curds are beginning to show up in fashionable restaurants. Fancy bakeshops are using them as fillings for meringue shells and spreading them between cake layers. And we love spooning a dollop on waffles for an easy dessert.

 Wrap a jar in a seasonal fabric, tie with a ribbon and attach the recipe and you have a wonderful gift.

LIST OF RECIPES

APRICOT GRAND MARNIER CONSERVE

A beautiful golden color, this conserve follows through with great apricot and orange flavors. Use as a savory accompaniment to meats, or to top piping-hot biscuits or crispy herb toast. For a simple yet splendid main dish, try it in Apricot Sauce for Chicken (page 324).

2 cups	diced dried apricots	500 mL
4½ cups	water	1.125 L
1	large tart apple, peeled, cored and chopped	1
1 tsp	finely grated lemon rind	5 mL
¼ cup	lemon juice	50 mL
4 cups	granulated sugar	1 L
⅓ cup	Grand Marnier or orange juice concentrate	75 mL
½ cup	slivered almonds	125 mL

1. Place apricots and water in a large stainless steel or enamel saucepan. Cover and let stand for at least 4 hours or overnight.

2. Add apple, lemon rind and lemon juice. Bring to a full boil over high heat, reduce heat, cover and boil gently for about 15 minutes or until fruit is tender, stirring occasionally.

3. Add sugar to saucepan. Return to a boil, reduce heat and boil gently, uncovered, until mixture will form a light gel*, about 25 minutes, stirring occasionally.

4. Add liqueur, return to a boil and boil gently for 5 minutes. Remove pan from heat and stir in almonds.

5. Ladle into sterilized jars and process as directed on page 21 (Shorter Time Processing Procedure).

Makes 5 cups (1.25 L).

 TIP *The dried apricots are soaked in water to soften them and obtain a better cooked yield.*

* To determine when mixture will form a gel, see page 19.

MAPLE BLUEBERRY CONSERVE WITH WALNUTS

Any kind of blueberries, especially wild ones, make a marvelous conserve. Combine this with the nectar of the maple tree and you have a real New England treat. Fold it into yogurt for a pancake or waffle topping, or just spread it on toast or muffins.

2 cups	fresh or frozen blueberries, crushed	500 mL
½ cup	water	125 mL
¼ cup	maple syrup	50 mL
1 tbsp	lemon juice	15 mL
1 cup	granulated sugar	250 mL
½ cup	raisins	125 mL
¼ cup	chopped walnuts	50 mL
½ tsp	each: ground allspice and ginger	2 mL

1. Combine blueberries, water, maple syrup and lemon juice in a medium stainless steel or enamel saucepan. Bring to a boil over high heat, cover, reduce heat and boil gently for about 5 minutes or until fruit is tender, stirring occasionally.

2. Stir in sugar and raisins. Return to a boil, reduce heat and boil gently, uncovered, until mixture will form a light gel*, about 15 minutes, stirring occasionally. Remove from heat and stir in walnuts, allspice and ginger.

3. Ladle into sterilized jars and process as directed on page 21 (Shorter Time Processing Procedure).

Makes 1½ cups (375 mL).

VARIATION:

Blueberry Honey
Another blueberry pleasure for morning toast.
Finely chop ½ cup (125 mL) blueberries in a food processor. Add 1 cup (250 mL) creamed honey and pulse until blended. Store in a tightly sealed container.
Makes 1⅓ cups (325 mL).

* To determine when mixture will form a gel, see page 19.

BRANDIED CRANBERRY CONSERVE

This spirited conserve with the bright taste of cranberries is adapted from a recipe given to Ellie by her professor at the University of Wisconsin, Dr. Maxine McDivitt, who has made the recipe for years to give as Christmas gifts to faculty and friends.

1	small orange	1
1	cinnamon stick, about 4 inches (10 cm) long	1
3	whole cloves	3
½ cup	water	125 mL
1 tbsp	lemon juice	15 mL
3 cups	cranberries, fresh or frozen	750 mL
1½ cups	granulated sugar	375 mL
⅓ cup	brandy	75 mL
¼ cup	slivered almonds	50 mL

1. Finely chop orange in a food processor. Combine with cinnamon stick, cloves, water and lemon juice in a medium stainless steel or enamel saucepan. Bring to a boil over medium-high heat, reduce heat, cover and boil gently for 10 minutes. Remove cinnamon and cloves.

2. Add cranberries and sugar. Return to a boil, reduce heat and boil gently, uncovered, until berries pop and mixture will form a light gel*, about 5 minutes, stirring frequently. Remove from heat and cool slightly; stir in brandy and almonds.

3. Ladle into sterilized jars and process as directed on page 21 (Shorter Time Processing Procedure).

Makes 3½ cups (875 mL).

* To determine when mixture will form a gel, see page 19.

CRANBERRY PORT CONSERVE

In memory of a good friend, Jane Hope, a Toronto home economist, this recipe was inspired using one of our favorite festive-season fruits, cranberries. It makes a dandy gift any time of the year for serving with hot tea biscuits, game or poultry. We remember her again with this wonderful recipe.

4 cups	fresh or frozen cranberries	1 L
2 cups	granulated sugar	500 mL
¾ cup	port	175 mL
½ cup	finely chopped peeled orange	125 mL
⅓ cup	raisins	75 mL
¼ cup	chopped walnuts	50 mL

1. Combine cranberries, sugar and port in a large stainless steel or enamel saucepan. Bring to a full boil over high heat and cook, uncovered, until berries pop.

2. Add orange and raisins. Return to a boil, reduce heat and boil gently, uncovered, until mixture will form a light gel*, about 15 minutes, stirring occasionally. Remove from heat and stir in nuts.

3. Ladle into sterilized jars and process as directed on page 21 (Shorter Time Processing Procedure).

Makes 4 cups (1 L).

VARIATION:

Raspberry Honey with Chambord
A delightful fruit honey with toast.
Stir together ¼ cup (50 mL) sieved fresh or frozen unsweetened raspberries, 1 tbsp (15mL) Chambord or Raspberry Schnapps and 1 cup (250 mL) creamed honey. Store in a tightly sealed container.
Makes 1 cup (250 mL).

  TIP   *Cranberry Port Conserve makes a delicious appetizer cheese spread (page 316).*

* To determine when mixture will form a gel, see page 19.

KIWIFRUIT CRANBERRY CONSERVE

Tart dried cranberries add a crimson touch to kiwifruit's cool green color and subtle sweet-tart flavor in this attractive sweet-and-sour conserve.

1¼ cups	finely chopped kiwifruit (about 8 kiwifruits)	425 mL
⅓ cup	water	75 mL
¼ cup	fresh lime juice	50 mL
¼ cup	dried cranberries	50 mL
1¾ cups	granulated sugar	425 mL
¼ cup	toasted pine nuts *	50 mL
⅛ tsp	ground nutmeg	0.5 mL

1. Place kiwifruit, water, lime juice and cranberries in a medium stainless steel or enamel saucepan. Bring to a boil over high heat, reduce heat, cover and boil gently for 10 minutes or until fruit is tender.

2. Add sugar. Return to a boil, reduce heat and boil gently, uncovered, until mixture will form a light gel**, about 15 minutes, stirring frequently. Remove from heat.

3. Ladle into sterilized jars and process as directed on page 21 (Shorter Time Processing Procedure).

Makes 2½ cups (625 mL).

To toast pine nuts, place on a shallow microwavable dish and microwave at Medium (50%) until lightly browned, stirring frequently.

** To determine when mixture will form a gel, see page 19.

KIWIFRUIT HONEY ALMOND CONSERVE

Sliced almonds suspended in an emerald gel entice us to taste this luxurious teaming of kiwifruit, honey and almonds. Amaretto adds a nice flavor note and a softer texture.

1½ cups	diced peeled kiwifruit	375 mL
1 cup	diced peeled and cored apple	250 mL
1	lemon	1
¼ cup	water	50 mL
⅔ cup	granulated sugar	150 mL
⅔ cup	liquid honey	150 mL
½ cup	raisins	125 mL
½ cup	sliced almonds	125 mL
2 tbsp	Amaretto liqueur (optional)	25 mL

1. Place kiwifruit and apple in a medium stainless steel or enamel saucepan.

2. Remove thin outer rind from lemon with vegetable peeler and cut into fine strips with scissors or sharp knife; or use a zester and add to saucepan. Remove and discard the remaining white rind. Finely chop the pulp with a knife or in a food processor with on/off motion. Add pulp and water to saucepan. Bring to a boil over high heat, cover, reduce heat and boil gently for 10 minutes or until fruit is tender.

3. Stir in sugar, honey and raisins. Return to a boil, reduce heat and boil gently, uncovered, until mixture will form a light gel*, about 25 minutes, stirring occasionally. Remove from heat; stir in nuts and liqueur (if using).

4. Ladle into sterilized jars and process as directed on page 21 (Shorter Time Processing Procedure).

Makes 3 cups (750 mL).

* To determine when mixture will form a gel, see page 19.

SOUR CHERRY HAZELNUT CONSERVE

Cherry pieces and hazelnut halves suspended in a ruby-red gel promise the rich flavors to come. Enjoy this conserve with toasted crumpets or English muffins at teatime.

4 cups	**coarsely chopped pitted fresh or frozen sour cherries (about 6 cups/1.5 L whole)**	**1 L**
1	**lemon**	**1**
1	**medium orange**	**1**
⅔ cup	**dry white wine**	**150 mL**
3 cups	**granulated sugar**	**750 mL**
½ cup	**halved hazelnuts (filberts)**	**125 mL**

1. Place chopped cherries in a large stainless steel or enamel saucepan.

2. Remove thin outer rind from lemon and orange with vegetable peeler or zester, chop finely and add to saucepan. Remove and discard remaining white rind from lemon and orange; chop pulp into small pieces. Add pulp and wine to cherries. Bring to a boil over high heat, cover, reduce heat and simmer for 10 minutes or until fruit is tender.

3. Stir in sugar. Return to a boil, reduce heat and boil gently, uncovered, until mixture will form a light gel*, about 20 minutes, stirring occasionally. Remove pan from heat and stir in nuts.

4. Ladle into sterilized jars and process as directed on page 21 (Shorter Time Processing Procedure).

Makes 4 cups (1 L).

Lemon-Scented Honey
A refreshing and tangy fruit honey with tea biscuits and toasted English muffins.
Combine ½ cup (125 mL) creamed honey, 2 tbsp (25 mL) lemon juice and 1 tsp (5 mL) grated lemon rind in a small saucepan. Heat briefly, stirring well. Store in a tightly sealed container.
Makes ½ cup (125 mL).

* To determine when mixture will form a gel, see page 19.

ISLAND PAPAYA PINEAPPLE CONSERVE WITH RUM

This conserve will remind you of a winter holiday somewhere in the tropics. (Usually nuts are added to conserves, but not always—this recipe is an example of the no-nut type.)

1	lime	1
2	papayas, peeled and finely chopped	2
½ cup	crushed pineapple with juice	125 mL
½ cup	water	125 mL
4	whole cloves	4
1	cinnamon stick about 4 inches (10 cm) long, broken	1
2½ cups	granulated sugar	625 mL
½ cup	chopped dried apricots	125 mL
2 tbsp	finely chopped Candied Ginger (page 301) or crystallized ginger	25 mL
1 tbsp	rum	15 mL

1. Remove thin outer rind from lime with a vegetable peeler or zester, chop finely and place in a medium stainless steel or enamel saucepan. Remove and discard remaining white rind from lime; chop lime pulp into small pieces.

2. Add lime pulp, papaya, pineapple, water, cloves and cinnamon stick to saucepan. Bring to a boil over high heat, reduce heat, cover and boil gently for 10 minutes or until fruit is tender. Remove and discard cloves and cinnamon stick.

3. Stir in sugar, apricots and ginger. Return to a boil, reduce heat and boil gently, uncovered, until mixture will form a light gel*, about 25 minutes. Remove from heat; stir in rum.

4. Ladle into sterilized jars and process as directed on page 21 (Shorter Time Processing Procedure).

Makes 3½ cups (875 mL).

* To determine when mixture will form a gel, see page 19.

GINGERED PEAR APRICOT CONSERVE

An adventure in fruit, nut and spice flavors, this conserve is great as a tart filling or over ice cream.

1	large lime	1
4 cups	finely chopped peeled and cored pears (4 large pears)	1 L
½ cup	water	125 mL
2½ cups	granulated sugar	625 mL
½ cup	chopped dried apricots	125 mL
¼ cup	finely chopped Candied Ginger (page 301) or crystallized ginger	50 mL
¼ cup	slivered almonds	50 mL

1. Remove thin outer rind from lime with vegetable peeler and cut into fine strips with scissors or sharp knife; or use a zester. Remove and discard remaining white rind. Finely chop lime pulp with a knife or in a food processor with on/off motion. Place lime rind and pulp in a large stainless steel or enamel saucepan; add pears and water. Bring to a boil over high heat, cover and boil gently for 10 minutes or until fruit is tender.

2. Stir in sugar, apricots and ginger. Return to a boil, reduce heat and boil gently, uncovered, until mixture will form a light gel*, about 20 minutes, stirring occasionally. Remove from heat and stir in almonds.

3. Ladle into sterilized jars and process as directed on page 21 (Shorter Time Processing Procedure).

Makes 4 cups (1 L).

* To determine when mixture will form a gel, see page 19.

PLUM CONSERVE WITH MAPLE SYRUP

This conserve is an outstanding example of using both maple syrup and sugar to provide sweetness and a "hint" of maple flavor. Blue plums are best to use in season, but other types may be substituted.

3 cups	chopped, pitted plums (about 1½ lb/750 g)	750 mL
3 cups	chopped, peeled, cored apples (about 3 large)	750 mL
1½ cups	water	375 mL
1	cinnamon stick, 4 inches (10 cm) long	1
2 cups	granulated sugar	500 mL
½ cup	maple syrup	125 mL
	Grated rind of 1 lemon	
1 tbsp	lemon juice	15 mL
¼ cup	chopped hazelnuts	50 mL

1. Combine plums, apples, water and cinnamon in a large stainless steel or enamel saucepan. Bring to a boil over high heat, cover, reduce heat and boil gently for 10 minutes.

2. Add sugar, maple syrup, lemon rind and juice. Return to a boil and boil rapidly, uncovered, until mixture will form a gel*, about 20 minutes. Remove from heat and stir in nuts.

3. Ladle into sterilized jars and process as directed on page 21 (Shorter Time Processing Procedure).

Makes 5 cups (1.25 L).

* To determine when mixture will form a gel, see page 19.

FESTIVE PEACH CONSERVE WITH HAZELNUTS

The fresh fruitiness of peaches contrasts with the texture and sweet, rich, nutty flavor of hazelnuts in this attractive conserve. Use either fresh or frozen peaches. We often find frozen peaches in bulk food stores or you may choose to freeze your own when fresh peaches are in season.

1	each: lemon and large orange	1
3 cups	finely chopped peeled peaches, fresh or frozen*	750 mL
½ cup	water or white wine	125 mL
2½ cups	granulated sugar	625 mL
½ cup	golden raisins	125 mL
¼ cup	chopped candied cherries	50 mL
¼ cup	coarsely chopped hazelnuts	50 mL

1. Remove thin outer rind from orange and lemon with vegetable peeler and cut into fine strips with scissors or sharp knife; or use a zester. Remove and discard remaining white rind and seeds.

2. Finely chop orange and lemon pulp with a knife or in a food processor with on/off motion. Place rinds and pulp in a large stainless steel or enamel saucepan; add peaches and water. Bring to a boil over high heat, boil gently, covered, for 10 minutes or until fruit is tender.

3. Stir in sugar, raisins and cherries. Return to a boil, reduce heat and boil gently, uncovered, until mixture will form a light gel**, about 25 minutes, stirring occasionally. Remove from heat and stir in hazelnuts.

4. Ladle into sterilized jars and process as directed on page 21 (Shorter Time Processing Procedure).

Makes 3½ cups (875 mL).

VARIATION:

Festive Nectarine Conserve with Almonds
Replace peaches with same amount of chopped nectarines, and replace hazelnuts with sliced almonds.

TIP   *If you freeze your own peaches, it is helpful to measure and label in the amount required for this recipe.*

** To determine when mixture will form a gel, see page 19.

WINTER DRIED FRUIT AND NUT CONSERVE

You will find this marvelous conserve fabulous with goose, turkey or chicken, duck and pork roasts. It reminds us of mincemeat, but for meats. We've been known to eat it with cheese and crackers also.

2	Granny Smith apples, peeled, cored and diced	2
2	winter pears, peeled, cored and diced	2
½ cup	finely chopped dates	125 mL
½ cup	raisins	125 mL
½ cup	dried cranberries	125 mL
½ cup	apple juice	125 mL
2 cups	lightly packed brown sugar	500 mL
3 tbsp	lemon juice	45 mL
½ cup	coarsely chopped pecans	125 mL
⅛ tsp	each: ground allspice, nutmeg and ginger	0.5 mL

1. Place apples, pears, dates, raisins, cranberries and apple juice in a large stainless steel or enamel saucepan. Bring to a full boil over high heat, cover, reduce heat and boil gently for 10 minutes or until fruit is tender, stirring occasionally.

2. Stir in sugar and lemon juice. Return to a boil, reduce heat and boil gently, uncovered, until mixture will form a light gel*, about 10 minutes, stirring frequently. Remove from heat and stir in nuts, allspice, nutmeg and ginger.

3. Ladle into sterilized jars and process as directed on page 21 (Shorter Time Processing Procedure).

Makes 3½ cups (875 mL).

* To determine when mixture will form a light gel, see page 19.

SWEET AND CHUNKY APPLE BUTTER

This fruit butter makes a quick dessert. It's also a great snack on bread or toast. We use it in a low-fat recipe—a moist Sweet and Chunky Apple Butter Spice Cake (page 342). We have found preserving in half-pint (250 mL) jars convenient, since this recipe calls for that amount of apple butter. But if you use larger jars, you'll have lots left for other uses.

2 lb	McIntosh apples, peeled and cored (6 large apples)	1 kg
2 lb	Granny Smith apples, peeled and cored (4 large apples)	1 kg
1 cup	apple cider	250 mL
2 cups	granulated sugar	500 mL
2 tbsp	lemon juice	25 mL

1. Cut McIntosh apples into 1-inch (2.5 cm) pieces. Cut Granny Smith apples into smaller dice.

2. Combine apples and cider in a very large stainless steel or enamel saucepan. Bring to a boil over medium-high heat, stirring occasionally. Reduce heat and boil gently for 20 minutes or until mixture is reduced by half.

3. Stir in sugar and lemon juice. Return to a boil, reduce heat and boil gently for about 25 minutes or until mixture is very thick. There should still be some tender apple chunks remaining. Remove from heat.

4. Ladle into sterilized jars and process as directed on page 21 (Shorter Time Processing Procedure).

Makes 7 cups (1.75 L).

VARIATION:

Spiced Apple Butter
Add 2 tsp (10 mL) ground cinnamon and ½ tsp (2 mL) each ground cloves and allspice with the sugar.

TIP   *Sweet and Chunky Apple Butter adds lots of flavor to Nippy Apple Cheddar Soup (page 321).*

APRICOT HONEY BUTTER

Spread this elegant ambrosia on English muffins, pancakes or waffles. You'll never miss butter again!

2 cups	chopped dried apricots	500 mL
2 tbsp	grated lemon rind	25 mL
2 cups	water	500 mL
½ cup	lemon juice	125 mL
¼ cup	finely chopped Candied Ginger (page 301) or crystallized ginger	50 mL
⅔ cup	liquid honey	150 mL

1. Combine apricots, lemon rind, water, lemon juice and ginger in a medium stainless steel or enamel saucepan. Bring to a boil over high heat, cover, reduce heat and boil gently for 35 minutes or until apricots are tender, stirring frequently.

2. Place apricot mixture in a food processor or blender and process until smooth; return to saucepan. Stir in honey. Return to a boil, reduce heat and boil gently, uncovered, until mixture is very thick, stirring frequently.

3. Ladle into sterilized jars and process as directed on page 21 (Shorter Time Processing Procedure).

Makes 2 cups (500 mL).

CRANBERRY MAPLE BUTTER

Use this thick ruby-red preserve as a filling for cakes or over pancakes, fresh fruits or ice cream as well as a fat replacement in muffins (page 312).

1 lb	cranberries (about 5 cups/1.25 L)	500 g
½ cup	apple juice	125 mL
½ cup	pure maple syrup	125 mL
¼ cup	liquid honey	50 mL
½ tsp	ground cinnamon	2 mL
1 tsp	vanilla extract	5 mL

1. Combine cranberries and apple juice in a medium stainless steel or enamel saucepan. Bring to a boil over medium-high heat, reduce heat, cover, and boil gently for 5 minutes or until cranberries pop, stirring frequently.

2. Remove from heat and purée mixture in a food processor until smooth. Press through a sieve and discard seeds. Return sieved mixture to saucepan; add maple syrup, honey and cinnamon and boil gently, uncovered, for 10 minutes or until thickened, stirring occasionally. Remove from heat and stir in vanilla.

3. Ladle into sterilized jars and process as directed on page 21 (Shorter Time Processing Procedure).

Makes 2½ cups (625 mL).

SPICED PLUM BUTTER

The Shorter Oxford Dictionary defines plum as a "good thing . . . the pick or best of a collection of things." This is an apt reflection of the high esteem held for the plum fruit. We think this recipe is a plum among butters. It works equally well with blue, red or purple plums.

10	plums, sliced	10
1 cup	water	250 mL
	Granulated sugar	
1	cinnamon stick, about 4 inches (10 cm) long	1
4	whole cloves	4
½ tsp	ground nutmeg (optional)	2 mL

1. Place plums and water in a medium stainless steel or enamel saucepan. Bring to a full boil over high heat, cover, reduce heat and simmer for 20 minutes or until plums are tender, stirring occasionally.

2. Place plum mixture in a food processor or blender and process until almost smooth. Measure and return to saucepan. For each 1 cup (250 mL) plums, add 1¼ cups (300 mL) sugar. Tie cinnamon and cloves in a spice bag and add to saucepan.

3. Return plum mixture to a boil, reduce heat and boil gently, uncovered, until mixture is very thick, stirring frequently.

4. Discard spice bag; stir in nutmeg (if using).

5. Ladle into sterilized jars and process as directed on page 21 (Shorter Time Processing Procedure).

Makes about 3 cups (750 mL).

VARIATION:

Spiced Pear Butter
Replace plums with 5 peeled, cored and sliced pears.

 TIP *Use this butter to make Spiced Plum Butter Bran Muffins (page 313).*

BAKER'S PRUNE BUTTER

Butters are used in many ways. This one is best used as a fat replacement in chocolate cakes and brownies. Its dark color makes it most suitable for darker-colored baking.

1¾ cups	boiling water	425 mL
2	tea bags	2
½ lb	pitted prunes	250 g
¼ cup	granulated sugar	50 mL
1 tsp	grated lemon rind	5 mL
½ tsp	vanilla extract	2 mL

1. Pour boiling water over tea bags and steep for 5 minutes; discard bags.

2. Combine tea and prunes in a medium stainless steel or enamel saucepan. Bring to a boil over medium-high heat, reduce heat, cover and boil gently for 5 minutes or until prunes are softened. Remove from heat and purée mixture in a food processor or blender until smooth.

3. Return prune mixture to saucepan, add sugar and lemon rind, and boil gently, uncovered, for 15 minutes or until thickened, stirring occasionally. Remove from heat and stir in vanilla.

4. Ladle into sterilized jars and process as directed on page 21 (Shorter Time Processing Procedure).

Makes about 2 cups (500 mL).

TIP *See page 337 for an excellent low-fat brownie recipe using Baker's Prune Butter.*

MICROWAVE LEMON CURD

Lemon curd has long been a staple in many English households. It is fast gaining popularity in North America as an easy dessert served in tart shells, as a filling for meringue shells or to spread between layers of a cake or on scones. Making it in the microwave oven is much easier than making it in the traditional double boiler. Just be careful not to overcook it or it will separate.

2–3	lemons	2–3
¼ cup	butter	50 mL
¾ cup	granulated sugar	175 mL
2	eggs	2

1. Finely grate thin outer rind of lemons. Squeeze lemons. Measure ½ cup (125 mL) lemon juice into a 4-cup (1 L) microwavable container.

2. Stir in rind, butter and sugar. Microwave, uncovered, on High (100%) for 1½ to 2 minutes or until butter is melted and mixture is hot.

3. Beat eggs in a bowl. Gradually add hot lemon mixture to eggs, stirring constantly. Return mixture to the microwavable container and microwave, uncovered, on Medium (50%) for 1 to 2 minutes or just until thickened, stirring every 30 seconds. (Do not allow it to boil; mixture will thicken as it cools). Let cool.

4. Pour curd into a tightly sealed container. Refrigerate up to 2 weeks or freeze for longer storage.

Makes 1⅔ cups (400 mL).

VARIATIONS:

Lime, Tangerine or Orange Curd
Use 1 lime, tangerine or orange in place of 1 lemon.

Spirited Curd
Stir 1 tbsp (15 mL) Amaretto or Grand Marnier into curd after cooking.

TIPS   *To get the maximum juice from citrus fruit, microwave fruit on High (100%) for 20 seconds before cutting.*

Use Lemon Curd in Lady Fingers with Lemon Mousse (page 344).

MICROWAVE ORANGE CURD WITH CANDIED PEEL

Old-fashioned fruit curds are back in style! Adding candied peel to this orange curd makes it utterly mouth-watering. It is wonderful spread on scones warm from the oven. Making any curd in the microwave oven is so much easier and more foolproof than using the traditional double boiler. Just be careful not to over-cook the curd or it will separate.

3	eggs	3
2	medium oranges	2
1	lemon	1
¼ cup	butter	50 mL
¾ cup	granulated sugar	175 mL
⅓ cup	candied orange peel, chopped	75 mL

1. Beat eggs in a 4-cup (1 L) microwavable container.

2. Finely grate thin outer rind from oranges and lemon and reserve. Squeeze juice from oranges and lemon. Measure combined juice to give ¾ cup (175 mL) and whisk into eggs. Add rind, butter and sugar. Microwave, uncovered, on High (100%) for 2 minutes or until butter is melted and mixture is hot; whisk until smooth.

3. Microwave, uncovered, on Medium (50%) for 2 to 3 minutes or just until thickened, stirring every 30 seconds. (Do not allow it to boil; mixture will thicken as it cools). Stir in candied peel; let cool.

4. Pour curd into a tightly sealed container. Refrigerate up to 2 weeks or freeze for longer storage.

Makes 2⅓ cups (575 mL).

VARIATION:

Lime or Tangerine Curd
Replace 2 oranges with 3 limes or 2 tangerines.

TIPS

To get maximum juice from citrus fruit, microwave fruit on High (100%) for 20 seconds before squeezing.

Use Orange Curd as a cake filling, folded into whipped cream to make a light dessert or fill pre-baked tart shells.

CHAPTER FIVE

LIGHT 'N' LOW SUGAR SPREADS

SOME people enjoy a less-sweet spread. Others make this choice for dietary reasons. In this chapter we offer ten spreads, so-called because they do not have enough sugar to be called a jam.

Some recipes call for "no sugar needed" dry fruit pectin which may be used with little or no sugar to make either cooked or uncooked spreads. Other recipes call for light fruit pectin. It is important to use the pectin specified in the recipe to achieve a proper gel. These two pectins are of special interest to those with diabetes or those who prefer a low-sugar breakfast spread since they can also be used with artificial sweeteners. Unlike sugar, sweeteners do not affect formation of the gel. You can add any amount to suit your personal taste.

This chapter has five recipes for cooked spreads and five for uncooked spreads. Except for Light Citrus Strawberry Spread (page 120), the cooked ones contain no added pectin and achieve their thickness from the natural pectin found in the fruits. They should be processed in a boiling water canner. The uncooked spreads require added pectin, as do all uncooked spreads. They can be stored in the refrigerator for up to three weeks or in the freezer for longer storage. Be aware that spreads made with little or no sugar have a softer set than jams made with sugar.

SERVING SUGGESTION:

Use these spreads as you would any jam. The nutrient analysis per serving is provided with each spread which will be of use to someone with diabetes.

LIST OF RECIPES

LIGHT BLUEBERRY PINEAPPLE SPREAD

This all-natural fruit spread uses blueberries in an interesting combination with chopped orange, apple and pineapple juice concentrate, which provides most of the natural sweetness.

1	large orange	1
2 cups	blueberries, fresh or frozen	500 mL
1	tart green apple, peeled, cored	1
½ cup	undiluted frozen pineapple juice concentrate	125 mL
2 tbsp	granulated sugar	25 mL
2 tsp	lemon juice	10 mL
½ tsp	rum extract	2 mL
⅛ tsp	ground nutmeg	0.5 mL

1. Grate 2 tsp (10 mL) rind from orange; place in a medium stainless steel or enamel saucepan. Remove and discard remaining white rind from orange. Finely chop pulp in a food processor and add to rind.

2. Finely chop blueberries and apple in a food processor. Add to saucepan with pineapple juice, sugar and lemon juice. Bring to a boil over high heat, reduce heat and boil gently, uncovered, for about 25 minutes or until mixture is thickened and spreadable, stirring frequently.

3. Remove from heat and stir in rum extract and nutmeg.

4. Ladle into sterilized jars and process as directed on page 21 (Shorter Time Processing Procedure). Once opened, these spreads are best kept in the refrigerator and used within 3 weeks.

Makes 2 cups (500 mL).

Nutritional Information per 1 tbsp (15 mL) serving
3 g carbohydrate, 0 g protein, 0 g fat,
0 g fiber, 0 mg sodium, 13 kcal (50 kJ)

TIP   *Should extra sweetness be desired, stir in either liquid or granular sweetener to taste before serving.*

LIGHT CITRUS STRAWBERRY SPREAD

The diced orange helps extend the strawberries, particularly useful if you are using more expensive out-of-season berries. The tangy spread is quite refreshing. If you find it too tart, add liquid sweetener to taste.

1	large orange	1
4 cups	strawberries, washed and hulled	1 L
1 tbsp	lemon juice	15 mL
2 tbsp	granulated sugar	25 mL
1	box light fruit pectin	1
1 cup	granular low-calorie sweetener	250 mL

1. Grate 2 tsp (10 mL) rind from orange; place in a large stainless steel or enamel saucepan. Remove and discard remaining white rind from orange. Chop pulp and place in a 4-cup (1 L) measuring cup.

2. Mash strawberries; add to orange. You should have 3 cups (750 mL) fruit.

3. Combine fruit, lemon juice, sugar and pectin in saucepan; mix well. Bring to a boil over high heat, stirring constantly. Stir in sweetener, return to a boil and boil hard for 1 minute, stirring constantly.

4. Ladle into sterilized jars and process as directed on page 21 (Shorter Time Processing Procedure). Once opened, this spread is best kept in the refrigerator and used within 3 weeks.

Makes 3 cups (750 mL).

Nutritional Information per 1 tbsp (15 mL) serving
3 g carbohydrate, 0 g protein, 0 g fat,
1 g fibre, 0 mg sodium, 11 kcal (50 kJ)

LIGHT STRAWBERRY PINEAPPLE SPREAD

This all-natural fruit spread uses ever-popular strawberries and pineapple juice concentrate for most of its sweetness.

5 cups	strawberries, washed and hulled	1.25 L
1	Granny Smith apple, peeled, cored and chopped	1
1 tsp	grated lemon rind	5 mL
½ cup	pineapple juice concentrate	125 mL
2 tbsp	granulated sugar	25 mL
2 tsp	lemon juice	10 mL
½ tsp	vanilla extract	2 mL

1. Mash strawberries in a medium stainless steel or enamel saucepan and measure; you should have about 3 cups (750 mL). Add apple, lemon rind, pineapple juice, sugar and lemon juice. Bring to a boil over high heat, reduce heat and boil gently, uncovered, for 20 minutes or until mixture is thickened and spreadable, stirring frequently.

2. Remove from heat and stir in vanilla extract.

3. Ladle into sterilized jars and process as directed on page 21 (Shorter Time Processing Procedure). Once opened, these spreads are best kept in the refrigerator and used within 3 weeks.

Makes 3½ cups (875 mL).

Nutritional Information per 1 tbsp (15 mL) serving
3 g carbohydrate, 0 g protein, 0 g fat,
1 g fibre, 0 mg sodium, 12 kcal (50 kJ)

LIGHT SPICED RASPBERRY SPREAD

This fresh-tasting spread uses a minimum of sugar and no sweetener. Its sweetness comes mainly from apple juice concentrate and the natural sweetness of the fruit.

3 cups	frozen unsweetened raspberries	750 mL
1	tart apple, peeled, cored and chopped	1
½ cup	apple juice concentrate	125 mL
2 tbsp	granulated sugar	25 mL
1 tsp	grated lemon rind	5 mL
2 tsp	lemon juice	10 mL
⅛ tsp	each: ground ginger, cinnamon and nutmeg	0.5 mL
½ tsp	almond extract	2 mL

1. Mash raspberries in a medium stainless steel or enamel saucepan and measure; you should have 2 cups (500 mL). Add apple, apple juice, sugar, lemon rind and lemon juice. Bring to a boil over high heat, reduce heat and boil gently, uncovered, for 20 minutes or until mixture is thickened and spreadable, stirring frequently.

2. Stir in ginger, cinnamon and nutmeg; simmer for 3 minutes. Remove from heat and add almond extract.

3. Ladle into sterilized jars and process as directed on page 21 (Shorter Time Processing Procedure). Once opened, this spread is best kept in the refrigerator and used within 3 weeks.

Makes 2 cups (500 mL).

Nutritional Information per 2 tsp (10 mL) serving
3 g carbohydrate, 0 g protein, 0 g fat,
1 g fibre, 1 mg sodium, 14 kcal (60 kJ)

LIGHT MICROWAVE PEACH PLUM BUTTER

This spread has great flavor and color with the thick consistency expected of a good fruit butter.

1 cup	finely chopped peeled peaches	250 mL
1 cup	finely chopped plums	250 mL
1 tbsp	water	15 mL
½ cup	granular low-calorie sweetener	125 mL
½ tsp	ground cinnamon	2 mL
¼ tsp	ground ginger	1 mL

1. Combine peaches, plums and water in a 4-cup (1 L) microwavable container. Microwave, uncovered, on High (100%) for 5 minutes, stirring once. Microwave, uncovered, on High for 10 minutes or until mixture is very thick, stirring every 3 minutes.

2. Stir in sweetener, cinnamon and ginger.

3. Spoon spread into clean jars or plastic containers to within ½ inch (1 cm) of rim. Cover with tight-fitting lids. Label jars and refrigerate for up to 1 week or freeze for longer storage.

Makes 1 cup (250 mL).

Nutritional Information per 2 tsp (10 mL) serving
3 g carbohydrate, 0 g protein, 0 g fat,
0 g fibre, 0 mg sodium, 11 kcal (50 kJ)

LIGHT NO-COOK KIWIFRUIT PINEAPPLE SPREAD

Lime, along with pineapple juice, gives an interesting background flavor to the distinctive taste of kiwifruit in this easy-to-make spread.

1 cup	finely chopped peeled kiwifruit	250 mL
1 cup	unsweetened pineapple juice	250 mL
1 tsp	grated lime rind	5 mL
2 tbsp	lime juice	25 mL
1 cup	granular low-calorie sweetener	250 mL
2 tbsp	granulated sugar	25 mL
1	box light fruit pectin	1

1. Combine kiwifruit, pineapple juice, lime rind and juice in a medium bowl; stir well.

2. Combine sweetener, sugar and pectin. Gradually stir into fruit. Let stand for 30 minutes, stirring occasionally.

3. Spoon spread into clean jars or plastic containers to within ½ inch (1 cm) of rim. Cover with tight-fitting lids. Label jars and refrigerate for up to 1 week or freeze for longer storage.

Makes 2¼ cups (550 mL).

 TIP   *Remember, the best flavor comes from fruit that is ripe but not too soft. Kiwifruit when purchased are often too firm. Wait for them to soften.*

Nutritional Information per 2 tsp (10 mL) serving
3 g carbohydrate, 0 g protein, 0 g fat,
0 g fibre, 0 mg sodium, 11 kcal (50 kJ)

LIGHT NO-COOK MANGO SPREAD

For full-flavored "touch of the tropics" mango preserves, be sure the mango you choose is slightly soft to the touch. If not, keep it at room temperature for several days and check daily. Mangoes are ripe when they have a fresh, fruity aroma and yield slightly to gentle pressure.

2	large ripe mangoes, peeled and finely chopped	2
1 cup	unsweetened orange juice	250 mL
1 cup	granular low-calorie sweetener	250 mL
2 tbsp	granulated sugar	25 mL
1 tsp	grated orange rind	5 mL
½ tsp	ground nutmeg	2 mL
1	box "no sugar needed" dry fruit pectin	1
1 cup	water	250 mL

1. Combine mangoes, orange juice, sweetener, sugar, orange rind and nutmeg in a large bowl. Let stand for 10 minutes.

2. Gradually stir pectin into water in a small saucepan (do not add pectin all at once). Use a wire whisk or fork to mix well. Bring to a full boil over medium-high heat. Boil for 1 minute, stirring constantly. Gradually stir into fruit mixture. Let stand for 30 minutes, stirring occasionally.

3. Spoon spread into clean jars or plastic containers to within ½ inch (1 cm) of rim. Cover with tight-fitting lids. Label jars and refrigerate for up to 1 week or freeze for longer storage.

Makes 4½ cups (1.125 L).

Nutritional Information per 1 tbsp (15 mL) serving
2 g carbohydrate, 0 g protein, 0 g fat,
1 g fiber, 0 mg sodium, 9 kcal (40 kJ)

LIGHT NO-COOK RASPBERRY PINEAPPLE SPREAD

Any fruit-based liqueur makes a nice addition to this fresh-tasting breakfast spread. The spread is excellent with English muffins or scones for afternoon tea.

4 cups	mashed raspberries	1 L
½ cup	pineapple juice	125 mL
1½ cups	water, divided	375 mL
1 cup	granular low-calorie sweetener	250 mL
2 tbsp	granulated sugar	25 mL
3 tbsp	peach brandy or Cointreau	45 mL
1 tsp	grated orange rind	5 mL
1	box "no sugar needed" dry fruit pectin	1

1. Combine raspberries, pineapple juice, ½ cup (125 mL) water, sweetener, sugar, brandy and orange rind in a large bowl. Let stand for 10 minutes.

2. Gradually stir pectin into remaining water in a small saucepan (do not add pectin all at once). Use wire whisk or fork to mix well. Bring to a full boil over medium-high heat, boil for 1 minute, stirring constantly. Gradually stir into fruit mixture. Let stand for 30 minutes, stirring occasionally.

3. Spoon spread into clean jars or plastic containers to within ½ inch (1 cm) of rim. Cover with tight-fitting lids. Label and refrigerate for up to 1 week or freeze for longer storage.

Makes about 4 cups (1 L).

Nutritional Information per 1 tbsp (15 mL) serving
2 g carbohydrate, 0 g protein, 0 g fat,
1 g fiber, 0 mg sodium, 12 kcal (50 kJ)

LIGHT NO-COOK STRAWBERRY DAIQUIRI SPREAD

A fruit spread version of the famous cocktail, its no-cook preparation gives it a really fresh taste. Also, it is possible to add liquid sweetener to suit your own taste.

4 cups	strawberries, washed and hulled	1 L
½ cup	unsweetened pineapple juice	125 mL
1 tsp	grated lime rind	5 mL
2 tbsp	lime juice	25 mL
2 tbsp	dark rum (optional)	25 mL
1½ cups	granular low-calorie sweetener	375 mL
2 tbsp	granulated sugar	25 mL
1	box light fruit pectin	1

1. Crush strawberries in a large bowl; you should have about 2 cups (500 mL). Add pineapple juice, lime rind, lime juice and rum (if using). Stir well.

2. Combine sweetener, sugar and pectin. Gradually stir into fruit mixture. Let stand for 30 minutes, stirring occasionally.

3. Spoon spread into clean jars or plastic containers to within ½ inch (1 cm) of rim. Cover with tight-fitting lids. Label and refrigerate for up to 1 week or freeze for longer storage.

Makes about 3 cups (750 mL).

Nutritional Information per 1 tbsp (15 mL) serving
3 g carbohydrate, 0 g protein, 0 g fat,
1 g fibre, 0 mg sodium, 14 kcal (60 kJ)

LIGHT NO-COOK STRAWBERRY KIWIFRUIT SPREAD

Another fresh-tasting freezer spread that uses two very popular and available fresh fruits. Raspberries may be used to replace strawberries for a delectable variation.

3 cups	small ripe strawberries	750 mL
4	kiwifruit, peeled and diced	4
½ cup	pineapple juice	125 mL
1½ cups	water, divided	375 mL
1 tsp	grated lime rind	5 mL
1 tbsp	lime juice	15 mL
1½ cups	granular low-calorie sweetener	375 mL
2 tbsp	granulated sugar	25 mL
1	box "no sugar needed" dry fruit pectin	1

1. Crush strawberries and kiwifruit in a large bowl; there should be about 3 cups (750 mL). Stir in pineapple juice, ½ cup (125 mL) water, lime rind and juice, sweetener and sugar. Let stand for 10 minutes.

2. Gradually stir pectin into remaining water in a small saucepan (do not add pectin all at once). Use a wire whisk or fork to mix well. Bring to a full boil over medium-high heat. Boil for 1 minute, stirring constantly.

3. Gradually stir into fruit mixture. Let stand for 30 minutes, stirring occasionally.

4. Spoon spread into clean jars or plastic containers to within ½ inch (1 cm) of rim. Cover with tight-fitting lids. Label and refrigerate for up to 1 week or freeze for longer storage.

Makes 3¼ cups (800 mL).

Nutritional Information per 1 tbsp (15 mL) serving
2 g carbohydrate, 0 g protein, 0 g fat,
1 g fiber, 15 mg sodium, 15 kcal (60 kJ)

CONDIMENTS OF CHOICE

Introduction To
Condiments of Choice

PICKLES, relishes, salsas, chutneys, mustards, ketchups—they all add the "spice of life" to our day-to-day meals. These savory, piquant, salty or spicy accompaniments are an easy way to make an otherwise ordinary meal special. Condiments are generally made by a pickling process. This process preserves the vegetable or fruit ingredients with an acid, usually vinegar. Good pickling technique is essential to creating great condiments.

Name that Condiment

Pickle is a piece of vegetable or fruit that has been preserved with a salt and/or a vinegar mixture. Pickles may be either sweet or sour and may use herbs or spices to provide extra heat and flavor.

Relish is a pickle that has been chopped rather than left whole. Relishes can be sweet or sour, mild or hot.

Salsa is a Mexican word for "sauce" and can be either cooked or fresh. It has come to refer to a blend of vegetables and/or fruits with spices and herbs.

Chutney is a spicy condiment made from fruit, vinegar, sugar and spices. It originated in India, where it was known by the Hindu word *chatni*. Chutneys can be smooth or chunky and range in spiciness from mild to very hot.

Mustard is a sauce made from seeds of the mustard plant. Its spiciness ranges from mild to hot depending on the method of preparation and the variety of mustard seed. "Prepared" mustards are mustards mixed with other ingredients.

Ketchup is a spicy mixture made from the juice of cooked vegetables and fruits. In North America it is typically made from tomatoes.

ESSENTIAL PICKLING INGREDIENTS

1. Vegetables and Fruits

Cucumber is the most common vegetable used in condiments. It is essential that cucumbers intended for pickling are not waxed. The thin coat of wax on the skin of the typical smooth green cucumber available in stores throughout the year prevents pickling brine from penetrating the cucumber. English seedless cucumbers are also unsuitable because of their very high water content. The smaller, squatter cucumbers with bumpy skins, sometimes called Kirbys, are the best cucumber for pickling. Remember to remove the blossom end of cucumbers before pickling. It contains enzymes that cause pickles to become soft.

Fruits as well as vegetables make interesting condiments. Whole pickled fruits add a tasty highlight to many meals. Many chutneys, salsas and relishes benefit from a variety of fruit flavors. Do not use frozen fruits or vegetables for making condiments, because freezing softens the texture. This affects the crispness and sometimes the flavor of the condiment. Whether vegetables or fruits are used, the best results come from the best produce. So choose the freshest and highest quality you can find.

2. Vinegar

Vinegar is the essential ingredient in the pickling process. It provides the acidity necessary to preserve produce as well as adding a piquant flavor. White vinegar is most commonly used because it does not affect the color of the condiment. Cider and malt vinegars do affect the color but are sometimes used for their interesting flavors. All our recipes are based on vinegars that have at least 5% acetic acid. Never use one with less. Check the label for the percentage, and avoid specialty vinegars as they often are lower in acid. Never reduce the amount of vinegar in a recipe. If you want a product that is less sour, add a bit of sugar instead.

The acid in the vinegar may change the color of some vegetables. All plant materials contain pigments, some of which are affected by acidity. One change frequently seen is the blue/green color that develops in garlic in a pickling brine. Don't worry—it is still safe to eat.

3. Salt

Salt affects both the flavor and texture of the finished condiment. It is important to use only pickling salt. Table salt contains iodine that can turn the condiment dark, as well as anti-caking agents that can give a cloudy appearance.

4. Sugar and Spice

Sugar is generally added for flavor, but it also helps to keep the preserved condiment firm. Most recipes call for white granulated sugar, but brown sugar and maple syrup may also be added for their flavors.

To maintain clarity of the pickling brine, spices added during cooking should be in their whole form. Either tie them in a small piece of cheesecloth or place them in a large tea ball for easy removal before processing. If you like a stronger spice flavor, add spices to the jar before packing the condiment ingredients. Ground spices are usually added to relishes and chutneys where clarity is not an issue. Always purchase spices in small quantities to keep them fresh, and store them in an airtight container away from heat, light and moisture. A spice rack over the stove may look attractive, but it is not a good place to keep spices fresh!

HOW TO'S OF PICKLING

The first step in pickling is either to sprinkle the vegetables with dry pickling salt or pour a salt brine (salt dissolved in water) over the vegetables. This draws out the moisture, resulting in a firmer product. The choice of method depends on the vegetable and the recipe. Soaking in brine requires more time but we find that generally it is the better method, especially for vegetables cut in pieces. It produces a less salty product than the dry-salt method. With either method, the soaked or sprinkled vegetable must be rinsed and drained to eliminate excess salt.

Preserving foods by pickling relies on exposing the food to an acid in the form of vinegar to discourage bacteria growth. The easiest way to do this is to pour a syrup made of vinegar combined with the salt, sugar or spices specified by the recipe over ingredients already packed into jars.

Condiments must be processed in a boiling-water canner. Grandmother may not have bothered, but it is absolutely essential to ensure the safety of your carefully made condiments. The heat produced by processing destroys the organisms that can grow in high-acid foods and spoil the product. The process also creates an airtight seal that prevents further contamination. The secret to crisp pickles is careful attention to pickling techniques and the right balance of the acid (vinegar) and salt.

ESSENTIAL PICKLING EQUIPMENT

Most of the equipment needed for pickling is found in the usual well-equipped kitchen. You need a large stainless steel or enamel saucepan for cooking and a boiling-water canner and jar lifter for processing. Since most condiments are quite thick, a jar filler or wide-mouth funnel is very helpful for filling the jars. Canning jars and lids of any size can be used, but we like the pint (500 mL) jars for pickles and the half-pint (250 mL) jars for salsas, relishes and chutneys. The very small half-cup (125 mL) jars are ideal for small amounts of savory sauces and for gift giving.

PROCEDURE FOR LONGER TIME PROCESSING

Below is the step-by-step procedure for the processing of foods that require 10 minutes or more processing time. Use this procedure for most condiments as directed in the recipes.

If the recipe requires a preparation and cooking time longer than 20 minutes, begin preparation of the ingredients first. Then bring the water and jars in the canner to a boil while the prepared food is cooking. If the ingredients require a shorter preparation and cooking time, begin heating the canner before you start your recipe. The jars do not need to be sterile if the processing time is 10 minutes or longer, but they do need to be hot. Have a kettle with boiling water handy to top up the water level in the canner after you have put in the jars.

STEPS FOR PERFECT PROCESSING

20 Minutes Before Processing

Partially fill a boiling-water canner with hot water. Place in the canner a sufficient number of clean canning jars to hold the quantity of food prepared by the recipe. Cover and bring the water to a boil over high heat. This step generally requires 15 to 20 minutes, depending on the size of your canner.

5 Minutes Before Processing

Place lids in boiling water 5 minutes before you are ready to fill the jars. Follow the manufacturer's directions.

Filling Jars

Remove jars from the canner and ladle or pack the food into hot jars to within ½ inch (1 cm) of top rim (head space). If the food is in large pieces, remove trapped air bubbles by sliding a clean small wooden or plastic spatula between glass and food; readjust the head space to ½ inch (1 cm). Wipe jar rim to remove any stickiness. Center lid on jar; apply screw band just until fingertip tight.

Remove air bubbles

Processing Jars

Place jars in canner and adjust water level to cover jars by 1 inch (2.5 cm). Cover canner and return water to boil. Begin timing when water returns to a boil. Process for the exact time specified in the recipe.

Remove jars from canner and cool for 24 hours. Check jar seals (sealed lids turn downward). Remove screw bands, dry and either replace loosely on jar or store separately. Label jars with contents and date and store in a cool, dark place.

Leave proper
'head space'

courtesy of Bernardin

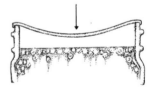

Cool jars 24 hours;
check for vacuum seal.
Sealed lids curve downward

CHAPTER SIX

PICKLE PERFECTION

PICKLING can be traced to India, over 4,000 years ago. Today, more than ever, we can revel in the marvelous versatility of pickles which is reflected in the variety of vegetables—and even a few fruits—in our recipes, including Madras Pickled Eggplant (page 159), which harkens back to the origins of this condiment.

North Americans are said to eat more than 20 billion pickles each year. The Japanese even eat them for dessert. While it will no doubt be a long time before the cucumber loses its popularity, we weren't surprised to learn that peppers account for more than 20% of specialty pickle sales. Fire-Roasted Pickled Sweet Red Peppers (page 156) are one of our favorite specialty pickle recipes since they have so many uses.

Many fruits and vegetables find their way into a pickle. Cucumbers, cauliflower and beets are favorites, but asparagus, sweet cherries and lemons offer interesting variety. Slightly less common, but in our opinion absolutely wonderful, are oranges, pumpkin and watermelon rind. All these can be made in sweet, sour or hot versions and flavored with such herbs as dill, mustard seeds, bay leaf, or peppercorns—the possibilities are endless.

Remember that you need perfect produce for perfect pickles. This means the very freshest produce available. Too long between harvest and preparation can result in hollowed or shriveled pickles. Most pickles need a few weeks to mellow before they are ready to eat.

TECHNIQUES FOR PRODUCING THE PERFECT PICKLE.

- Fresh produce is a must when making a batch of pickled anything.

- Always use pickling salt.

- Salt vegetables before making them into pickles. This draws out some of the moisture, producing a firmer pickle.

- Cut a thin slice from the blossom end of cucumbers to remove an enzyme that may cause pickles to soften.

- Process pickles in a boiling-water canner to destroy organisms that can cause pickles to soften.

- Check the label on vinegar to make sure that it has at least 5% acetic acid.

- Store prepared pickles a few weeks before sampling.

- Serve pickles cold and refrigerate pickles after opening.

SERVING SUGGESTIONS:

Pickles are a great way to add interest to just about any meal. They are a wonderful accompaniment to richer meats like pork and ham, helping to cut the fat taste. What self-respecting Rueben sandwich would adorn a plate without a kosher dill pickle? Any of our pickles make handy and welcome gifts, so make extra jars to give to friends.

LIST OF RECIPES

FAST FAVORITE GARLIC DILL PICKLES

Often called kosher-style dill pickles, these are quick to make. Use either small whole cucumbers or cut larger ones into quarters. For an additional interesting flavor, tuck a small dried hot red pepper into each jar.

8–10	small pickling cucumbers	8–10
	(about 3 lb/1.5 kg)	
2 cups	white vinegar	500 mL
2 cups	water	500 mL
2 tbsp	pickling salt	25 mL
4	heads fresh dill or	4
	4 tsp dill seeds (20 mL)	
4	small cloves garlic	4

1. Cut a thin slice from the ends of each cucumber.

2. Meanwhile, combine vinegar, water and salt in a saucepan and bring to a boil.

3. Remove hot jars from canner. Place 1 head fresh dill or 1 tsp (5 mL) dill seeds and 1 clove garlic into each jar; pack in cucumbers. Pour boiling vinegar mixture over cucumbers to within ½ inch (1 cm) of rim (head space). Process 10 minutes for pint (500 mL) jars and 15 minutes for quart (1 L) jars as directed on page 133 (Longer Time Processing Procedure).

Makes 4 pint (500 mL) jars.

TIP *Garlic may turn blue or green in the jar. Nothing to be alarmed about, it is only the effect of the acid on the natural pigments in the garlic.*

Sweet Garlic Dills

Among pickle lovers, we're absolutely convinced that no other pickle is a greater favorite than the dill pickle. These crisp garlicky ones are a fine example.

12–16	small pickling cucumbers (about 4 lb/2 kg)	12–16
4	large cloves garlic	4
4	heads fresh dill or 4 tsp (20 mL) dill seeds	4
½ tsp	celery seeds	2 mL
2 cups	white vinegar	500 mL
⅔ cup	water	150 mL
1 cup	granulated sugar	250 mL
3 tbsp	pickling salt	45 mL
⅛ tsp	turmeric	0.5 mL

1. Cut a thin slice from the ends of each cucumber. Cut cucumbers lengthwise into quarters.

2. Remove hot jars from canner. Place 1 clove garlic, 1 head fresh dill or 1 tsp (5 mL) dill seeds and ⅛ tsp (0.5 mL) celery seeds into each jar; pack in cucumbers.

3. Meanwhile, combine vinegar, water, sugar, salt and turmeric in a small saucepan and bring to a boil. Pour boiling vinegar mixture over cucumbers to within ½ inch (1 cm) of rim (head space). Process 10 minutes for pint (500 mL) jars and 15 minutes for quart (1 L) jars as directed on page 133 (Longer Time Processing Procedure).

Makes 4 pint (500 mL) jars.

TIPS

If you can find small cucumbers approximately 6 inches (15 cm) long, they fit neatly into wide-mouth pint (500 mL) jars.

Many old recipes call for alum as a crisping agent for pickles. Alum is crystals of potassium aluminum sulfate and is no longer recommended for pickling. It can give a bitter flavor to pickles and may cause digestive upsets. Modern pickling procedures make it unnecessary.

SALT-FREE DILLS WITH HORSERADISH

This is the pickle for those who need to reduce their salt intake. Fresh grape leaves are used to produce the crispness traditionally obtained with the use of salt. Either wild or cultivated grape leaves are appropriate.

12–16	small pickling cucumbers (about 3 lb/1.5 kg)	12–16
1	3 x 1-inch (7.5 x 2.5 cm) piece fresh peeled horseradish *	1
2½ cups	white vinegar	625 mL
2 cups	water	500 mL
4	fresh grape leaves, washed	4
4	cloves garlic	4
4	heads fresh dill or 4 tsp (20 mL) dill seeds	4
2 tsp	mustard seeds	10 mL

1. Cut a thin slice from the ends of each cucumber. Cut horseradish into 4 lengthwise pieces and reserve.

2. Combine vinegar and water in a saucepan and bring to a boil over high heat.

3. Remove hot jars from canner. Place 1 piece horseradish, 1 grape leaf, 1 garlic clove, 1 head dill and ½ tsp (2 mL) mustard seeds in each jar. Pack cucumbers in jars.

4. Pour boiling vinegar mixture over cucumbers to within ½ inch (1 cm) of rim (head space). Process 10 minutes for pint (500 mL) jars and 15 minutes for quart (1 L) jars as directed on page 133 (Longer Time Processing Procedure).

Makes 4 pint (500 mL) jars.

TIP *Horseradish adds a bit of flavor, but if you can't find the fresh root, just leave it out.*

CURRY PICKLE SLICES

All curry lovers will be happy with this interesting flavor variation to a traditional pickle.

2 quarts	pickling cucumbers	2 L
4	small onions, sliced	4
1 tbsp	pickling salt	15 mL
2½ cups	cider vinegar	625 mL
1⅔ cups	granulated sugar	400 mL
1 tbsp	curry powder	15 mL
2 tsp	pickling spice *	10 mL
1 tsp	each: celery seeds and mustard seeds	5 mL

1. Cut a thin slice from the ends of each cucumber and cut into thick slices. Place with onions in a non-reactive container, sprinkle with salt and let stand for 24 hours; drain. Rinse twice and drain thoroughly.

2. Combine vinegar, sugar, curry powder, pickling spice, celery seeds and mustard seeds in a large stainless steel or enamel saucepan. Bring to a boil over high heat. Add vegetables and return just to a boil. Remove from heat.

3. Remove hot jars from canner. Remove vegetables from liquid with a slotted spoon; pack into jars. Pour liquid over vegetables to within ½ inch (1 cm) of rim (head space). Process 10 minutes for pint (500 mL) jars and 15 minutes for quart (1 L) jars as directed on page 133 (Longer Time Processing Procedure).

Makes 4 pint (500 mL) jars.

Pickling Spice Blend
* *Pickling spice is a blend of various spices. Since we have had trouble finding it when it's not what stores call "the preserving season," here is a recipe.*
Combine 2 tbsp (25 mL) each: allspice berries, cardamom seeds, coriander seeds, whole cloves, mustard seeds and peppercorns. Add 2 bay leaves, crumbled; 2 cinnamon sticks, broken; 2 small pieces dried gingerroot, chopped, and 2 small dried red chilies, crushed (1-2 tsp/5-10 mL hot pepper flakes). Store in a tightly sealed container until ready to use.

CUCUMBER PICKLES WITH LEMON

These pickles will find favor with those who don't like the sharp bite of most pickles. Fresh lemon juice gives a nice lift to the cucumbers.

2 lb	small cucumbers	1 kg
1 tbsp	pickling salt	15 mL
1⅓ cups	white vinegar	325 mL
1 cup	granulated sugar	250 mL
⅔ cup	lemon juice	150 mL
1½ tsp	peppercorns	7 mL
½ tsp	whole allspice	2 mL
3	slices fresh lemon	3
3	cloves garlic	3
3	bay leaves	3

1. Cut a thin slice from the ends of each cucumber and cut into thick slices. You should have about 7 cups (1.75 L). Place in a non-reactive container, sprinkle with salt and let stand for 3 hours; drain. Rinse twice and drain thoroughly.

2. Combine vinegar, sugar, lemon juice, peppercorns and allspice in a large stainless steel or enamel saucepan and bring to a boil over high heat.

3. Remove hot jars from canner. Place 1 slice lemon, 1 garlic clove and 1 bay leaf in each pint jar.

4. Add cucumbers to boiling liquid and return just to a boil, stirring constantly. Remove from heat. Remove cucumbers from liquid with a slotted spoon and pack into jars. Pour hot liquid over cucumbers to within ½ inch (1 cm) of rim (head space). Process 10 minutes for pint (500 mL) jars and 15 minutes for quart (1 L) jars as directed on page 133 (Longer Time Processing Procedure).

Makes 3 pint (500 mL) jars.

BEST BREAD-AND-BUTTER PICKLES

Most of our grandmothers made their own versions of bread-and-butter pickles.
If you yearn for this bit of nostalgia, try our favorite version.

4 lb	small pickling cucumbers	2 kg
4	small onions, thinly sliced	4
1	sweet green pepper, cut in thin strips	1
1	sweet red pepper, cut in thin strips	1
2 tbsp	pickling salt	25 mL
4 cups	cider vinegar	1 L
3 cups	granulated sugar	750 mL
2 tbsp	mustard seeds	25 mL
1 tsp	celery seeds	5 mL
½ tsp	turmeric	2 mL
¼ tsp	ground cloves	1 mL

1. Cut a thin slice from the ends of each cucumber and cut into medium thick slices,
   about ³⁄₁₆ inch (4 mm). Place cucumbers, onions and peppers in a non-reactive
   container, sprinkle with salt and let stand for 3 hours; drain. Rinse twice and drain
   thoroughly.

2. Combine vinegar, sugar, mustard seeds, celery seeds, turmeric and cloves in a large
   stainless steel or enamel saucepan. Bring to a boil over high heat. Add vegetables and
   return to a boil for 30 seconds or just until cucumbers are no longer bright green.

5. Remove hot jars from canner. Remove vegetables from liquid with a slotted spoon;
   pack into jars. Pour liquid over vegetables to within ½ inch (1 cm) of rim (head
   space). Process 10 minutes for pint (500 mL) jars and 15 minutes for quart (1 L)
   jars as directed on page 133 (Longer Time Processing Procedure).

Makes 6 pint (500 mL) jars.

TIP   *On a hot summer day you may want to keep the pickles cool during the salting.
Adding ice cubes to the top of the cucumbers after sprinkling with salt is an
easy way to do this.*

FREEZER BREAD AND BUTTER PICKLES

A fast variation of a traditional favorite, this easy recipe requires little preparation and no processing time. Either English or small pickling cucumbers can be used.

4 cups	thinly sliced cucumbers (about ³⁄₁₆ inch/4 mm thick)	1 L
1 cup	thinly sliced onion	250 mL
1	sweet red pepper, thinly sliced	1
2 tsp	pickling salt	10 mL
1½ cups	cider vinegar	375 mL
⅔ cup	granulated sugar	150 mL
1 tsp	mustard seeds	5 mL
½ tsp	celery seeds	2 mL
½ tsp	turmeric	2 mL

1. Place cucumbers, onion and red pepper in a large non-reactive container. Sprinkle with salt and mix well. Let stand for 3 hours, stirring occasionally; drain. Rinse twice and drain thoroughly.

2. Heat vinegar in microwave oven for 30 seconds or warm slightly on the stove top. Combine vinegar, sugar, mustard seeds, celery seeds and turmeric in a small bowl stirring until sugar is dissolved. Pour over vegetables and mix well.

3. Pack vegetables into small freezer containers. Divide liquid and pour over pickles. Seal tightly and freeze.

4. Store pickles in freezer up to 6 months. Once thawed, use them within several days before they lose their crunch.

Makes about 3 cups (750 mL).

NINE-DAY ICICLE PICKLES

Icicle pickles have a long tradition. You probably remember your grandmother making them. Don't let the nine days deter you. The steps are simple—the rewards are well worth the effort.

2 quarts	pickling cucumbers, 4 to 6 inches (10 to 15 cm) long	2 L
4 cups	boiling water	1 L
½ cup	pickling salt	125 mL
2 cups	white vinegar	500 mL
3 cups	granulated sugar, divided	750 mL
1 tbsp	pickling spice	15 mL

Days 1–3
- Cut a thin slice from the ends of each cucumber. Cut cucumbers lengthwise into quarters. Cut each quarter crosswise in half. Place in a large non-reactive container. Combine boiling water and salt; pour over cucumbers. Place a weight such as a plate on top of cucumbers to keep them submerged. Stir once a day for 3 days.

Day 4
- Drain cucumbers and discard liquid. Cover cucumbers with fresh boiling water. Replace weight and let stand for 24 hours.

Day 5
- Drain cucumbers and discard liquid. Cover cucumbers with fresh boiling water. Replace weight and let stand for 24 hours.

Day 6
- Drain cucumbers and discard liquid.
- Prepare a brine: combine vinegar and 1½ cups (375 mL) sugar in a stainless steel or enamel saucepan. Place pickling spice in a large tea ball or tie in a piece of cheesecloth; add to saucepan. Bring to a full boil over high heat. Pour over cucumbers and let stand for 24 hours.

Day 7
- Drain brine into a large saucepan; add ½ cup (125 mL) sugar. Bring to a full boil over high heat. Pour over pickles and let stand for 24 hours.

Day 8
- Repeat Day 7, adding ½ cup (125 mL) sugar to the brine.

Day 9

- Drain brine into large saucepan and add ½ cup (125 mL) sugar. Bring to a boil over high heat.
- Remove hot jars from canner and pack pickles into jars. Pour hot brine over pickles to within ½ inch (1 cm) of rim (head space). Process 10 minutes for pint (500 mL) and quart (1 L) jars as directed on page 133 (Longer Time Processing Procedure).

Makes 3 or 4 pint (500 mL) jars.

TIP   *The secret to crisp sweet pickles is adding the sugar gradually during the brining process.*

WINTER SALAD PICKLE

Make this pickle when all the fresh vegetables are plentiful. Keep lots on hand for a quick wintertime salad.

2 cups	cauliflower florets	500 mL
1 cup	peeled pearl onions, or larger onions cut into quarters	250 mL
1 cup	thickly sliced celery	250 mL
1 cup	sliced carrot	250 mL
1 cup	thickly sliced zucchini	250 mL
1 cup	yellow beans, trimmed and cut into 1-inch (2.5 cm) pieces	250 mL
2	medium sweet red peppers, cut into squares	2
3 cups	white wine vinegar or Herb Vinegar (page 267)	750 mL
1½ cups	granulated sugar	375 mL
1⅓ cups	water	325 mL
2 tsp	pickling salt	10 mL
⅛ tsp	paprika	0.5 mL

1. Combine cauliflower, onions, celery and carrot in a large bowl. Combine zucchini, beans and peppers in a separate bowl.

2. Combine vinegar, sugar, water, salt and paprika in a large stainless steel or enamel saucepan. Bring to a full boil over high heat. Add cauliflower, onions, celery and carrot and return just to a boil. Remove from heat and stir in zucchini, beans and peppers.

3. Remove hot jars from canner. Remove vegetables from liquid with a slotted spoon; pack into jars. Pour liquid over vegetables to within ½ inch (1 cm) of rim (head space). Process 10 minutes for pint (500 mL) jars and 15 minutes for quart (1 L) jars as directed on page 133 (Longer Time Processing Procedure).

Makes 4 pint (500 mL) jars.

VARIATION:

Use any combination of vegetables for a total of 8 cups (2 L).

MIXED VEGETABLE MUSTARD PICKLES

This pickle is the original version of chow chow, Chinese pickled vegetables preserved in a sweet-tart syrup. This name has evolved to refer to any mixed vegetable pickle or relish made with mustard. Amazingly easy to make, it is a great way to convert a deluge of summer vegetables so they can be enjoyed later.

1 quart	pickling cucumbers (about 1¼ lb/625 g)	1 L
4 cups	cauliflower florets	1 L
	(about 1 small cauliflower)	
1 cup	peeled pearl onions	250 mL
½ cup	pickling salt	125 mL
6 cups	lukewarm water	1.5 L
3 cups	granulated sugar	750 mL
½ cup	all-purpose flour	125 mL
3 tbsp	dry mustard	45 mL
1 tbsp	celery seeds	15 mL
1½ tsp	turmeric	7 mL
3 cups	white vinegar	750 mL
½ cup	water	125 mL

1. Cut a thin slice from the ends of each cucumber and cut into thick slices. Place cucumbers, cauliflower and onions in a large non-reactive container. Combine salt with lukewarm water, stirring until dissolved. Pour over vegetables and let stand for 24 hours; drain. Rinse twice and drain thoroughly.

2. Combine sugar, flour, mustard, celery seeds and turmeric in a large saucepan; stir until well mixed. Whisk in vinegar and water. Bring to a boil over high heat, stirring constantly, until smooth and thickened. Add vegetables and return to a boil for 30 seconds.

3. Remove hot jars from canner. Remove vegetables from liquid with a slotted spoon; pack into jars. Pour liquid over vegetables to within ½ inch (1 cm) of rim (head space). Process 10 minutes for pint (500 mL) jars and 15 minutes for quart (1 L) jars as directed on page 133 (Longer Time Processing Procedure).

Makes 5 pint (500 mL) jars.

EASY SPICED PICKLED BEETS

Pickled beets have long been a favorite in our families. Tiny beets are the most attractive, but larger ones cut into pieces are just as delicious.

10–15	fresh beets (about 2 lb/900 g)	10–15
2 cups	granulated sugar	500 mL
2 cups	white vinegar	500 mL
⅓ cup	water	75 mL
16	whole cloves	16
8	whole allspice berries	8
2	cinnamon sticks, about 4 inches (10 cm) long	2
2 tsp	pickling salt	10 mL

1. Trim beets, leaving 1 inch (2.5 cm) of stem and tap root attached. Place beets in a large saucepan and cover with water. Bring to a boil over high heat, reduce heat, cover and simmer for 25 to 45 minutes or until tender. Drain and rinse under cold water. Remove skins and cut beets into large pieces.

2. Combine sugar, vinegar and water in a large saucepan. Bring to a boil over high heat, stirring occasionally.

3. Remove hot jars from canner and place 4 whole cloves, 2 allspice berries, ½ cinnamon stick and ½ tsp (2 mL) salt in each jar. Pack beet pieces into jars.

4. Pour hot liquid over beets to within ½ inch (1 cm) of rim (head space). Process 30 minutes for pint (500 mL) jars and 35 minutes for quart (1 L) jars as directed on page 133 (Longer Time Processing Procedure).

Makes 4 pint (500 mL) jars.

VARIATION:

For an interesting variation, add ¼ tsp (1 mL) hot pepper flakes to each jar.

PICKLED BEETS AND ONIONS

This pickled beet variation with caraway and mustard seeds adds new interest to a traditional favorite. Use tiny beets and onions for a pickle with a more elegant appearance. But larger ones cut into quarters work just as well.

10–15	small fresh beets	10–15
2 cups	cider vinegar	500 mL
1½ cups	granulated sugar	375 mL
½ cup	water	125 mL
1 cup	peeled small whole onions (about 4 oz/250 g)	250 mL
2 tsp	pickling salt	10 mL
2 tsp	caraway seeds	10 mL
1 tsp	mustard seeds	5 mL

1. Trim beets, leaving 1 inch (2.5 cm) of stem and tap root attached. Place beets in a large saucepan, cover with water and bring to a boil over high heat. Reduce heat, cover and simmer for 25 to 40 minutes or until tender. Drain and rinse under cold water. Remove skins and cut beets into serving-sized pieces if necessary.

2. Combine vinegar, sugar and water in a saucepan. Bring to a boil over high heat, stirring occasionally.

3. Remove hot jars from canner. Divide onions, caraway seeds and mustard seeds equally among jars; add beet pieces.

4. Pour boiling vinegar mixture over beets to within ½ inch (1 cm) of rim (head space). Process 30 minutes for pint (500 mL) jars and 35 minutes for quart (1 L) jars as directed on page 133 (Longer Time Processing Procedure).

Makes 4 pint (500 mL) jars.

LEMON SPICED BEAN PICKLE

Green and yellow beans pickled with a bit of lemon are nice with cold meats or on a relish tray. Pack the beans into wide-mouth jars placed on their sides.

1 lb	green beans	500 g
1 lb	yellow beans	500 g
2½ cups	cider vinegar	625 mL
1¼ cups	water	300 mL
1 tbsp	pickling salt	15 mL
1 tbsp	granulated sugar	15 mL
1 tbsp	pickling spice	15 mL
3	strips lemon rind	3

1. Wash and trim beans into 4-inch (10 cm) lengths to fit into jars.

2. Combine vinegar, water, salt and sugar in a medium saucepan and bring to a boil over high heat. Add beans, cover and return to a boil; boil for 1 minute. Remove from heat and drain, reserving liquid. Return liquid to saucepan and bring to a boil.

3. Remove hot jars from canner and place 1 tsp (5 mL) pickling spice and 1 strip lemon rind into each jar. Pack in beans and pour boiling liquid into jars to within ½ inch (1 cm) of rim (head space). Process 10 minutes for pint (500 mL) jars as directed on page 133 (Longer Time Processing Procedure).

Makes 3 pint (500 mL) jars.

SERVING SUGGESTION:

Easy Three Bean Salad
A quick salad to serve with barbecued or cold meats.
In a medium bowl, combine 1 cup (250 mL) drained Lemon Spiced Bean Pickle cut into small pieces, ½ cup (125 mL) each: diced celery, drained kidney beans and ¼ cup (50 mL) finely chopped red onion. Bring ½ cup (125 mL) brine drained from pickles, 1 tbsp (15 mL) each: sugar and olive oil to a boil. Pour over bean mixture, cover and refrigerate for several hours, stirring occasionally.
Makes 2 cups (500 mL).

HERBED ASPARAGUS PICKLES

Tarragon appears in the spring just as asparagus begins to push out of the ground. The two combine to make a savory pickle that is quite out-of-the-ordinary.

2½-3 lb	asparagus spears	1.2-1.5 kg
4	sprigs fresh tarragon	4
2	small dry shallots, halved	2
2 cups	white wine vinegar	500 mL
1½ cups	white vinegar	375 mL
1 cup	water	250 mL
¼ cup	granulated sugar	50 mL
1 tsp	pickling salt	5 mL

1. Wash asparagus and cut each spear 4¼ inches (11 cm) long or long enough to fit a wide-mouth pint (500 mL) jar leaving ¾ inch (2 cm) head space.

2. Remove hot jars from canner and pack asparagus into jars with tips down. Tuck a sprig of tarragon and half a shallot among the spears.

3. Combine wine vinegar, white vinegar, water, sugar and salt in a medium saucepan and bring to a boil. Pour boiling vinegar mixture over asparagus to within ½ inch (1 cm) of rim (head space). Process 15 minutes for pint (500 mL) jars as directed on page 133 (Longer Time Processing Procedure).

Makes 4 pint (500 mL) jars.

PICKLED BABY CARROTS WITH OREGANO AND PEPPERS

Take advantage of packaged tiny peeled carrots to make this easy and interesting pickle.

3 tbsp	finely chopped fresh oregano or 1 tbsp (15 mL) dried	45 mL
2 tbsp	each: chopped sweet red and green pepper	25 mL
¼ tsp	hot pepper flakes	1 mL
2	small cloves garlic	2
1 lb	peeled baby carrots	500 g
1½ cups	white vinegar	375 mL
½ cup	granulated sugar	125 mL
⅓ cup	water	75 mL
1 tsp	pickling salt	5 mL

1. Combine oregano, peppers and hot pepper flakes. Remove hot jars from canner and divide pepper mixture between them. Add 1 clove garlic to each jar and fill each with half the carrots leaving ½ inch (1 cm) head space. (There may be a few carrots left over).

2. Meanwhile, combine vinegar, sugar, water and salt in a small saucepan and bring to a boil.

3. Pour hot liquid over carrots to within ½ inch (1 cm) of rim (head space). Process 15 minutes for pint (500 mL) jars as directed on page 133 (Longer Time Processing Procedure).

Makes 2 pint (500 mL) jars.

CARROT ZUCCHINI PICKLE STRIPS

Here is a neat pickle to make when zucchini are taking over the garden. Carrots and a hint of dill add interest.

1 lb	carrots, peeled and cut into short strips	500 g
1 lb	zucchini, cut into short strips	500 g
1 tsp	pickling salt	5 mL
1¼ cups	white vinegar	425 mL
⅔ cup	water	150 mL
⅓ cup	granulated sugar	75 mL
2 tbsp	chopped fresh dill	25 mL
2 tbsp	chopped fresh parsley	25 mL
½ tsp	each: freshly ground pepper and dried thyme	2 mL

1. Cook carrots in boiling water for 2 minutes; drain and refresh in cold water. Combine carrots and zucchini; sprinkle with salt. Let stand for 4 hours; drain and rinse twice.

2. Mix vinegar, water, sugar, dill, parsley, pepper and thyme in a small saucepan. Bring to a boil, stirring until sugar has dissolved.

3. Remove hot jars from canner and pack vegetables into jars. Pour liquid over vegetables to within ½ inch (1 cm) of rim (head space). Process 15 minutes for half-pint (250 mL) jars and 20 minutes for pint (500 mL) jars as directed on page 133 (Longer Time Processing Procedure).

Makes 5 half-pint (250 mL) jars.

Refrigerator Pickles

Add this easy refrigerator pickle to your condiment recipes. They are really delicious.
Thinly slice 1 unpeeled English cucumber. Layer ½ of cucumber with ½ thinly sliced small onion; repeat layers. In small saucepan combine ½ cup (125 mL) granulated sugar, ½ cup (125 mL) white vinegar, ¼ cup (50 mL) cider vinegar, pinch each: salt, mustard seeds, celery seeds and ground turmeric. Bring to a boil for 1 minute. Pour over cucumber and onion; let cool. Cover and marinate in refrigerator for 4 days. These crisp pickles keep in the refrigerator for up to 1 month.

MULTI-COLORED GINGER PICKLED PEPPERS

Allow these pickles to sit for several weeks for the full flavor to develop. Serve them with cold cuts or roasted meats and salads.

1	sweet green pepper, sliced lengthwise	1
1	sweet red pepper, sliced lengthwise	1
1	sweet yellow pepper, sliced lengthwise	1
2	jalapeño peppers, seeded and thinly sliced	2
1	2-inch (5 cm) piece gingerroot, peeled and thinly sliced	1
1½ cups	rice vinegar	375 mL
½ cup	water	125 mL
2 tbsp	granulated sugar	25 mL
1 tsp	pickling salt	5 mL

1. Place peppers and gingerroot in a shallow bowl. Combine vinegar, water, sugar and salt; stir well to dissolve. Pour over peppers. Cover and refrigerate overnight.

2. Drain peppers, reserving liquid. Remove hot jars from canner. Pack peppers into jars.

3. Bring drained liquid to a boil over high heat. Pour over peppers to within ½ inch (1 cm) of rim (head space). Process 15 minutes for half-pint (250 mL) jars and 20 minutes for pint (500 mL) jars as directed on page 133 (Longer Time Processing Procedure).

Makes 3 half-pint (250 mL) jars.

Radish Refrigerator Pickles
Serve radishes as a colorful side-salad pickle. The color from the radishes bleeds after assembling, so make them no longer than 2 hours before serving.
Combine ½ cup (125 mL) rice vinegar, 2 tbsp (25 mL) granulated sugar, 2 tsp (10 mL) finely chopped gingerroot and 1 tsp (5 mL) chopped fresh dill in a small bowl. Wash, trim and slice 2 bunches radishes; toss with dressing, cover and refrigerate up to 2 hours before serving.
Makes 2 cups (500 mL).

FIRE-ROASTED PICKLED SWEET RED PEPPERS

Roasted red peppers are fast becoming popular for everything from antipasto to pizzas, from garnishing a fresh mozzarella salad to enhancing a robust Italian spaghetti sauce. This recipe lets you roast peppers in the summer when they are plentiful to enjoy during the winter months.

6–8	small sweet red peppers (about 2 lb/900 g)	6–8
1	large clove garlic, unpeeled	1
½ cup	dry white wine	125 mL
½ cup	white vinegar	125 mL
¼ cup	cider vinegar	50 mL
½ cup	coarsely chopped onion	125 mL
2 tbsp	granulated sugar	25 mL
½ tbsp	dried oregano leaves or 1 tbsp (15 mL) fresh	7 mL
1 tsp	pickling salt	5 mL

1. Roast peppers and garlic on the barbecue grill or on a rack under the broiler until skins are blistered and starting to blacken. Place peppers in a paper bag until cool enough to handle; set garlic aside. When peppers are cool, remove skins, cores and seeds. Cut lengthwise into strips about 1 inch (2.5 cm) wide; set aside.

2. Combine wine, vinegars, onion, sugar, oregano and salt in a small stainless steel or enamel saucepan. Squeeze roasted garlic to remove from skin, mash and add to saucepan. Bring mixture to a boil over high heat, reduce heat and boil gently for 5 minutes.

3. Remove hot jars from canner and pack peppers into jars to within ¾ inch (2 cm) of top rim, being careful not to pack too tightly. Pour boiling vinegar mixture including onion to within ½ inch (1 cm) of rim (head space). Process 15 minutes for half-pint (250 mL) and pint (500 mL) jars as directed on page 133 (Longer Time Processing Procedure).

Makes 4 half-pint (250 mL) jars.

PICKLED JALAPEÑO PEPPERS

People who enjoy lots of heat with their meals will keep these preserved jalapeños for the time an extra spice accompaniment to a meal is needed. Try Pickled Jalapeño Peppers in a variety of appetizers: Jalapeño Cheddar Canapés (page 315) or Piquant Cream Cheese Dip (page 316). They also add lots of flavor to Apricot Red Pepper Relish (page 169) and to Jalapeño Quesadillas (page 319).

1 cup	cider vinegar	250 mL
¼ cup	water	50 mL
4 tsp	liquid honey	20 mL
2 tsp	pickling spice	10 mL
½ tsp	pickling salt	2 mL
2	cloves garlic, halved	2
½ lb	jalapeño peppers, seeded and thinly sliced	250 g

1. Combine vinegar, water, honey, pickling spice and salt in a small saucepan. Bring to a boil over high heat, remove from heat and let stand for 10 minutes.

2. Remove hot jars from canner. Place ½ clove garlic in each jar. Divide peppers between jars. Add ½ clove garlic.

3. Return pickling liquid to a boil. Pour over peppers to within ½ inch (1 cm) of rim (head space). Process 10 minutes for half-pint (250 mL) jars and 15 minutes for pint (500 mL) jars as directed on page 133 (Longer Time Processing Procedure).

Makes 2 half-pint (250 mL) jars.

For extra eye-appeal, strips of either hot (cayenne, de Arbol and Mirasol are generally available) or sweet red peppers may be placed in jars with jalapeño slices before liquid is added.

Other hot peppers may be processed in the same way. Scotch Bonnet (Habanero) are very hot and so a little will go a long way to add heat to meals. De Arbol and Mirasol are mid-heat peppers. See the Chile Pepper Heat Scale (page 186) and process them as for jalapeños.

MIXED JAPANESE PICKLE STICKS

Mirin, a sweet Japanese rice wine, gives these vegetable sticks an interesting flair. This low-alcohol golden wine adds flavor to a variety of Japanese dishes, sauces and glazes. It can be found in any Japanese market as well as the gourmet section of many supermarkets.

4	small zucchini, (about 1 lb/500 g)	4
4	medium pickling cucumbers, about 1 lb (500 g)	4
1	piece peeled Japanese white radish (daikon or lobok, about 1 lb/500 g)	1
2 cups	rice vinegar	500 mL
1 cup	water	250 mL
¼ cup	mirin	50 mL
2 tbsp	pickling salt	25 mL
16	black peppercorns	16
8	whole allspice	8

1. Cut zucchini, cucumbers and radish into lengthwise spears. Set aside.

2. Combine vinegar, water, mirin and salt in a small saucepan and bring to a boil.

3. Remove hot jars from canner. Place 4 peppercorns and 2 allspice in each jar. Pack vegetables into jars. Pour hot vinegar mixture into jars to within ½ inch (1 cm) of rim (head space). Process 10 minutes for pint (500 mL) jars as directed on page 133 (Longer Time Processing Procedure).

Makes 4 pints (500 mL).

MADRAS PICKLED EGGPLANT

A friend of Margaret's daughter Martha, brought this wonderful family recipe with her from Calicut, India, when she came to live in Canada. It has unique Indian flavors that are quite delightful. Our only change has been to reduce the amount of oil. The heat level can be controlled to suit your own taste buds (see Tip).

2 lb	eggplant (2 large)	1 kg
3 tbsp	white vinegar	45 mL
2	large cloves garlic, minced	2
2 tbsp	chili powder	25 mL
2 tsp	each: ground ginger and turmeric	10 mL
⅓ cup	canola oil	75 mL
1 tbsp	each: cumin seeds and fenugreek seeds	15 mL
1¼ cups	white vinegar	300 mL
1 cup	granulated sugar	250 mL
2–4	finely chopped and seeded small hot red chile or jalapeño peppers	2–4
¼ cup	finely chopped gingerroot	50 mL
2 tbsp	pickling salt	25 mL

1. Cube unpeeled eggplant into bite-sized pieces and reserve.

2. Combine 3 tbsp (45 mL) vinegar, garlic, chili powder, ginger and turmeric in a small bowl to form a paste and reserve.

3. Heat oil on medium-high heat in a large saucepan. Add cumin and fenugreek seeds and sauté for 1 minute. Add eggplant and sauté for about 10 minutes or until eggplant is just tender. Reduce heat and add reserved paste and 1¼ cups (300 mL) vinegar, sugar, chile peppers, gingerroot and salt. Stir over medium heat for about 5 minutes or until boiling.

4. Remove hot jars from canner and ladle pickles into jars to within ½ inch (1 cm) of rim (head space). Process 15 minutes for half-pint (250 mL) jars and 20 minutes for pint (500 mL) jars as directed on page 133 (Longer Time Processing Procedure).

Makes 3 pint (500 mL) jars.

TIP *Whether to use milder jalapeño peppers or 2–4 of the smaller and hotter red chile peppers depends on the heat level you enjoy.*

PICKLED GINGER

Keep a jar of this easy-to-make pickle on your shelf to make speedy additions to stir-fries. Pickled ginger and its jalapeño and garlic variations also add zest to antipasto plates, meat loaf and any other dishes in need of a pickled spice lift.

1	large piece fresh gingerroot (about 10 oz/280 g)	1
¾ cup	rice wine vinegar	175 mL
½ cup	white vinegar	125 mL
2 tsp	soy sauce	10 mL
1 tsp	granulated sugar	5 mL

1. Peel ginger and cut into pieces no larger than 1 inch (2.5 cm). Remove hot jars from canner and pack ginger into jars.

2. Bring vinegars, soy sauce and sugar to a boil in a small saucepan. Pour over ginger to within ½ inch (1 cm) of rim (head space). Process 10 minutes for half-pint (250 mL) and half-cup (125 mL) jars as directed on page 133 (Longer Time Processing Procedure).

Makes 2 half-pint (250 mL) jars or 4 half-cup (125 mL) jars.

VARIATIONS:

Pickled Jalapeños
Replace ginger with 10-12 jalapeño peppers, depending on their size. Omit soy sauce and add ½ tsp (2 mL) salt.

Pickled Garlic
Replace ginger with 3-4 heads garlic, depending on their size. Omit soy sauce and add ½ tsp (2 mL) salt plus 2 tsp (10 mL) pickling spice, if desired.

TIP   *Fresh gingerroot may be frozen to have on hand to add to a variety of dishes. Cut in pieces and freeze in a tightly sealed freezer bag. When needed, the frozen gingerroot may be easily peeled and grated.*

Piquant Tomato Sauce (page 235), Grandma's Chili Sauce (page 242)

Red Pepper Peach Chutney (page 223), Fruit Chili Sauce (page 243),
Peach Lavender Jam (page 41)

Cucumber Pickles with Lemon (page 142), Easy Spiced Pickled Beets (page 149)
Your Basic Multi-Use Tomato Sauce (page 236)

Salsa Bruschetta-Style (page 195)

PICKLED SWEET CHERRIES

This unusual and colorful pickle with its sweet-sour taste makes an excellent condiment for game and poultry as well as other roasted meats.

1¾ cups	white vinegar	425 mL
1¾ cups	granulated sugar	425 mL
¾ cup	water	175 mL
2	cinnamon sticks, about 4 inches (10 cm) long	2
2 tsp	whole cloves	10 mL
1 tsp	whole allspice	5 mL
2 lb	dark sweet cherries with stems	1 kg

1. Combine vinegar, sugar, water, cinnamon, cloves and allspice in a small saucepan. Bring to a boil, reduce heat and boil gently, uncovered, for 20 minutes.

2. Remove hot jars from canner and pack cherries into jars. Pour hot syrup over cherries to within ½ inch (1 cm) of rim (head space). Process 10 minutes for pint (500 mL) jars as directed on page 133 (Longer Time Processing Procedure).

Makes 3 pint (500 mL) jars.

SPICED PICKLED PEACHES

Both the peach and the pineapple version of this condiment is a wonderful accompaniment to many meals. Look for very small peaches. If you can find only large ones, cut them into quarters.

21–24	small peaches (about 4 lb/2 kg)	21–24
3½ cups	granulated sugar	875 mL
1¼ cups	white vinegar	425 mL
1¼ cup	water	300 mL
3	cinnamon sticks, 3 inches (8 cm) long, broken	3
1 tbsp	whole cloves	15 mL
½ tsp	whole allspice	2 mL

1. Bring a saucepan of water to a boil over high heat. Dip peaches into boiling water for about 30 seconds or until skins will slip off easily. Peel peaches and place in a solution of 8 cups (2 L) water and 1 tsp (5 mL) lemon juice.

2. Bring sugar, vinegar and water to a boil over high heat in a large stainless steel or enamel saucepan, stirring until sugar is dissolved. Tie cinnamon, cloves and allspice in a cheesecloth bag; add to sugar. Reduce heat, cover and boil gently for 15 minutes.

3. Drain peaches and add to syrup. Return to a boil and boil gently for 5 minutes. Discard spice bag.

4. Remove hot jars from canner. Remove peaches from liquid with a slotted spoon; pack into jars. Pour liquid over peaches to within ½ inch (1 cm) of rim (head space). Process for 20 minutes for pint (500 mL) jars and 25 minutes for quart (1 L) jars as directed on page 133 (Longer Time Processing Procedure).

Makes 3 quart (1 L) jars, depending on size of peaches.

VARIATION:

Spiced Pineapple Pickles
Use 1 peeled and cored pineapple cut into chunks in place of the peaches. Increase water to 3 cups (750 mL) for syrup.

PUMPKIN PICKLES

This famous pickle comes from a friend of a friend. She suggests putting a light rather than a candle inside your Hallowe'en pumpkin so you can recycle it into pickles. Better still, paint a face on the pumpkin with magic markers.

1	large pumpkin	1
6 cups	granulated sugar	1.5 L
3 cups	white or cider vinegar	750 mL
1 tsp	whole cloves	5 mL
1	cinnamon stick, about 4 inches (10 cm) long, broken	1
2	pieces Candied Ginger (page 301) or crystallized ginger	2

1. Peel pumpkin, remove seeds and cut into 2-inch (5 cm) cubes.

2. Bring sugar and vinegar to a boil over high heat in a large stainless steel or enamel saucepan, stirring until sugar is dissolved. Tie cloves, cinnamon and ginger tightly in cheesecloth bag; add to sugar. Reduce heat and boil gently for 5 minutes.

3. Add pumpkin pieces and return to a boil. Reduce heat, cover, and boil gently for 25 minutes or until pumpkin is tender but pieces still hold their shape, stirring frequently. Discard spice bag.

4. Remove hot jars from canner. Remove pumpkin from liquid with a slotted spoon; pack tightly into jars. Pour liquid over pumpkin to within ½ inch (1 cm) of rim (head space). Process 15 minutes for pint (500 mL) jars and 20 minutes for quart (1 L) jars as directed on page 133 (Longer Time Processing Procedure).

Makes 5 pint (500 mL) jars.

TIP   *Depending on the size of the pumpkin, you may need to make more of the syrup. Always use the same proportions called for in the recipe: 2 parts sugar to 1 part white vinegar.*

SPICED ORANGE SLICES

We were served these unusual orange pickle slices on recent trips to Australia. They came as an accompaniment to a cheese tray. Since they are a sweet-sour condiment, they are not a traditional main course pickle. Try them in Spiced Orange-Slice Salad (page 333).

4	large oranges	4
8 cups	hot water	2 L
1 tsp	salt	5 mL
1 cup	granulated sugar	250 mL
½ cup	lightly packed brown sugar	125 mL
½ cup	each: cider vinegar and water	125 mL
¼ cup	corn syrup	50 mL
8	whole cloves	8
4	cardamom pods	4
4	cinnamon sticks, 3 inches (8 cm) long	4
½ tsp	peppercorns	2 mL

1. Combine whole unpeeled oranges, 8 cups (2 L) hot water and salt in a large saucepan. Bring to a boil, reduce heat, cover and simmer for 45 minutes or until fruit is tender. Drain oranges, discarding liquid, and cool.

2. Cut oranges in half crosswise and then into very thin slices.

3. Combine granulated sugar, brown sugar, vinegar, water, corn syrup, cloves, cardamom, cinnamon and peppercorns in a large saucepan. Stir over high heat until sugars have dissolved. Reduce heat and cook for 10 minutes. Add orange slices, cover and cook gently for 20 minutes. Remove from heat and let stand for 5 minutes. Remove and discard cardamom and cinnamon.

4. Remove hot jars from canner. Remove orange slices from liquid with a slotted spoon; pack into jars. Pour liquid and whole cloves over oranges to within ½ inch (1 cm) of rim (head space). Process 10 minutes for half-pint (250 mL) jars and 15 minutes for pint (500 mL) jars as directed on page 133 (Longer Time Processing Procedure).

Makes 4 half-pint (250 mL) jars.

WATERMELON RIND PICKLES

Make this delightful pickle from a part of the watermelon that is often discarded. Leave a small amount of the pink flesh to give a bit of color. Cut interesting shapes with canapé cutters. The secret of the crisp texture is to add the sugar gradually during the pickling process. The extra two days this requires is well worth the wait.

4 cups	peeled watermelon rind, cut into 1-inch (2.5 cm) cubes	1 L
¼ cup	pickling salt	50 mL
4 cups	water	1 L
2 cups	granulated sugar, divided	500 mL
1 cup	white vinegar	250 mL
1	lemon or lime, thinly sliced	1
1 tsp	whole cloves	5 mL
1 tsp	whole allspice	5 mL
2	cinnamon sticks, 3 inches (8 cm) long	2

Day 1
- Place watermelon rind in a large non-reactive bowl. Dissolve salt in the water and pour over rind. Let stand for 4 hours; drain and rinse twice.
- Place rind in a large stainless steel or enamel saucepan; cover with cold water. Bring to a boil over high heat, reduce heat, cover, and boil gently for 8 minutes, or just until tender. Drain; place in a large non-reactive bowl.
- Combine 1 cup (250 mL) sugar, vinegar, lemon slices, cloves, allspice and cinnamon in a saucepan. Bring to a boil, stirring until sugar is dissolved, and pour over rind. Place a weight such as a plate on top of rind to keep it submerged. Let stand for 24 hours.

Day 2
- Drain liquid from rind into a saucepan; add ½ cup (125 mL) sugar. Bring to a boil and pour over rind. Replace weight and let stand for 24 hours.

Day 3
- Drain liquid from rind into a saucepan; add ½ cup (125 mL) sugar. Bring to a boil. Add rind and return to a boil. Remove from heat.
- Remove hot jars from canner. Remove cinnamon sticks from liquid and place one in each jar. Remove rind from liquid with a slotted spoon; pack into jars. Pour liquid over rind to within ½ inch (1 cm) of rim (head space). Process 10 minutes for half-pint (250 mL) jars, 10 minutes for pint (500 mL) jars and 15 minutes for quart (1 L) jars as directed on page 133 (Longer Time Processing procedure).

Makes 2 pint (500 mL) jars.

CHAPTER SEVEN

RAVISHING RELISHES

RELISHES have been around for so long that many have interesting histories. One of these is the chow chow relish. It is thought by some to have been created for Europeans residing in China. Another story has it that the chef to Napoleon developed the original chow chow relish and yet another that Chinese railroad laborers brought it to America. Whatever the origin, chow chow is a popular relish and we trust our Cauliflower Chow Chow (page 183) will win your heart.

Relishes are made from many different fruits and vegetables with added herbs and spices. It is best to chop the ingredients into equal-sized pieces so they have similar cooking times. And, like pickles, relishes should be processed in a boiling water canner.

All relishes in this chapter are cooked and then processed. Storage allows their flavors to mellow and continue to develop. For best flavor, allow relishes to wait a few weeks before tasting.

Relish ingredients with a high water content, like zucchini, onions and cucumbers, should first be put in salt water or layered with pickling salt to draw off some of their moisture. They are then drained and rinsed well before being cooked. Relish vegetables and fruits are cooked only until they are just tender to maintain their crisp texture. Most relish ingredients are available year round.

Serving Suggestions:

Many great creamy salad dressings benefit from a spoonful of relish. Potato salad is also much tastier with a dollop of Sun Relish (page 177) stirred in. Look for the Caramelized Red Onion and Tomato Pizza on page 317 and Zucchini Corn Salad made with Fiesta Corn Relish (page 176). Did you ever consider adding some relish to a meat loaf? You may never again make one without! Try it with hamburger patties too. And, of course, there is that combination of mustard and relish that transforms the lowly hot dog and hamburger.

The Antipasto Relish (page 168) is one of our favorites. The recipe contains directions for converting the relish to an antipasto by adding anchovies, tuna, olives and mushrooms at serving time. This is a very quick and convenient way to make an antipasto and eliminates the preserving problems associated with the low-acid nature of this condiment.

List of Recipes

ANTIPASTO RELISH

This recipe becomes antipasto when you add tuna, olives, mushrooms and anchovies.

2	large cloves garlic, minced	2
¾ cup	white vinegar	175 mL
½ cup	each: water and tomato sauce	125 mL
¼ cup	granulated sugar	50 mL
2 tsp	pickling spice	10 mL
6	peppercorns	6
3	bay leaves	3
1 tsp	dried oregano	5 mL
1 cup	each: small broccoli and cauliflower florets	250 mL
¾ cup	bottled small pickled onions, drained	175 mL
½	each: large sweet red, yellow and green pepper, diced	½
2	carrots, peeled and thinly sliced	2
1	jalapeño pepper, seeded and finely chopped	1

1. Combine garlic, vinegar, water, tomato sauce and sugar in large stainless steel or enamel saucepan. Tie pickling spice, peppercorns and bay leaves in a cheesecloth bag. Add spice bag and oregano to saucepan. Bring to a boil over high heat, reduce heat and stir until sugar is dissolved. Add broccoli and cauliflower florets, pickled onions, sweet peppers, carrots and jalapeño pepper. Return to a boil, reduce heat and boil gently for 1 hour or until mixture has thickened. Discard spice bag.

2. Remove hot jars from canner and ladle relish into jars to within ½ inch (1 cm) of rim (head space). Process 10 minutes for half-pint (250 mL) jars and 15 minutes for pint (500 mL) jars as directed on page 133 (Longer Time Processing Procedure).

Makes 3½ cups (875 mL).

SERVING SUGGESTION:

Antipasto Appetizer

To 1 cup (250 mL) Antipasto Relish, add 1 can (6.5 oz/184 g) flaked and drained tuna, ½ cup (125 mL) each: black and green olives, ½ cup (125 mL) canned sliced mushrooms and 2 flat anchovy fillets, minced. Keep refrigerated for up to 1 week or freeze for longer storage.
Makes about 3 cups (750 mL).

APRICOT RED PEPPER RELISH

This gourmet relish is superb both as a topping to cream cheese spread on crackers and as a zippy complement to roasts.

1½ cups	cider vinegar	375 mL
1 cup	diced sweet red pepper	250 mL
¼ cup	drained Pickled Jalapeño Peppers (page 157)	50 mL
1¼ cups	chopped dried apricot halves	300 mL
3½ cups	granulated sugar	875 mL
1	pouch liquid fruit pectin	1

1. Combine vinegar, red pepper and jalapeño pepper in blender or food processor. Process with on/off motion until finely chopped but not puréed. Transfer to large saucepan.

2. Add apricots and sugar. Bring to a boil, reduce heat and cook for 5 minutes. Remove from heat and stir in pectin.

3. Ladle relish into sterilized jars to within ½ inch (1 cm) of rim (head space). Process as directed on page 21 (Shorter Time Processing Procedure).

Makes 5 cups (1.25 L).

VARIATION:

For extra spirit, add 2 tbsp (25 mL) port to mixture during cooking.

GREEN AND RED PEPPER RELISH

We think this pepper relish is vastly superior to any commercial one. In fact, when sweet green and red peppers are in season, we always try to make our winter's supply.

4	sweet green peppers, chopped	4
4	sweet red peppers, chopped	4
4	medium onions, finely chopped	4
1 cup	white vinegar, divided	250 mL
1 cup	granulated sugar	250 mL
1 tsp	pickling salt	5 mL

1. Combine peppers, onions and ¾ cup (175 mL) boiling water in a large stainless steel or enamel saucepan. Cover and let stand for 5 minutes.

2. Drain vegetables and return to saucepan. Stir in ⅓ cup (75 mL) each vinegar and water. Bring to a boil, cover and reduce heat; simmer for 5 minutes.

3. Drain vegetables and return to saucepan. Heat remaining ⅔ cup (150 mL) vinegar, sugar and salt in a 2-cup (500 mL) microwavable container on High (100%) until sugar is dissolved. Add to vegetables and return mixture to a boil. Boil gently, uncovered, for 25 minutes or until liquid is reduced and vegetables are tender-crisp.

4. Remove hot jars from canner and ladle relish into jars to within ½ inch (1 cm) of rim (head space). Process 10 minutes for half-pint (250 mL) and pint (500 mL) jars as directed on page 133 (Longer Time Processing Procedure).

Makes 4 cups (1 L).

TIP   *Store empty canning jars with the used lids in place to keep them clean for the next use.*

BARBECUE RELISH

This easy-to-make relish is so right with everything from hot dogs and hamburgers to egg salad or cold meat sandwiches.

4 cups	finely chopped zucchini (about 2 large)	1 L
1 cup	finely chopped onion	250 mL
1	medium sweet red, green or yellow pepper, finely chopped	1
½ cup	finely chopped celery	125 mL
2 tbsp	pickling salt	25 mL
1½ cups	granulated sugar	375 mL
1¼ cups	white vinegar *	300 mL
1 tbsp	celery seed, optional	15 mL
1 tsp	mustard seed	5 mL
½ tsp	each: dry mustard and ground cloves	2 mL

1. Combine zucchini, onion, pepper and celery in a large non-reactive bowl. Sprinkle with salt and cover with cold water; let stand for 1 hour. Drain vegetables in a sieve, pressing out excess moisture; reserve vegetables.

2. Combine sugar, vinegar, celery seed (if using), mustard seed, dry mustard and cloves in a large stainless steel or enamel saucepan. Bring to a boil over high heat; add reserved vegetable mixture. Return to a boil, reduce heat and boil gently, uncovered, for 45 minutes or until mixture is thickened.

3. Remove hot jars from canner and ladle relish into jars to within ½ inch (1 cm) of rim (head space). Process 10 minutes for half-pint (250 mL) jars and 15 minutes for pint (500 mL) jars as directed on page 133 (Longer Time Processing Procedure).

Makes 3¼ cups (800 mL).

TIP   *Replace one half of the white vinegar with cider vinegar for a change of taste.*

BEET RELISH WITH HORSERADISH

Horseradish gives this savory beet relish extra zest to enhance any meat dish.

5	medium beets (about 1 lb/500g)	5
1	large onion, finely chopped	1
2	sweet red peppers, finely chopped	2
1 cup	white vinegar	250 mL
½ cup	granulated sugar	125 mL
1 tsp	pickling salt	5 mL
⅔ cup	grated fresh horseradish	150 mL

1. Cook beets in boiling water until tender, about 20 minutes. Drain beets, remove skins and chop finely. There should be about 2 cups (500 mL). Mix beets with onions and peppers.

2. Combine vinegar, sugar, salt and horseradish in a large stainless steel or enamel saucepan. Bring to a boil over high heat. Add vegetables. Return to a boil, reduce heat and simmer, uncovered, for 20 minutes, stirring occasionally.

3. Remove hot jars from canner and ladle relish into jars to within ½ inch (1 cm) of rim (head space). Process 15 minutes for half-pint (250 mL) jars and 20 minutes for pint (500 mL) jars as directed on page 133 (Longer Time Processing Procedure).

Makes 3½ cups (875 mL).

A can (14 oz/398 mL) of beets may be used in place of fresh for this relish.

Commercially prepared horseradish may be substituted for the fresh, but double the amount.

CRANBERRY APPLE PEAR RELISH

The combination of apples and pears gives this versatile relish a lovely freshness as well as extending the cranberries. Orange liqueur and juice add a citrus flavor. We like using this relish with poultry or as an appetizer with crackers and Cheddar cheese.

3 cups	fresh or frozen cranberries	750 mL
3	apples, peeled, cored and diced	3
2	pears, peeled, cored and diced	2
1½ cups	golden raisins	375 mL
2 cups	granulated sugar	500 mL
1 cup	orange juice	250 mL
2 tbsp	grated orange rind	25 mL
2 tsp	ground cinnamon	10 mL
¼ tsp	ground nutmeg	1 mL
½ cup	orange liqueur	125 mL

1. Combine cranberries, apples, pears, raisins, sugar, orange juice and rind, cinnamon and nutmeg in a very large stainless steel or enamel saucepan. Bring to a boil over high heat, stirring frequently. Reduce heat and boil gently, uncovered, for about 25 minutes or until mixture thickens, stirring occasionally. Remove from heat and stir in liqueur.

2. Remove hot jars from canner and ladle relish into jars to within ½ inch (1 cm) of rim (head space). Process 10 minutes for half-pint (250 mL) jars and 15 minutes for pint (500 mL) jars as directed on page 133 (Longer Time Processing Procedure).

Makes 6 cups (1.5 L).

SERVING SUGGESTIONS:

Oven-Baked Carrots
This vegetable casserole using Cranberry Apple Pear Relish makes a tasty accompaniment for roasted meats.
Coarsely grate 6 carrots and place in a lightly greased 6-cup (1.5 L) casserole. Stir in ¾ cup (175 mL) Cranberry Apple Pear Relish; dot with 1 tbsp (15 mL) butter or margarine. Add 2 tbsp (25 mL) water, cover and bake in a 325°F (160°C) oven for 45 minutes. Uncover and continue to bake 10 minutes longer or until carrots are tender. Makes 6–8 servings.

CRANBERRY RUM RELISH

Take this tangy cranberry relish to your next turkey dinner. We love it as an accompaniment to grilled chicken breasts and it is also splendid with pâté and crackers.

⅓ cup	dark rum	75 mL
¼ cup	finely chopped shallots	50 mL
	Grated rind of 1 orange	
3 cups	fresh or frozen cranberries	750 mL
1 cup	granulated sugar	250 mL
½ tsp	freshly ground pepper	2 mL

1. Combine rum, shallots and orange rind in a medium saucepan. Bring to a boil over high heat, reduce heat and simmer for a few minutes until rum has reduced and mixture is a syrupy glaze.

2. Add cranberries and sugar. Stirring constantly, cook until cranberries pop and sugar is dissolved. Remove from heat and stir in pepper.

3. Remove hot jars from canner and ladle relish into jars to within ½ inch (1 cm) of rim (head space). Process 10 minutes for half-pint (250 mL) jars and 15 minutes for pint (500 mL) jars as directed on page 133 (Longer Time Processing Procedure).

Makes 2 cups (500 mL).

Kiwifruit Relish
Kiwifruit makes an interesting refrigerated relish to serve with cold meats.
In a small saucepan, combine 1 cup (250 mL) each: granulated sugar and white vinegar, ¼ cup (50 mL) water and 1 tsp (5 mL) each: mustard seeds and peppercorns. Bring to a boil over high heat; remove from heat and cool. Meanwhile, place ½ cup (125 mL) diced shallots and 1 sweet red pepper, cubed, in a bowl. Cover with boiling water and let stand for 2 minutes; drain, refresh in cold water and pat dry. Peel and slice 5 firm kiwifruit. Combine kiwifruit, shallot mixture and vinegar mixture. Place in a clean jar and refrigerate for at least 5 days before tasting.
Makes 2½ cups (625 mL).

EASY OVEN RELISH

A fruity oven-prepared relish makes a delicious accompaniment to cold meats, meat loaves and roasts, and goes well with sandwiches. See page 332 for Garden Pasta Salad with this relish used in the dressing.

3	large peaches, peeled, pitted and coarsely chopped	3
3	pears, peeled, cored and coarsely chopped	3
4	large tomatoes, peeled and chopped	4
2	large onions, finely chopped	2
1	large sweet green pepper, chopped	1
1	stalk celery, finely chopped	1
1½ cups	granulated sugar	375 mL
1½ cups	cider vinegar	375 mL
1 tbsp	whole allspice (tied in cheesecloth)	15 mL
1 tbsp	pickling salt	15 mL

1. Combine peaches, pears, tomatoes, onions, green pepper, celery, sugar, vinegar, allspice and salt in a large metal roasting pan.

2. Bring to a boil over medium heat, stirring occasionally. Transfer roasting pan to a 375°F (190°C) oven and bake, uncovered, for about 1½ hours or until mixture is thickened; stir occasionally. Remove from oven and discard allspice bag.

3. Remove hot jars from canner and ladle relish into jars to within ½ inch (1 cm) of rim (head space). Process 10 minutes for half-pint (250 mL) jars and 15 minutes for pint (500 mL) jars as directed on page 133 (Longer Time Processing Procedure).

Makes 5 cups (1.25 L).

SERVING SUGGESTION:

Easy Seafood Sauce
Stir 2 tbsp (25 mL) ketchup, 1 tbsp (15 mL) horseradish and a splash of lemon juice into ½ cup (125 mL) of the Easy Oven Relish.

FIESTA CORN RELISH

We especially like serving this colorful relish with cold meats and barbecued burgers. There is a hint of the Southwest in its flavors and its bit of heat. Frozen corn is almost as delicious as fresh corn, so this relish can be made any time of year.

5–6	large ears fresh corn *	5–6
1	hot yellow pepper, seeded and finely chopped	1
2	cloves garlic, minced	2
1½ cups	cider vinegar	375 mL
¾ cup	granulated sugar	175 mL
½ cup	chopped red onion	125 mL
½ cup	chopped sweet red pepper	125 mL
⅓ cup	chopped green onions	75 mL
1 tsp	ground cumin	5 mL
1 tsp	pickling salt	5 mL
½ tsp	freshly ground black pepper	2 mL
2 tbsp	chopped fresh cilantro	25 mL

1. Bring a large pot of water to a boil over high heat. Add corn, cover and cook for 6 minutes. Drain and cool until easy to handle. With a sharp knife cut kernels from cob and measure 4 cups (1 L) corn into a large stainless steel or enamel saucepan.

2. Add hot pepper, garlic, vinegar, sugar, onion, red pepper, green onions, cumin, salt and black pepper to saucepan. Bring to a boil over high heat, reduce heat and boil gently, uncovered, for 20 minutes. Stir in cilantro and cook 2 minutes longer. Remove from heat.

3. Remove hot jars from canner and ladle relish into jars to within ½ inch (1 cm) of rim (head space). Process 15 minutes for half-pint (250 mL) jars and pint (500 mL) jars as directed on page 133 (Longer Time Processing Procedure).

Makes 4½ cups (1.125 L).

TIP

To make this relish when fresh corn is unavailable, you can use 4 cups (1 L) frozen corn.

SUN RELISH

Combining peaches and yellow peppers gives this relish its sweet and hot flavors and its "sunny" color. It is an inspired addition to cream cheese or to a wedge of Canadian Cheddar. While best with cheeses, it also goes well with warm biscuits and omelets.

6	peaches, peeled, pitted and chopped	6
6	sweet yellow peppers, seeded and chopped	6
1	hot yellow pepper, seeded and chopped	1
1	lemon, halved	1
½ cup	white wine vinegar	125 mL
2½ cups	granulated sugar	625 mL
1½ tsp	pickling salt	7 mL

1. Place peaches, peppers, lemon and vinegar in a large stainless steel or enamel saucepan. Bring to a boil over medium-high heat, reduce heat and boil gently, uncovered, for 30 minutes or until softened. Remove and discard lemon, add sugar and salt; return to a boil. Cook, uncovered, for about 20 minutes or until mixture thickens, stirring frequently.

2. Remove hot jars from canner and ladle relish into jars to within ½ inch (1 cm) of rim (head space). Process 10 minutes for half-pint (250 mL) jars and 15 minutes for pint (500 mL) jars as directed on page 133 (Longer Time Processing Procedure).

Makes 4 cups (1 L).

CARAMELIZED RED ONION RELISH

Balsamic vinegar is the magic ingredient in this recipe. It adds a pungent sweetness to the caramelized onions. Serve with barbecued or broiled meats such as steak, lamb chops and chicken. See page 317 for an easy appetizer pizza using this spread.

2	large red onions, peeled	2
¼ cup	firmly packed brown sugar	50 mL
1 cup	dry red wine	250 mL
3 tbsp	balsamic vinegar	45 mL
⅛ tsp	each: salt and freshly ground pepper	0.5 mL

1. Slice onions into very thin slices. Combine onions and sugar in a heavy non-stick skillet. Cook, uncovered, over medium-high heat for about 25 minutes or until onions turn golden and start to caramelize, stirring frequently.

2. Stir in wine and vinegar. Bring to a boil over high heat, reduce heat to low and cook for about 15 minutes or until most of the liquid has evaporated, stirring frequently.

3. Season to taste with salt and pepper. Spoon into a clean wide-mouthed jar and cool briefly.

4. Remove hot jars from canner and ladle relish into jars to within ½ inch (1 cm) of rim (head space). Process 10 minutes for half-pint (250 mL) jars as directed on page 133 (Longer Time Processing Procedure).

Makes 2 cups (500 mL).

 TIP *This small-batch recipe probably won't last long enough to bother processing in a hot-water bath. If you follow these instructions, you may refrigerate it for up to 3 weeks or even freeze for longer storage.*

SWEET ONION AND FENNEL RELISH

Fennel's sweet, delicate hint of licorice is evident in this unique relish. It complements cold meats.

1	large sweet onion, such as Spanish or Vidalia (about 8 oz/250 g)	1
1	fennel bulb (about 10 oz/275 g)	1
1	sweet red pepper, sliced into thin strips	1
2½ tsp	pickling salt, divided	12 mL
1½ cups	white wine vinegar	375 mL
½ cup	water	125 mL
¼ cup	granulated sugar	50 mL
2	bay leaves	2
8	black peppercorns	8

1. Slice onion in half lengthwise, then in very thin slices crosswise to form half circles. Cut fennel bulb in half lengthwise and remove core; thinly slice crosswise to form half circles. Place onion, fennel and pepper in a non-reactive bowl and sprinkle with 2 tsp (10 mL) salt. Toss and let stand for 4 hours. Rinse twice and drain thoroughly.

2. Combine vinegar, water, sugar and ½ tsp (2 mL) salt in a large stainless steel or enamel saucepan. Bring to a boil over high heat. Add vegetables and return just to a boil, stirring constantly. Remove from heat.

3. Remove vegetables from liquid with a slotted spoon and pack into hot jars. Pour liquid over vegetables to within ½ inch (1 cm) of rim (head space). Add bay leaves and peppercorns.

4. Process 10 minutes for half-pint (250 mL) and pint (500 mL) jars as directed on page 133 (Longer Time Processing Procedure).

Makes 4 cups (1 L).

ZUCCHINI GARDEN PEPPER RELISH

Zucchini lends a lightness and freshness to traditional pepper relish. Zucchini growers will love to have another such tasty use for their fast-growing vegetable.

4	medium zucchini (about 1¼ lb/625 g), finely chopped	4
2	medium onions, finely chopped	2
½	sweet red pepper, finely chopped	½
½	sweet green pepper, finely chopped	½
2 tbsp	pickling salt	25 mL
1¼ cups	granulated sugar	300 mL
¾ cup	cider vinegar	175 mL
1 tsp	each: dry mustard and celery seeds	5 mL
½ tsp	each: hot pepper flakes and turmeric	2 mL
1 tbsp	water	15 mL
2 tsp	cornstarch	10 mL

1. Toss together zucchini, onions and red and green peppers in a large non-reactive bowl. Sprinkle with salt and stir well. Let stand for 1 hour, stirring occasionally.

2. Drain vegetables in a sieve and rinse; drain again, pressing out excess moisture.

3. Combine drained vegetables, sugar, vinegar, mustard, celery seeds, hot pepper flakes and turmeric in large stainless steel or enamel saucepan. Bring to a boil over high heat, reduce heat and boil gently, uncovered, for 15 minutes or until vegetables are tender.

4. Blend water and cornstarch; stir into vegetables. Cook for 5 minutes or until liquid clears and thickens, stirring often.

5. Remove hot jars from canner and ladle relish into jars to within ½ inch (1 cm) of rim (head space). Process 10 minutes for half-pint (250 mL) jars and 15 minutes for pint (500 mL) jars as directed on page 133 (Longer Time Processing Procedure).

Makes 4 cups (1 L).

BRINJAL PICKLE RELISH

Ellie first tasted this relish in Australia and immediately set about finding a way to duplicate it. She found the secret of the relish's flavor in an old cookbook given to her by a visitor from Sri Lanka—sautéing the diced eggplant in "½ bottle of oil" before mixing it with "spiced pickle."

⅓ cup	vegetable oil	75 mL
1	eggplant, cut into ¼-inch (5mm) cubes	1
2–3	hot red chile peppers, seeded and finely chopped	2–3
3	large cloves garlic, finely chopped	3
¾ cup	white vinegar	175 mL
4 tsp	chili powder	20 mL
1 tbsp	whole fenugreek	15 mL
1 tsp	ground coriander	5 mL
½ tsp	dry mustard	2 mL
¼ tsp	each: turmeric and salt	1 mL
½ cup	brown sugar	125 mL

1. Heat oil over medium heat in a large nonstick skillet. Add eggplant and fry gently for about 10 minutes. (At first the oil is completely absorbed, but then is gradually released as the eggplant becomes fairly firm). Stir in chile peppers and garlic; cook for 3 minutes.

2. Stir in vinegar, chili powder, fenugreek, coriander, mustard, turmeric and salt. Bring to a boil, reduce heat and boil gently for about 10 minutes. Add sugar and cook for 2 minutes.

3. Remove hot jars from canner and ladle relish into jars to within ½ inch (1 cm) of rim (head space). Process 15 minutes for half-pint (250 mL) jars and 20 minutes for pint (500 mL) jars as directed on page 133 (Longer Time Processing Procedure).

Makes 2 cups (500 mL).

TIP

Be sure to label your jars after processing and include the date. It's amazing how easy it is to forget what is inside and the year it was made.

INDIAN-STYLE CUCUMBER RELISH

Seasoned with traditional spices, cumin, and black and yellow mustard seeds, this relish shows its East Indian heritage. Use it to pep up meats or poultry. Mixed with yogurt it becomes *raita*, a salad that is served with Indian food as a cool counterpoint to spicy dishes.

6 cups	diced peeled cucumber	1.5 L
	(about 8–12 medium pickling cucumbers)	
2 cups	thinly sliced onions	500 mL
1 tbsp	pickling salt	15 mL
2 cups	white vinegar	500 mL
½ cup	granulated sugar	125 mL
1 tbsp	whole cumin seeds	15 mL
2 tsp	black mustard seeds	10 mL
2 tsp	yellow mustard seeds	10 mL

1. Place cucumber and onion in a non-reactive bowl and sprinkle with salt. Let stand for 4 hours, stirring occasionally. Drain vegetables in a sieve, rinse twice and drain thoroughly.

2. Combine vinegar, sugar, cumin seeds and mustard seeds in a very large stainless steel or enamel saucepan. Bring to a boil over high heat. Add vegetables and return to a boil for 30 seconds.

3. Remove hot jars from canner. Remove vegetables from liquid with a slotted spoon; pack into jars. Pour liquid over cucumber to within ½ inch (1 cm) of rim (head space).

4. Process 10 minutes for pint (500 mL) jars as directed on page 133 (Longer Time Processing Procedure).

Makes 6 cups (1.5 L).

CAULIFLOWER CHOW CHOW

Originally chow chow was a Chinese condiment made from ginger, fruits and peels preserved in a heavy syrup. More recently, it has come to refer to a relish of mixed vegetables in a mustard sauce

3 cups	cauliflower florets, coarsely chopped (about ½ head)	750 mL
2	small pickling cucumbers, peeled and chopped	2
1	sweet green pepper, seeded and chopped	1
1	small hot red chile pepper, seeded and chopped	1
1	onion, chopped	1
3 tbsp	pickling salt	45 mL
3 cups	lukewarm water	750 mL
⅔ cup	granulated sugar	150 mL
3 tbsp	all-purpose flour	45 mL
2 tsp	each: dry mustard and celery seeds	10 mL
½ tsp	each: curry powder and turmeric	2 mL
⅔ cup	each: cider vinegar and white vinegar	150 mL
⅓ cup	water	75 mL

1. Toss together cauliflower, cucumbers, green pepper, chile pepper and onion in a large non-reactive bowl. Stir salt and lukewarm water together and pour over vegetables. Let stand for 8 to 10 hours. Drain vegetables in a sieve; rinse twice and drain thoroughly.

2. Combine sugar, flour, mustard, celery seeds, curry powder and turmeric in a large stainless steel or enamel saucepan. Add vinegars and water, stirring to blend well. Bring to a boil over high heat, stirring constantly until mixture thickens. Add the drained vegetables, return to a boil, reduce heat and boil gently, uncovered, for 10 minutes.

3. Remove hot jars from canner and ladle relish into jars to within ½ inch (1 cm) of rim (head space). Process 10 minutes for half-pint (250 mL) jars and pint (500 mL) jars as directed on page 133 (Longer Time Processing Procedure).

Makes 3½ cups (875 mL).

CAPONATA

Caponata is a Sicilian dish served as a salad, side dish or relish. We also like it as an appetizer spread on toasted baguette slices.

1	small eggplant, cut into ¼-inch (5 mm) cubes	1
1½ tbsp	pickling salt	20 mL
2	large tomatoes, peeled and chopped	2
1	medium sweet red pepper, diced	1
1 cup	diced zucchini	250 mL
½ cup	chopped onion	125 mL
3	large cloves garlic, chopped	3
¼ cup	chopped stuffed olives	50 mL
1 tbsp	capers, rinsed	15 mL
1	bay leaf	1
1 tsp	fresh thyme or ¼ tsp (1 mL) dried	5 mL
¼ tsp	each: salt and freshly ground pepper	1 mL
⅓ cup	red wine vinegar	75 mL
2 tsp	each: granulated sugar and olive oil	10 mL
2 tbsp	tomato paste	25 mL

1. Place eggplant in a non-reactive bowl. Sprinkle with salt and stir well. Let stand for 2 hours. Drain eggplant in a sieve and rinse twice, draining thoroughly; press out excess moisture.

2. Place eggplant, tomatoes, red pepper, zucchini, onion, garlic, olives, capers, bay leaf, thyme, salt and pepper in a large roasting pan.

3. Heat vinegar, sugar and oil in a microwavable container until hot, about 1 minute; stir into vegetables. Bake in a 350°F (180°C) oven for about 1½ hours (1 hour for a convection oven), or until vegetables are softened and liquid has evaporated, stirring every 20 minutes. Remove pan from oven, discard bay leaf and stir in tomato paste.

4. Remove hot jars from canner and spoon relish into jars to within ½ inch (1 cm) of rim (head space). Process 15 minutes for half-pint (250 mL) jars and 20 minutes for pint (500 mL) jars as directed on page 133 (Longer Time Processing Procedure).

Makes 5 cups (1.25 L).

CHAPTER EIGHT

SALSA SENSATIONS

RARELY do we open a food magazine without finding a mention of salsa. Salsas, the name given to a Mexican sauce, are either cooked or fresh mixtures of fruits and vegetables. The more salsas we make, the better we like them. Spicy or mild, chunky or smooth, and in colors of gold, green or red, salsas transform an otherwise plain meal into a dinner to remember.

Chile peppers of one type or another are usually added to salsa for flavor and to give authenticity. Some chiles can be positively fiery while others are quite mild. Just how mouth-searing a chile is depends on the amount of capsaicin, an acidic chemical, concentrated in the veins and seeds. That's why removing veins and seeds lower the heat level. As a rule of thumb, the smaller and more pointed the chile, the hotter it is. Remember to always wear rubber gloves when handling all hot chile peppers and never touch your mouth or eyes. Chile peppers are interchangeable in most recipes, so experiment with their differing flavors and heat levels. See the Chile Pepper Heat Scale on the following page.

Tomatillos are another Mexican specialty. We love to make our Tomatillo Mexican Salsa (page 193) whenever they are available. Fresh cilantro also gives an authentic Mexican flavor to salsa. It is easily found today in supermarkets, sometimes referred to as Chinese parsley, other times as fresh coriander.

Fresh uncooked salsas should be kept refrigerated and consumed quickly, as you would with any other fresh food. Most salsas are made from assorted vegetables. But fruit salsas are gaining popularity, so we have added several including Fresh Pineapple Jalapeño Salsa (page 208) and Papaya Mango Salsa (page 196).

SERVING SUGGESTIONS:

Salsas really jazz up plain old ground beef, whether in a meat loaf or in patties. Fajitas, enchiladas and Tacos wouldn't be the same without salsa. Add some salsa to low-fat sour cream or plain yogurt to make a light dip. Be adventurous and mix salsa with pasta for a speedy supper. And perhaps the best way to eat salsa is alone with your favorite dippers!

♪ CHILE PEPPER HEAT SCALE ♫

Rating	Varieties
10 (hottest)	Habanero, Scotch Bonnet
9	Santaka, Chiltepin, Thai
8	Aji, Rocoto, Piquin, Cayenne, Tabasco
7	de Arbol
6	Yellow Hot Wax, Serrano
5	Jalapeño, Mirasol
4	Sandia, Cascabel
3	Ancho, Pasilla, Espanola
2	NuMex Big Jim
1	Mexi-Bell, Cherry
0	Sweet Bell, Pimiento, Sweet Banana

LIST OF RECIPES

YOUR BASIC CHUNKY TOMATO SALSA

Make this basic salsa in the fall when ingredients are at their freshest. We believe its many variations will suit your family's preferences.

4	medium tomatoes, peeled and chopped (about 1 lb/500 g)	4
1	medium onion, finely chopped	1
½	sweet green pepper, chopped	½
1–4	jalapeño peppers, halved, seeded and chopped	1–4
3	cloves garlic, minced	3
½ cup	tomato sauce	125 mL
½ cup	red wine vinegar	125 mL
½ cup	chopped fresh parsley	125 mL
2 tsp	granulated sugar	10 mL
½ tsp	pickling salt	2 mL
½ tsp	ground cumin	2 mL

1. Combine tomatoes, onion, green pepper, jalapeño peppers, garlic, tomato sauce, vinegar, parsley, sugar, salt and cumin in a medium stainless steel or enamel saucepan. Bring to a boil over high heat, reduce heat and boil gently, uncovered, for 25 minutes or until desired consistency, stirring frequently.

2. Remove hot jars from canner and ladle salsa into jars to within ½ inch (1 cm) of rim (head space). Process 20 minutes for half-pint (250 mL) and pint (500 mL) jars as directed on page 133 (Longer Time Processing Procedure).

Makes 2½ cups (625 mL).

VARIATIONS:

Mild Salsa: Use 1 jalapeño pepper
Medium Salsa: Use 2 or 3 jalapeños
Hot Salsa: We guess the sky's the limit. Choose 1 Scotch bonnet, habanero or Jamaican chile pepper to replace the jalapeño peppers.
Basil or Thyme Tomato Salsa: Replace parsley with fresh basil or thyme.
Sherry Vinegar Salsa: Replace red wine vinegar with Sherry Vinegar (page 272).

BEYOND HOT SALSA

Commonly known as piquant, this salsa is not for the timid. If it's too piquant for your taste, cut the heat by reducing the amount of red hot chile peppers. If it's not piquant enough, be our guest and replace some of the jalapeño peppers with more hot chiles.

8	plum tomatoes (about 2lb/1kg)	8
1	large onion	1
4	large cloves garlic	4
4–5	jalapeño peppers, seeded *	4–5
2	small hot red chile peppers, seeded	2
¼ cup	cider vinegar	50 mL
2 tsp	dried oregano leaves or 2 tbsp (25 mL) fresh	10 mL
1 tsp	each: pickling salt and granulated sugar	5 mL

1. Combine tomatoes, onion, garlic and peppers in a food processor or blender; process until smooth. Transfer to a medium stainless steel or enamel saucepan.

2. Add vinegar, oregano, salt and sugar. Bring to a boil over high heat, reduce heat and boil gently, uncovered, for about 15 minutes or until the salsa is thickened.

3. Remove hot jars from canner and ladle salsa into jars to within ½ inch (1 cm) of top rim (head space). Process 20 minutes for half-pint (250 mL) and pint (500 mL) jars as directed on page 133 (Longer Time Processing Procedure).

Makes 3 cups (750 mL).

TIP   *Jalapeño peppers vary in heat level from hot to very hot, but you cannot tell the heat level from their appearance.*

FIERY YELLOW PEPPER SALSA

This salsa has lots of heat. If you don't like your salsa this hot, use more sweet pepper in place of the hot ones. Just don't change the total amount of peppers. Remember that the heat of individual peppers can vary greatly. This salsa is a peppery dip for nacho chips or a bold accompaniment to grilled chicken, beef or pork.

2 cups	chopped sweet yellow pepper	500 mL
2 cups	chopped peeled ripe tomatoes	500 mL
	(about 2 medium tomatoes)	
½ cup	finely chopped red onion	125 mL
¼ cup	finely chopped hot yellow pepper	50 mL
¼ cup	finely chopped jalapeño pepper	50 mL
2	large cloves garlic, minced	2
¼ cup	lime juice	50 mL
2 tbsp	white vinegar	25 mL
½ tsp	pickling salt	2 mL
2 tbsp	finely chopped fresh cilantro	25 mL

1. Combine sweet pepper, tomatoes, onion, hot peppers, garlic, lime juice, vinegar and salt in a medium stainless steel or enamel saucepan. Bring to a boil over high heat, reduce heat and boil gently, uncovered, for about 15 minutes or until mixture is thickened, stirring frequently. Stir in cilantro and cook for 2 minutes.

2. Remove hot jars from canner and ladle sauce into jars to within ½ inch (1 cm) of rim (head space). Process 20 minutes for half-pint (250 mL) and pint (500 mL) jars as directed on page 133 (Longer Time Processing Procedure).

Makes 3 cups (750 mL).

Tomato Salsa Tortillas
Add a new twist to Sunday brunch. Serve tortillas! Roll them up with scrambled eggs and top with a Fresh Vegetable Salsa (pages 199–205). It's the perfect way to start a week.
Heat 1 tbsp (15 mL) butter or margarine in a large skillet. Add 2 chopped green onions and 6 sliced mushrooms; sauté for 5 minutes. Beat 5 eggs with 2 tbsp (25 mL) milk and salt and pepper to taste. Pour into skillet and scramble eggs until soft, about 5 minutes. Add 2 chopped tomatoes and cook for 2 minutes. Place one quarter of filling on each of 4 tortillas, roll up and place seam-side down. Spoon your choice of salsa on top. Serve immediately.
Makes 4 servings.

GARDEN PATCH SALSA

This mixed vegetable salsa is an excellent accompaniment to burgers and cheese nachos or as a low-fat topping for a baked potato. Try it as a zesty dip.

6	tomatoes, peeled and diced (1½ lb/750g)	6
4	jalapeño peppers, seeded and minced	4
2	cloves garlic, minced	2
1 cup	chopped onion	250 mL
1 cup	each: shredded carrot and shredded zucchini	250 mL
½ cup	each: chopped sweet green pepper and chopped sweet yellow pepper	125 mL
½ cup	chopped Italian (flat-leaf) parsley	125 mL
½ cup	white vinegar	125 mL
⅓ cup	tomato paste	75 mL
¼ cup	chopped fresh oregano or 1 tbsp (15 mL) dried	50 mL
½ tsp	pickling salt	2 mL

1. Place all ingredients in a large stainless steel or enamel saucepan. Bring to a boil over high heat, reduce heat and simmer, uncovered, for 30 minutes or until thickened.

2. Remove hot jars from canner and ladle salsa into jars to within ½ inch (1 cm) of rim (head space). Process 20 minutes for half-pint (250 mL) and pint (500 mL) jars as directed on page 133 (Longer Time Processing Procedure).

Makes 5½ cups (1.375 L).

Mexican Vegetable Salsa Pizza
Place a 12 inch (30 cm) pizza crust or flatbread round on a baking sheet and spread with your favorite tomato salsa. Spoon 1 drained can (14 oz/398 mL) black beans or lentils over top and sprinkle with 2 finely chopped jalapeño peppers and ½ tsp (2 mL) cumin. Bake at 450°F (230°C) for 10 minutes. Sprinkle with 2 cups (500 mL) shredded mozzarella cheese and bake 10 minutes or until cheese is melted and golden.

GAZPACHO SALSA

Gazpacho, that great Spanish cold soup from Andalucia, always makes us think of summertime. So does this salsa. However, this salsa can be made anytime but the flavors are always at their best in summer, when garden-ripened produce is used.

1 tbsp	olive oil	15 mL
½ cup	finely chopped onion	125 mL
2	cloves garlic, minced	2
4	large tomatoes, peeled and chopped (about 3 cups/750 mL)	4
½ cup	diced peeled seedless cucumber	125 mL
½ cup	diced sweet green pepper	125 mL
2 cups	tomato juice	500 mL
⅓ cup	red wine vinegar	75 mL
1 tbsp	Worcestershire sauce	15 mL
1 tsp	each: ground cumin and paprika	5 mL
2 tbsp	chopped fresh basil	25 mL
	Salt and freshly ground pepper, to taste	

1. Heat oil in a large stainless steel or enamel saucepan and sauté onion on medium heat for 5 minutes. Add garlic and cook for 1 minute.

2. Stir in tomatoes, cucumber, green pepper, tomato juice, vinegar, Worcestershire sauce, cumin and paprika. Bring to a boil over high heat, reduce heat and boil gently, uncovered, for about 30 minutes or until mixture is thickened, stirring occasionally. Stir in basil, salt and pepper and cook for 2 minutes.

3. Remove hot jars from canner and ladle salsa into jars to within ½ inch (1 cm) of rim (head space). Process 20 minutes for half-pint (250 mL) and pint (500 mL) jars as directed on page 133 (Longer Time Processing Procedure).

Makes 4 cups (1 L).

TIP   *Salsas are so popular, you will probably find yourself using them with beef or chicken fajitas and with all types of fish.*

Mango Chutney Vinaigrette (page 334) and Honey Mustard Dressing (page 335)

Winter Salad Pickle (page 147)

Fast Favorite Garlic Dill Pickles (page 138)

Your Basic Chunky Tomato Salsa (page 188)

TOMATILLO MEXICAN SALSA

Tomatillos are finding favor with salsa lovers for their fresh tart flavor and hint of lemon and apple. These little green fruits are covered with a thin papery husk. They belong to the same family as tomatoes and the cape gooseberry. Popular in Mexican and Southwestern cooking, they make one of our favorite salsas. Choose tomatillos that have their husks intact and are still green. They may be kept in a paper bag in the refrigerator for up to a month. If you can't find tomatillos, green tomatoes may be substituted. Choose pale green rather than dark green tomatoes to avoid solanine, a potentially toxic substance that disappears as the tomato ripens.

½ lb	tomatillos (about 7 tomatillos)	250 g
2	hot green chile peppers, seeded and chopped	2
2	cloves garlic, minced	2
½ cup	chopped sweet red pepper	125 mL
½ cup	chopped onion	125 mL
½ cup	chopped carrot	125 mL
¼ cup	each: apple juice and cider vinegar	50 mL
¾ tsp	pickling salt	4 mL
½ tsp	each: ground cumin and dried oregano	2 mL
1 tbsp	granulated sugar	15 mL

1. Remove husks from tomatillos and discard. Wash tomatillos and coarsely chop in a food processor or by hand. Transfer to a medium stainless steel or enamel saucepan; add chiles, garlic, red pepper, onion, carrot, apple juice, vinegar, salt, cumin and oregano. Bring to a boil over high heat, reduce heat, cover and boil gently for 10 minutes.

2. Stir in sugar, return to a boil and boil gently, uncovered, for 20 minutes or until mixture is thickened. Remove from heat.

3. Remove hot jars from canner and ladle salsa into jars to within ½ inch (1 cm) of rim (head space). Process 20 minutes for half-pint (250 mL) and pint (500 mL) jars as directed on page 133 (Longer Time Processing Procedure).

Makes 2 cups (500 mL).

SOUTHWEST SALSA

Here is your basic recipe for salsa. The original asked for the juice of a Seville orange. Since these bitter oranges are not always available, we substituted a blend of lime and sweet orange juice. The salsa is best made when field-ripened tomatoes are in season. Make enough to last till they are available again!

4 cups	chopped peeled tomatoes (about 2 lb/1 kg)	1 L
1 cup	chopped onion	250 mL
3	cloves garlic, minced	3
½ cup	chopped sweet red pepper	125 mL
2–4	jalapeño peppers, seeded and minced *	2–4
½ cup	red wine vinegar	125 mL
¼ cup	chopped fresh cilantro **	50 mL
2 tbsp	orange juice	25 mL
1 tbsp	lime juice	15 mL
1 tsp	each: granulated sugar and pickling salt	5 mL
¼ cup	tomato paste	50 mL

1. Combine tomatoes, onion, garlic, peppers, vinegar, cilantro, orange and lime juice, sugar and salt in a large stainless steel or enamel saucepan. Bring to a boil over high heat, reduce heat and boil gently, uncovered, for 30 minutes or until mixture is thickened, stirring occasionally. Stir in tomato paste and cook for 2 minutes.

2. Remove hot jars from canner and ladle salsa into jars to within ½ inch (1 cm) of rim (head space). Process 20 minutes for half-pint (250 mL) and pint (500 mL) jars as directed on page 133 (Longer Time Processing Procedure).

Makes 4 cups (1 L).

*Jalapeño peppers vary in heat level—you may wish less or more depending on your preference.

** Cilantro is perhaps the world's most popular herb. It really makes salsa sing. Store fresh cilantro with its root ends in water and covered with a plastic bag. Change the water every few days. Wash the cilantro and remove the root ends just before using.

SALSA BRUSCHETTA-STYLE

Bruschetta has its origins in ancient Rome. During the December and January holidays, Romans celebrated by eating flat buns soaked in olive oil still fresh from the fall harvest. The name bruschetta comes from the Italian *bruscare*, meaning "to roast over coals." This topping is a favorite of ours to have on hand for making a quick appetizer.

3 cups	chopped peeled Italian plum tomatoes (1½ lb/750 g)	750 mL
2	large cloves garlic, minced	2
2	shallots, minced	2
1 cup	chopped fresh basil	250 mL
1 tbsp	red wine vinegar	15 mL
1 tsp	lemon juice	5 mL
½ tsp	pickling salt	2 mL
¼ tsp	coarsely ground black pepper	1 mL
2	green onions, minced	2
3 tbsp	tomato paste	45 mL

1. Combine tomatoes, garlic, shallots, basil, vinegar, lemon juice, salt and pepper in a medium stainless steel or enamel saucepan. Bring to a boil over high heat, reduce heat and boil gently for 5 minutes, stirring frequently. Stir in green onion, tomato paste and return to a boil.

2. Remove hot jars from canner and ladle salsa into jars to within ½ inch (1 cm) of rim (head space). Process 35 minutes for half-pint (250 mL) jars and 40 minutes for pint (500 mL) jars as directed on page 133 (Longer Time Processing Procedure).

Makes 3 cups (750 mL).

SERVING SUGGESTIONS:

Bruschetta
These popular appetizers can be ready at a moment's notice with this salsa on hand.
Toast sliced Italian bread and rub with cut surface of a garlic clove. Brush lightly with olive oil and spoon on salsa. If desired, sprinkle with Parmesan cheese and place under a broiler for several minutes to warm.

PAPAYA MANGO SALSA

This is a true fruit salsa and it's processed to keep on the shelf. Its papaya, mango and pineapple flavors go particularly well with fish.

1	papaya, peeled, seeded and chopped	1
1	mango, peeled and chopped	1
1	jalapeño pepper, seeded and finely chopped	1
	Juice and grated rind of 1 lime	
¼ cup	unsweetened pineapple juice	50 mL
1 tbsp	finely chopped Candied Ginger (page 301) or crystallized ginger	15 mL
1 tbsp	rice wine vinegar	15 mL
¼ tsp	pickling salt	1 mL
2 tbsp	chopped fresh mint	25 mL

1. Place papaya, mango, jalapeño pepper, lime juice and rind, pineapple juice, ginger, vinegar and salt in a medium saucepan. Bring to a boil over high heat, reduce heat and boil gently for 1 minute. Stir in mint, return to a boil and cook for 1 minute.

2. Remove hot jars from canner and ladle salsa into jars to within ½ inch (1 cm) of rim (head space). Process 20 minutes for half-pint (250 mL) and pint (500 mL) jars as directed on page 133 (Longer Time Processing Procedure).

Makes 2 cups (500 mL).

PEACH MINT SALSA

The sunny taste of peaches and the cool freshness of mint combine in this lovely fruit salsa to say "summer." Make this quick salsa when peaches are at their flavor peak. Its fresh taste beautifully complements grilled chicken and fish.

2 cups	chopped peeled peaches	500 mL
	(about 4 medium peaches)	
¼ cup	finely chopped red onion	50 mL
¼ cup	finely chopped sweet green pepper	50 mL
1 tbsp	finely chopped jalapeño pepper	15 mL
2 tbsp	liquid honey	25 mL
¼ tsp	pickling salt	1 mL
	Grated rind and juice of 1 lime	
2 tbsp	finely chopped fresh mint	25 mL

1. Combine peaches, onion, peppers, honey, salt, lime rind and juice in a medium stainless steel or enamel saucepan. Bring to a boil over high heat, reduce heat and boil gently, uncovered, for 5 minutes, stirring occasionally.

2. Stir in mint and cook for 1 minute.

3. Remove hot jars from canner and ladle salsa into jars to within ½ inch (1 cm) of rim (head space). Process 10 minutes for half-pint (250 mL) or pint (500 mL) jars as directed on page 133 (Longer Time Processing Procedure).

Makes 2 cups (500 mL).

FRESH AND DRIED CRANBERRY SALSA

Dried cranberries are added to fresh or frozen ones in this salsa to create a more concentrated cranberry flavor. They are then cooked with the rest of the ingredients to bring out their best flavor. Use this salsa as an alternative to cranberry sauce or jelly.

1 cup	fresh or frozen cranberries, coarsely chopped	250 mL
¼ cup	dried cranberries	50 mL
¼ cup	chopped red onion	50 mL
2 tbsp	chopped fresh parsley	25 mL
1–2 tbsp	liquid honey	15–25 mL
1 tbsp	each: red wine vinegar and lemon juice	15 mL
2 tsp	granulated sugar	10 mL
¼ tsp	each: pickling salt and hot pepper flakes	1 mL

1. Combine cranberries, onion, parsley, honey, vinegar, lemon juice, sugar, salt and pepper flakes in a medium stainless steel or enamel saucepan. Bring to a boil over medium heat, reduce heat and boil gently, uncovered, for about 10 minutes or until mixture is thickened, stirring frequently.

2. Remove hot jars from canner and ladle salsa into jars to within ½ inch (1 cm) of rim (head space). Process 20 minutes for half-pint (250 mL) and pint (500 mL) jars as directed on page 133 (Longer Time Processing Procedure).

Makes 1¼ cups (300 mL).

 Extra honey may be added if a sweeter salsa is desired.

SERVING SUGGESTION:

Cranberry Salad Dressing
Combine ½ cup (125 mL) Fresh and Dried Cranberry Salsa, ¼ cup (50 mL) red wine vinegar, 3 tbsp (45 mL) extra virgin olive oil, 1 clove garlic, minced, pinch of salt and pinch of freshly ground pepper in a tightly sealed container. Shake well to blend. Store in the refrigerator.
Makes ¾ cup (175 mL).

Fresh Vegetable Salsas

Salsas originated in Mexico, where they are always served fresh and so are best eaten immediately or at the most in a day or two. Fresh tomato salsas are by far the most common, but more and more ingredients, particularly fruits and other vegetables, are finding their way into this popular condiment.

Vegetable salsas are the everyday salsas of the salsa-eating world. Made and used fresh, or refrigerated for a short time, these salsas do not require as much vinegar as those that are canned and stored for later use.

Pico de Gallo Salsa

Pico de Gallo is a blend of hot chile peppers and other fresh vegetables. Variations of this salsa can be found on every Mexican restaurant table to eat with crisp corn or flour tortillas. It is excellent as a dip, and also as a salsa on tacos and enchiladas and with grilled meats and poultry. We hope it will become as popular in your home as in ours.

4	plum tomatoes, chopped (about 2 cups/500 mL)	4
½ cup	chopped red onion	125 mL
½ cup	chopped cucumber	125 mL
1	large clove garlic, minced	1
1	small jalapeño pepper, seeded and minced	1
¼ cup	chopped fresh cilantro	50 mL
¼ cup	lime juice	50 mL

1. Combine tomatoes, onion, cucumber, garlic, jalapeño pepper, cilantro and lime juice. Stir well.

2. Cover and refrigerate for 30 minutes (longer is unnecessary as this salsa is best when freshly made).

Makes about 3 cups (750 mL).

Fresh Tomato and Black Olive Salsa

The olives convert this basic Mexican dish to something more Spanish or maybe Italian. It's good as an appetizer with crackers or squares of toasted Italian bread and is best served at room temperature.

2 cups	diced plum tomatoes (about 4)	500 mL
½ cup	chopped pitted black olives (preferably Kalamata)	125 mL
⅓ cup	chopped red onion	75 mL
2 tbsp	red wine vinegar	25 mL
1	clove garlic, minced	1
1 tbsp	Dijon mustard Freshly ground black pepper	15 mL

Combine tomatoes, olives, onion, vinegar, garlic, mustard and pepper to taste. Stir well. Cover and let stand at room temperature for a few hours. Or place in tightly sealed containers and refrigerate up to 2 weeks.

Makes about 2½ cups (625 mL).

Tomato Freezer Salsa

Take advantage of all those wonderful field tomatoes available in late summer by making this freezer salsa. Enjoy some before you freeze it.

5	large field tomatoes, peeled	5
2 tbsp	olive oil	25 mL
6	green onions, finely chopped	6
1	jalapeño pepper, seeded and finely chopped	6
4	medium cloves garlic, finely chopped	4
¼ cup	chopped fresh cilantro	50 mL
2 tbsp	lime juice	25 mL
¼ tsp	each: salt and freshly ground pepper	1 mL

1. Coarsely chop tomatoes and place in a sieve over a bowl to allow extra juice to drain.

2. Heat oil on medium heat in a nonstick skillet. Add onions, jalapeño pepper and garlic; cook for 7 minutes or until softened but not brown, stirring often. Let cool. Stir into drained tomatoes.

3. Stir in lime juice, salt and pepper. Spoon into tightly sealed plastic containers and freeze for up to 4 months.

Makes about 5 cups (1.25 L).

TOMATO BASIL SALSA

We like to make this salsa when great field tomatoes and lots of fresh basil are plentiful. Enjoy it with cooked fettucine, fusilli or shell pasta topped with freshly grated Parmesan cheese.

2 cups	chopped unpeeled tomatoes (about 2 large tomatoes)	500 mL
¾ cup	chopped fresh basil	175 mL
½ cup	finely chopped red onion	125 mL
¼ cup	tomato paste	50 mL
2	cloves garlic, crushed	2
2 tbsp	Dijon mustard	25 mL
2 tbsp	sherry or red wine vinegar	25 mL
1 tbsp	walnut or vegetable oil	15 mL

Combine tomatoes, basil, onion, tomato paste, garlic, mustard, vinegar and oil in a small bowl. Cover and let stand at room temperature for several hours or place in plastic containers with tight-fitting lids and freeze for longer storage.

Makes about 2½ cups (625 mL).

GARLIC TOMATO SALSA

An easy-to-make fresh salsa chock full of flavor. Even non-garlic lovers may become addicted.

2	ripe medium tomatoes, chopped	2
2	cloves garlic, crushed	2
2 tbsp	lime juice	25 mL
1 tbsp	chopped fresh cilantro or parsley	15 mL
1 tbsp	finely chopped red onion	15 mL
1 tsp	capers, drained and chopped	5 mL
⅛ tsp	salt	0.5 mL

Combine tomatoes, garlic, lime juice, cilantro, onion, capers and salt in a small bowl. Cover and let stand in refrigerator for 15 minutes.

Makes 1 cup (250 mL).

TRIPLE TOMATO SALSA

Three kinds of tomatoes—cherry, tomatillo and common—are the basis of this appealing salsa. It has become one of our favorite dips for tortilla chips. If you can find orange or yellow cherry tomatoes, they add interesting color.

1 tbsp	extra virgin olive oil	15 mL
½ cup	chopped red onion	125 mL
2 tbsp	dry white wine	25 mL
8	green tomatillos, husked, cored and diced *	8
4	ripe medium tomatoes, seeded and diced	4
2 cups	yellow, orange or red cherry tomatoes, diced	500 mL
	Salt and freshly ground pepper	
6	sprigs fresh basil, chopped	6

1. Heat oil in a large non-stick skillet over medium-high heat. Add onion and cook for 2 minutes. Add wine and tomatillos; stir to combine. Remove from heat.

2. Add tomatoes to skillet while it is still warm. Season to taste with salt and pepper; stir in basil.

3. Place mixture in a medium bowl. Cover and let stand for 20 minutes. Refrigerate until serving time, but use within 6 hours.

Makes 3 cups (750 mL).

TIP *If you are unable to buy tomatillos, replace with diced pale green tomatoes.*

ROASTED CORN AND SWEET PEPPER SALSA

Roasting sweet corn caramelizes the sugar in the kernels into a wonderful woodsy flavor that is highlighted by balsamic vinegar and sweet peppers.

1½ cups	fresh corn kernels (about 3 ears)	375 mL
1 tsp	olive oil	5 mL
¼ cup	each: diced sweet orange pepper and sweet green pepper	50 mL
¼ cup	diced red onion	50 mL
2 tbsp	chopped fresh Italian parsley	25 mL
2 tsp	each: balsamic vinegar and lime juice	10 mL
⅛ tsp	salt	0.5 mL

1. Heat a large non-stick skillet over medium-high heat. Add corn and oil and cook until corn turns a light brown, stirring constantly.

2. Remove from heat and cool for 5 minutes.

3. Stir in peppers, onion, parsley, vinegar, lime juice and salt.

4. Cover and let stand for 30 minutes before serving.

Makes 1½ cups (375 mL).

SOUTHWEST BLACK BEAN AND CORN SALSA

Cilantro, cumin and jalapeño peppers deliver flavors reminiscent of the Southwest. And mix it with rice and green pepper for a fast salad (page 333).

1 cup	cooked black beans	250 mL
1 cup	frozen or fresh corn niblets	250 mL
½ cup	finely chopped celery	125 mL
2	jalapeño peppers, seeded and finely chopped	2
2	cloves garlic, chopped	2
2 tbsp	each: lime juice and balsamic vinegar	25 mL
1 tbsp	red wine vinegar	15 mL
¼ tsp	each: cumin, coarsely ground black pepper and salt	1 mL
½ cup	each: finely chopped sweet red pepper and green onion	125 mL
1 tbsp	olive oil	15 mL
½ cup	chopped fresh cilantro	125 mL

1. Place beans, corn, celery, jalapeño peppers, garlic, lime juice, balsamic vinegar, red wine vinegar, cumin, pepper and salt in a large saucepan. Bring to a boil, reduce heat and boil gently for 5 minutes.

2. Stir in red pepper, green onion, olive oil and cilantro.

3. Spoon salsa into clean jars or plastic containers to within ½ inch (1 cm) of rim. Cover with tight-fitting lids. Label jars and refrigerate for up to 1 week or freeze for longer storage.

Makes 2¾ cups (675 mL).

TIP

To cook beans: Place washed dried beans in a large saucepan and add 3 times the amount of cold water. Cover and bring to a boil; boil for 2 minutes. Remove from heat and let stand for 1 hour; drain. Cover beans with cold water and bring to a boil; reduce heat, cover and boil gently, covered, for 30 minutes or until beans are tender; drain.

TAPENADE-STYLE SALSA

This salsa has a more paste-like consistency than most and with its olive and garlic flavors reminds us of the French tapenade. It is marvelous spread on sliced crusty Italian bread or on crackers.

¾ cup	chopped pitted Kalamata olives	175 mL
⅔ cup	chopped pitted green olives	150 mL
½	sweet red pepper, chopped	½
¼ cup	chopped sun-dried tomatoes in olive oil	50 mL
¼ cup	chopped Italian (flat-leaf) parsley	50 mL
¼ cup	olive oil	50 mL
2	cloves garlic, chopped	2
1 tbsp	each: red wine vinegar and balsamic vinegar	15 mL
	Freshly ground black pepper	

1. Place olives, red pepper, dried tomatoes, parsley, oil, garlic, red wine vinegar and balsamic vinegar in a food processor and process with on/off motion until finely chopped. Add black pepper to taste.

2. Spoon salsa into clean jars or plastic containers to within ½ inch (1 cm) of rim. Cover with tight-fitting lids.

3. Label jars and refrigerate for up to 1 week or freeze for longer storage.

Makes 2 cups (500 mL).

FRESH FRUIT SALSAS

Although vegetable salsas are by far the most common, trendy fresh fruit salsas are appearing more frequently. Their uses are many—and everyone eats large amounts as a side dish, so make lots. They are refreshing.

FRESH SPICY TROPICAL FRUIT SALSA

Tropical flavors abound in this fresh fruit salsa. We found that its fresh and minty flavors beautifully complement grilled sausages, pork chops, pork tenderloin and chicken.

1	kiwifruit, peeled and diced	1
¼	mango, peeled and diced	¼
¼	papaya, peeled, seeded and chopped	¼
½ cup	quartered strawberries	125 mL
½ cup	diced cantaloupe	125 mL
½	jalapeño or other hot pepper, seeded and finely chopped	½
2 tbsp	finely chopped fresh mint	25 mL
1 tbsp	each: granulated sugar and lime juice	15 mL

1. Gently stir together kiwifruit, mango, papaya, strawberries, cantaloupe and jalapeño.

2. Add mint, sugar and lime juice; stir to blend.

3. Refrigerate for about 10 minutes to allow flavors to develop.

Makes 3 cups (750 mL).

FRESH SWEET PEPPER AND PEACH SALSA

Peaches are to summer as apples are to fall, and this salsa is certainly a celebration of the summer peach season. It is also marvelous made with nectarines. Serve it with pork tenderloin or barbecued pork chops. We also like it with chicken breasts and chicken burgers.

4 cups	chopped peeled peaches (4 medium)	1 L
½	small sweet red pepper, chopped	½
½	small sweet green pepper, chopped	½
¼ cup	finely chopped red onion	50 mL
¼ cup	chopped fresh cilantro	50 mL
1 tbsp	chopped jalapeño or other hot pepper	15 mL
1	clove garlic, crushed	1
1 tbsp	each: lime juice and rice vinegar	15 mL
1 tsp	liquid honey	5 mL

Combine peaches, sweet peppers, onion, cilantro, jalapeño pepper and garlic in a medium bowl. Stir in lime juice, vinegar and honey. Cover and refrigerate for 30 minutes for flavors to develop.

Makes about 3½ cups (875 mL).

MANGO CILANTRO SALSA

Make this salsa whenever fresh mangoes are plentiful and inexpensive, usually from mid June till the end of July.

1	ripe medium mango	1
3 tbsp	chopped fresh cilantro	45 mL
2	green onions, thinly sliced	2
1–2 tbsp	finely chopped jalapeño pepper	15–25 mL
1 tsp	lime juice	5 mL
½ tsp	granulated sugar	2 mL
⅛ tsp	each: salt and ground ginger	0.5 mL

Peel and dice mango into small pieces. Combine mango, cilantro, onions, jalapeño pepper, lime juice, sugar, salt and ginger in a small bowl. Adjust seasonings, if desired. Serve immediately or cover and refrigerate for up to 1 day.

Makes about 1¼ cups (300 mL).

FRESH PINEAPPLE JALAPEÑO SALSA

Hot jalapeño pepper and sweet, cooling pineapple blend to produce a salsa to serve with grilled chicken or fish. We did, and everyone wanted the recipe.

3	plum tomatoes, diced	3
1 cup	diced pineapple	250 mL
1 cup	diced papaya	250 mL
¼ cup	chopped fresh cilantro	50 mL
2	green onions, chopped	2
2	small jalapeño peppers, seeded and finely chopped	2
2 tbsp	lime juice	25 mL
⅛ tsp	each: salt and freshly ground pepper	0.5 mL

1. Combine tomatoes, pineapple, papaya, cilantro, onions and jalapeño in a bowl.

2. Stir in lime juice, salt and pepper. Cover and refrigerate for 3 hours before serving. Stir again and transfer to a serving bowl.

Makes 2½ cups (625 mL).

PARADISE PAPAYA SALSA

Colorful as well as flavorful, this salsa goes well with fruit salads, cottage cheese and chicken.

2 cups	diced peeled papaya	500 mL
½ cup	chopped sweet red pepper	125 mL
2	green onions, chopped	2
4 tsp	lime juice	20 mL
2 tsp	balsamic vinegar	10 mL
1	clove garlic, minced	1
	Salt and freshly ground pepper	

Combine papaya, red pepper, onions, lime juice, vinegar and garlic. Cover and let stand for about 1 hour. Add salt and pepper to taste.

Makes 2½ cups (625 mL).

TRI-COLOR CITRUS MINT SALSA

Multi-hued citrus gives a pleasing appearance as well as a refreshing flavor to this delightful salsa. It is particularly good with fish and chicken entrées.

2	medium pink grapefruit	2
2	large oranges	2
2	limes	2
1	jalapeño pepper, seeded and minced	1
2 tsp	finely minced shallots	10 mL
1 tsp	liquid honey	5 mL
⅛ tsp	salt	0.5 mL
3-4 drops	hot pepper sauce	3-4 drops

1. Remove outside rind from grapefruit, oranges and limes with a sharp knife, exposing the pulp of the fruit. Carefully cut on both sides of each inner membrane and gently lift out fruit sections. Cut each section into several pieces and place in a bowl. Drain off extra juice and reserve for another use.

2. Stir in pepper, shallots, honey, salt and hot pepper sauce. Refrigerate for about an hour to allow flavors to blend. Salsa may be prepared up to 1 day ahead.

Makes 2 cups (500 mL).

CHAPTER NINE

CHOICE CHUTNEYS

CHUTNEYS offer a whole new dimension to foods. Whereas salsas have a light and fresh, lively taste, chutneys have a rich, smooth, mellow, sweet-sour taste. They are a perfect accompaniment to spicy and strong-flavored foods. Like salsas, chutneys can range in texture from chunky to smooth and in spiciness from mild to hot.

Traditionally, apples and onions are the base of chutney ingredients, with raisins and sometimes dates added. Since dried fruits are often a main ingredient, many chutneys can be made at any time of the year. Chopping can be done with a food processor because all the ingredients become very soft during the cooking. Long, slow cooking is the general rule in making chutneys in order to develop their mellow flavor. Chutneys get better with age, so allow a few weeks in the jar after processing.

Mango Chutney (page 218) is probably the best known of all the chutneys. The addition of papaya in our Mango Papaya Chutney (page 219) is a new approach to this all-time favorite. Hellfire Chutney (page 227), a unique chutney made from dried dates, is probably our most authentic recipe since it was brought with a family moving to Canada from India where chutneys were first created. Juniper Berry Chutney (page 217) has Scottish origins.

SERVING SUGGESTIONS:

Chutneys are traditionally served as an accompaniment to hot meals like curries, rice dishes, stews and casseroles. But don't hesitate to pair them with roast chicken, lamb, beef, pork and game. Some chutneys greatly enhance fish. You can offer a selection of chutneys with barbecued meats as well as with salads and cold meats. We often serve them with such cheeses as Stilton, Brie, Camembert and Gorgonzola. Be sure to try them with a cottage cheese salad and the sweeter ones make delicious bread and cracker spreads. One day, a small amount of chutney remained in the bottom of a jar when a dip was needed. We stirred in an equal amount of plain low-fat yogurt and *voilà*—the chutney became a delicious dip for raw veggies!

LIST OF RECIPES

APPLE PLUM CHUTNEY

Autumn flavors of apples, blue plums and tomatoes shine in this traditionally spiced chutney.

5 cups	chopped peeled and cored apples (about 5 medium apples)	1.25 L
2½ cups	chopped peeled tomatoes (about 3 large tomatoes)	625 mL
2 cups	chopped pitted blue plums (about 8–10 plums)	500 mL
2 cups	sultana raisins	500 mL
2 cups	cider vinegar	500 mL
⅔ cup	chopped onion	150 mL
2	cloves garlic, minced	2
2½ cups	demerara or lightly packed dark brown sugar	625 mL
2 tsp	curry powder	10 mL
¼ tsp	ground allspice	1 mL
¼ tsp	pickling salt	1 mL
⅛ tsp	cayenne	0.5 mL

1. Combine apples, tomatoes, plums, raisins, vinegar, onion and garlic in a very large stainless steel or enamel saucepan. Bring to a boil over high heat, reduce heat and boil gently, uncovered, for 30 minutes.

2. Add sugar, return to a boil and boil gently for 30 minutes or until thickened, stirring occasionally. Add curry powder, allspice, salt and cayenne; cook for 5 minutes, stirring frequently.

3. Remove hot jars from canner and ladle chutney into jars to within ½ inch (1 cm) of rim (head space). Process 10 minutes for half-pint (250 mL) jars and 15 minutes for pint (500 mL) jars as directed on page 133 (Longer Time Processing Procedure).

Makes about 6 cups (1.5 L).

QUICK APPLE CRANBERRY CHUTNEY

This colorful recipe is a breeze! Cooking time is particularly short because of the high pectin content of both fruits. It's wonderfully spicy with lamb, chicken, pork and game.

2 cups	chopped cranberries	500 mL
1 cup	finely chopped apple	250 mL
½ cup	each: finely chopped red onion and sweet red pepper	125 mL
½ cup	cider vinegar	125 mL
2	cloves garlic, minced	2
1 tbsp	finely chopped gingerroot	15 mL
½ cup	packed brown sugar	125 mL
¼ tsp	each: cumin and salt	1 mL
⅛ tsp	each: freshly ground pepper and hot pepper flakes	0.5 mL

1. Combine cranberries, apple, onion, red pepper, vinegar, garlic and gingerroot in a medium stainless steel or enamel saucepan. Bring to a boil over high heat, reduce heat and boil gently, covered, for 5 minutes or until cranberries pop.

2. Add sugar, cumin, salt, pepper and hot pepper flakes. Cook for 5 minutes or until thickened.

3. Remove hot jars from canner and ladle chutney into jars to within ½ inch (1 cm) of rim (head space). Process 10 minutes for half-pint (250 mL) jars and 15 minutes for pint (500 mL) jars as directed on page 133 (Longer Time Processing Procedure).

Makes 2 cups (500 mL).

MICROWAVE METHOD:

1. Combine cranberries, apple, onion, red pepper, vinegar, garlic and gingerroot in a shallow 4-cup (1 L) microwavable container. Microwave, covered, at High (100%) for 5 minutes or until cranberries pop.

2. Stir in sugar, cumin, salt, pepper and hot pepper flakes. Microwave, covered, at Medium-High (70%) for 5 minutes or until thickened, stirring once. Proceed from step 3 above.

SPICED KIWIFRUIT APPLE CHUTNEY

We enjoy making this chutney when few other fresh fruits are available. Try it as an appetizer with cream cheese. Its delicate flavor pairs well with fish.

7	kiwifruit, peeled and chopped (about 3 cups/750 mL)	7
2	apples, peeled, cored and chopped	2
¾ cup	finely chopped onion	175 mL
¾ cup	granulated sugar	175 mL
¾ cup	cider vinegar	175 mL
¼ cup	brown sugar	50 mL
⅓ cup	golden raisins	75 mL
2	cloves garlic, crushed	2
1 tsp	minced peeled gingerroot	5 mL
½ tsp	each: cinnamon and mustard seeds	2 mL
¼ tsp	each: cayenne pepper, ground cloves, nutmeg and salt	1 mL

1. Combine kiwifruit, apples, onion, granulated sugar, vinegar, brown sugar, raisins, garlic and gingerroot in a large stainless steel or enamel saucepan. Bring to a boil over high heat, reduce heat and boil gently, uncovered, for 25 minutes or until thickened and fruit is tender, stirring occasionally. Add cinnamon, mustard seeds, cayenne, cloves, nutmeg and salt; boil gently for a few minutes longer.

2. Remove hot jars from canner and ladle chutney into jars to within ½ inch (1 cm) of rim (head space). Process 10 minutes for half-pint (250 mL) jars and 15 minutes for pint (500 mL) jars as directed on page 133 (Longer Time Processing Procedure).

Makes 4 cups (1 L).

SERVING SUGGESTION:

Chicken Salad with Chutney Cream Dressing
Dressing: In a blender combine ½ cup (125 mL) plain yogurt or light sour cream, ¼ cup (50 mL) Spiced Kiwifruit Apple Chutney, 2 tbsp (25 mL) light mayonnaise, 1 tbsp (15 mL) Dijon mustard and 1 tsp (5 mL) dry sherry; process until smooth. Makes about 1 cup (250 mL).
Salad: Combine 1 cup (250 mL) diced cold cooked chicken and ½ cup (125 mL) each: chopped celery and apple in a bowl. Toss with enough dressing to moisten.

CHERRY CURRANT CHUTNEY

Rich and thick, this exciting combination of cherries, currants and peppers makes an exquisite accompaniment to duck, roasted turkey and chicken, and even to sausages.

1	medium orange	1
3 cups	fresh or frozen chopped cherries	750 mL
¾ cup	finely chopped onion	175 mL
½	finely chopped sweet green pepper	½
½	finely chopped sweet red pepper	½
⅓ cup	dried currants	75 mL
½ cup	lightly packed brown sugar	125 mL
¼ cup	balsamic vinegar	50 mL
1	1-inch (2.5 cm) piece gingerroot, peeled and chopped	1
¼–½ tsp	dried red pepper flakes	1–2 mL
½ tsp	each: ground cardamom and salt	2 mL
¼ tsp	ground allspice	1 mL

1. Remove 3 thin strips, about 2 inches (5 cm) long, of outer rind from orange and finely chop; reserve orange pulp for another use. Combine rind, cherries, onion, peppers, currants, sugar, vinegar, gingerroot and seasonings in a medium stainless steel or enamel saucepan. Bring to a boil, reduce heat and boil gently, covered, for 20 minutes. Uncover and continue to boil gently for 30 minutes or until thickened, stirring frequently.

2. Remove hot jars from canner and ladle chutney into jars to within ½ inch (1 cm) of rim (head space). Process 10 minutes for half-pint (250 mL) jars and 15 minutes for pint (500 mL) jars as directed on page 133 (Longer Time Processing Procedure).

Makes about 2 cups (500 mL).

SERVING SUGGESTION:

Chicken Breast with Cherry Currant Chutney
Coat boneless chicken breasts lightly with chutney mixed with water to thin to spreading consistency. Bake in a 350°F (180°C) oven for about 20 minutes or until chicken is no longer pink and juices run clear. Pork chops may also receive a similar treatment.

INDIAN CHUTNEY

Along the lines of the commercial chutney known as Major Gray, this recipe has a somewhat zippier flavor than some of our others. We love it with curries and also as a light appetizer combined with low-fat sour cream or plain yogurt served with crackers or raw vegetables.

1 cup	chopped onion	250 mL
¾ cup	raisins	175 mL
¾ cup	cider vinegar	175 mL
1	medium orange, peeled and chopped	1
1	medium lemon, peeled and chopped	1
1	lime, peeled and chopped	1
¼ cup	each: lightly packed brown sugar and molasses	50 mL
¼ cup	finely chopped gingerroot	50 mL
4	cloves garlic, crushed	4
1 tbsp	mustard seeds	15 mL
½ tsp	each: hot pepper flakes and cinnamon	2 mL
¼ tsp	each: ground cloves and allspice	1 mL
⅛ tsp	cayenne pepper	0.5 mL

1. Combine onion, raisins, vinegar, orange, lemon, lime, brown sugar, molasses, gingerroot, garlic and mustard seeds in a large stainless steel or enamel saucepan. Bring to a boil over high heat, reduce heat and boil gently, uncovered, for 30 minutes or until fruit is tender and mixture is thickened, stirring occasionally. Add hot pepper flakes, cinnamon, cloves, allspice and cayenne; boil gently for 5 minutes.

2. Remove hot jars from canner and ladle chutney into jars to within ½ inch (1 cm) of rim (head space). Process 10 minutes for half-pint (250 mL) jars and 15 minutes for pint (500 mL) jars as directed on page 133 (Longer Time Processing Procedure).

Makes 3 cups (750 mL).

SERVING SUGGESTION:

Indian Chutney Cheese Spread
Blend ⅓ cup (75 mL) chutney with ⅔ cup (150 mL) light cream cheese. Use as a spread for crackers or to fill celery sticks and hollowed-out cherry tomatoes.
Makes 1 cup (250 mL).

JUNIPER BERRY CHUTNEY

This unusual chutney was inspired by a gift jar that Margaret's friend Janine brought her from Scotland. The flavor of juniper berries makes it a natural accompaniment to game, curry dishes and ham. Juniper berries are usually sold dry for flavoring meats, sauces and stuffings.

3	large tomatoes, peeled and chopped (about 2½ cups/625 mL)	3
1	large tart green apple, peeled, cored and chopped	1
1	medium onion, chopped	1
½ cup	sultana raisins	125 mL
½ cup	light brown sugar	125 mL
½ cup	each: liquid honey and cider vinegar	125 mL
¼ cup	water	50 mL
1 tbsp	juniper berries, crushed *	15 mL
¼ tsp	salt	1 mL
⅛ tsp	hot pepper sauce	0.5 mL

1. Combine tomatoes, apple, onion, raisins, sugar, honey, vinegar, water and juniper berries in a large stainless steel or enamel saucepan. Bring to a boil over high heat, reduce heat and boil gently, uncovered, for 25 minutes or until thickened, stirring occasionally. Add salt and pepper sauce and cook for 2 minutes.

2. Remove hot jars from canner and ladle chutney into jars to within ½ inch (1 cm) of rim (head space). Process 10 minutes for half-pint (250 mL) jars and 15 minutes for pint (500 mL) jars as directed on page 133 (Longer Time Processing Procedure).

Makes 4 cups (1 L).

TIP   *Look for juniper berries in specialty or bulk stores carrying a selection of spices. Crushing the berries helps release their flavor.*

MANGO CHUTNEY

Mango Chutney is the one we think of as the "original" and most traditional of all chutneys. It goes well with curries, chicken, pork, lamb and game. See also the Mango Chutney Vinaigrette on page 334.

3	medium apples, peeled, cored and chopped	3
2	large mangoes, peeled and chopped	2
½	medium sweet red pepper, chopped	½
1½ cups	granulated sugar	375 mL
1 cup	finely chopped onion	250 mL
½ cup	golden raisins	125 mL
½ cup	white vinegar	125 mL
¼ cup	finely chopped peeled gingerroot	50 mL
1 tbsp	lemon juice	15 mL
2 tsp	curry powder	10 mL
½ tsp	each: ground nutmeg, cinnamon and salt	2 mL

1. Combine apples, mangoes, red pepper, sugar, onion, raisins, vinegar and gingerroot in a large stainless steel or enamel saucepan. Bring to a boil over high heat, reduce heat and boil gently, uncovered, for 20 minutes or until fruit is tender and mixture is thickened, stirring occasionally. Add lemon juice, curry powder, nutmeg, cinnamon and salt; boil gently for 5 minutes.

2. Remove hot jars from canner and ladle chutney into jars to within ½ inch (1 cm) of rim (head space). Process 10 minutes for half-pint (250 mL) jars and 15 minutes for pint (500 mL) jars as directed on page 133 (Longer Time Processing Procedure).

Makes 5 cups (1.25 L).

SERVING SUGGESTION:

Chutney Butter
Serve with grilled or barbecued chicken parts.
Combine 3 tbsp (45 mL) Mango Chutney and 1 tbsp (15 mL) softened butter or margarine. Stir in 2 tsp (10 mL) chopped fresh cilantro and a pinch of cayenne pepper.
Makes ¼ cup (50 mL).

MANGO PAPAYA CHUTNEY

These two magnificent tropical fruits, mango and papaya, make this chutney such a wonderful accompaniment to cottage cheese and fruit salad, or to any Caribbean chicken or pork dish. It is also excellent served with fish.

½ cup	granulated sugar	125 mL
¼ cup	water	50 mL
¼ cup	cider vinegar	50 mL
3 cups	finely chopped papaya and mango	750 mL
1–2 tbsp	minced jalapeño or hot yellow peppers	15–25 mL
1 tbsp	minced gingerroot	15 mL
½ tsp	ground coriander	2 mL
¼ tsp	salt	1 mL

1. Combine sugar and water in a heavy stainless steel or enamel saucepan. Bring to a boil, uncovered, over medium-high heat; reduce heat and boil gently for about 8 minutes or until mixture has become syrupy, without stirring.

2. Remove from heat and carefully add vinegar (mixture may bubble). Add papaya, mango, peppers, gingerroot, coriander and salt. Return to a boil, reduce heat to medium low and boil gently for 10 minutes or until fruit is tender and chutney has thickened, stirring occasionally.

3. Remove hot jars from canner and ladle chutney into jars to within ½ inch (1 cm) of rim (head space). Process 10 minutes for half-pint (250 mL) jars or 15 minutes for pint (500 mL) jars as directed on page 133 (Longer Time Processing Procedure).

Makes about 2¼ cups (550 mL).

SERVING SUGGESTION:

Chutney Salad Dressing
Use 2–3 tbsp (25-45 mL) Mango Papaya Chutney with ⅓ cup (75 mL) low-fat plain yogurt as a dressing for torn romaine leaves.

MIXED FRUIT CHUTNEY

This zesty chutney was shared with us by Sheila Whyte of Thyme and Again Creative Catering and Take Home Foods in Ottawa and her chef, Robert Jutres. Robert created this recipe one fall when apples, pears and plums were abundant. It has become one of their best-sellers. Robert suggests serving it with grilled chicken and curries. He says, "Don't be tempted to taste it for at least 2 weeks. Allow the flavors to mellow."

6 cups	diced cored peeled tart apples (about 2 lb/1 kg)	1.5 L
3 cups	coarsely chopped peeled tomatoes (about 1 lb/500 g)	750 mL
2 cups	diced cored peeled firm pears (about 1 lb/500 g)	500 mL
1 cup	diced prune plums (about ½ lb/250 g)	250 mL
1 cup	raisins or currants	250 mL
5 cups	lightly packed dark brown sugar	1.25 L
2½ cups	cider or malt vinegar	625 mL
½ tsp	each: ground ginger, mace*, ground cloves, cayenne pepper, coarsely ground black pepper and salt	2 mL

1. Combine apples, tomatoes, pears, plums and raisins in a large stainless steel or enamel saucepan. Stir in brown sugar, vinegar, ginger, mace, cloves, cayenne pepper, black pepper and salt.

2. Bring to a boil over high heat, stirring constantly. Reduce heat and boil gently for 1 hour or until chutney is very thick and golden brown, stirring frequently.

3. Remove hot jars from canner and ladle chutney into jars to within ½ inch (1 cm) of rim (head space). Process 15 minutes for half-pint (250 mL) and pint (500 mL) jars as directed on page 133 (Longer Time Processing Procedure).

Makes 4½ cups (1.125 L).

TIPS *Tomatoes peel easily after being dipped into boiling water for 30 seconds.*

*   * *Mace is the red covering of the nutmeg seed, dried and usually sold in a ground form. It has a fuller, spicier flavor than the nutmeg seed, but you may substitute ground nutmeg in recipes calling for mace.*

ORCHARD CHUTNEY

Roasted garlic gives richness to this flavorful multi-fruit chutney that always adds interest to everyday meals. Served as an appetizer with soft Brie or Camembert cheese on crackers, it is quite magnificent!

2	heads garlic	2
2½ cups	chopped peeled tart apples (about 3 medium apples)	625 mL
2 cups	chopped peeled peaches (about 4 medium peaches)	500 mL
1 cup	chopped onions	250 mL
1 cup	golden raisins	250 mL
½ cup	chopped dried apricots	125 mL
1 cup	lightly packed brown sugar	250 mL
1¼ cups	cider vinegar	300 mL
¼ cup	balsamic vinegar	50 mL
1 tbsp	finely chopped gingerroot	15 mL
½ tsp	each: ground allspice and pickling salt	2 mL
¼ tsp	ground cloves	1 mL

1. Wrap each head of garlic in a double thickness of foil. Bake in a 400°C (200°C) oven for 40 minutes or until garlic is very soft. Cool and remove foil. With scissors, snip the tip from each clove and carefully squeeze out garlic, removing any pieces of the paper husk. Chop garlic paste finely with a knife.

2. Add garlic, apples, peaches, onions, raisins, apricots, sugar, vinegars, gingerroot, allspice, salt and cloves to a large stainless steel or enamel saucepan. Bring to a boil over high heat, reduce heat and boil gently, uncovered, for 30 minutes or until thickened.

3. Remove hot jars from canner and ladle chutney into jars to within ½ inch (1 cm) of rim (head space). Process 10 minutes for half-pint (250 mL) and pint (500 mL) jars as directed on page 133 (Longer Time Processing Procedure).

Makes 5½ cups (1.375 L).

RHUBARB, DATE AND APRICOT CHUTNEY

Dates and apricots give a rich flavor to the sweet-sour taste of rhubarb. It pairs especially well with ham, but also complements other dishes.

4 cups	sliced rhubarb	1 L
1 cup	chopped dried dates	250 mL
1 cup	lightly packed brown sugar	250 mL
½ cup	chopped dried apricots	125 mL
½ cup	cider vinegar	125 mL
¼ cup	finely chopped onion	50 mL
¼ cup	finely chopped Candied Ginger (page 301) or crystallized ginger	50 mL
1 tsp	curry powder	5 mL
¼ tsp	ground nutmeg	1 mL
¼ tsp	pickling salt	1 mL

1. Combine rhubarb, dates, sugar, apricots, vinegar, onion, ginger, curry powder, nutmeg and salt in a medium stainless steel or enamel saucepan. Bring to a boil over medium-high heat; reduce heat and cook, uncovered, for 8 minutes, or until thickened and fruit is soft, stirring frequently.

2. Remove hot jars from canner and ladle chutney into jars to within ½ inch (1 cm) of rim (head space). Process 10 minutes for half-pint (250 mL) jars and 15 minutes for pint (500 mL) jars as directed on page 133 (Longer Time Processing Procedure).

Makes about 3 cups (750 mL).

RED PEPPER APRICOT CHUTNEY

This light, fresh chutney goes well with pork curries, and with duck, poultry and lamb. Enjoy it in a Cheddar cheese sandwich or with cream cheese and melba toast. Wonderful plump Turkish apricots for this recipe are readily found in most food stores.

1 cup	diced sweet red pepper (about ½ large pepper)	250 mL
1 cup	chopped dried apricots	250 mL
¾ cup	chopped onion	175 mL
1	apple, peeled, cored and chopped (1 cup/250 mL)	1
⅔ cup	granulated sugar	150 mL
½ cup	golden raisins	125 mL
½ cup	cider vinegar	125 mL
¼ cup	water	50 mL
1 tbsp	minced Candied Ginger (page 301) or crystallized ginger	15 mL
¼ tsp	each: ground cinnamon, mace and salt	1 mL
⅛ tsp	cayenne	0.5 mL

1. Combine red pepper, apricots, onion, apple, sugar, raisins, vinegar, water and ginger in a medium stainless steel or enamel saucepan. Bring to a boil over high heat, reduce heat, cover and boil gently for 10 minutes, stirring occasionally. Add cinnamon, mace, salt and cayenne. Cook, uncovered, for about 5 minutes, stirring frequently.

2. Remove hot jars from canner and ladle chutney into jars to within ½ inch (1 cm) of rim (head space). Process 10 minutes for half-pint (250 mL) jars and 15 minutes for pint (500 mL) jars as directed on page 133 (Longer Time Processing Procedure).

Makes about 2½ cups (625 mL).

VARIATION:

Red Pepper Peach Chutney
Replace apricots with 1 cup (250 mL) chopped peeled peaches and omit water.

ROASTED TOMATO CHUTNEY

Roasting the ingredients gives this chutney a nice mellow, roasted taste that is unusual in chutneys. Serve on cooked pasta, with crackers, as an appetizer or in a pasta salad. It also matches well with grilled beef, chicken or pork. Since this chutney is not processed, it must be frozen for longer storage. So make lots and freeze it when plum tomatoes are in season and inexpensive.

1 cup	fresh cilantro leaves, packed tightly	250 mL
10	plum tomatoes, quartered *	10
	(about 2½ lb/1 kg)	
10	cloves garlic, peeled	10
1	2-inch (5 cm) piece hot yellow or jalapeño	1
	pepper	
2 tbsp	olive oil	25 mL
½ tsp	each: ground cumin, mustard seeds,	2 mL
	salt and freshly ground pepper	

1. Place cilantro in a shallow ovenproof casserole. Top with tomatoes, garlic and hot pepper. Drizzle with oil and sprinkle with seasonings.

2. Roast, uncovered, in a 350°F (180°C) oven for about 35 minutes. Remove from oven, stir to combine and cool slightly. Place in a food processor and pulse with on/off motion until coarsely chopped.

3. Spoon chutney into jars or plastic containers to within ½ inch (1 cm) of rim (head space). Cover with tight-fitting lids. Label jars and refrigerate for up to 1 week or freeze for longer storage.

Makes 3 cups (750 mL).

VARIATION:

Fennel Seed Chutney
Replace mustard seeds with 1 tbsp (15 mL) fennel seeds in Step 1.

TIP

Tomatoes are best when stored at room temperature. Cold temperatures are usually the "kiss of death" to their fresh flavor and texture. However, if tomatoes are starting to over-ripen and will be used for cooking, not eating fresh, store them briefly in the refrigerator until you have time to work with them. And, of course, they may be frozen during the bountiful season to use in cooking during the colder months.
As for green tomatoes, they will ripen if kept out of the refrigerator. So, if you want them to stay green, the refrigerator is the place for them.

SUN-DRIED TOMATO CHUTNEY

Two kinds of tomatoes, sun-dried and fresh, are used to create this exciting chutney. It has some spice level for further interest. Perfect with cooked rice, pasta, curries and egg and cheese dishes, it can also be served with grilled meats and chicken.

4	large tomatoes, peeled and chopped (about 3 cups/750 mL)	4
1 cup	finely chopped onion	250 mL
½ cup	chopped sun-dried tomatoes (not oil-packed)	125 mL
½ cup	dried currants	125 mL
½ cup	lightly packed brown sugar	125 mL
½ cup	water	125 mL
¼ cup	balsamic vinegar	50 mL
1	2-inch (5 cm) piece gingerroot, finely chopped	1
2	cloves garlic, minced	2
2 tsp	curry powder	10 mL
¼ tsp	each: salt and hot pepper flakes	1 mL

1. Combine tomatoes, onion, sun-dried tomatoes and currants in a large stainless steel or enamel saucepan. Stir in sugar, water, vinegar, gingerroot, garlic, curry powder, salt and pepper flakes.

2. Bring to a boil over high heat, stirring occasionally. Reduce heat to low and boil gently, uncovered, for 30 minutes or until chutney is very thick, stirring frequently.

3. Remove hot jars from canner and ladle chutney into jars to within ½ inch (1 cm) of rim (head space). Process 10 minutes for half-pint (250 mL) jars and 15 minutes for pint (500 mL) jars as directed on page 133 (Longer Time Processing Procedure).

Makes 3½ cups (875 mL).

ALL-YEAR DRIED FRUIT CHUTNEY

All chutneys do not need to be prepared in the growing season. This one, using fruits available at any time of the year, is a marvelous addition to pork, poultry, beef and game. We have also used it as an appetizer with soft Brie or Camembert cheese on crackers.

1	large banana, mashed	1
1	large apple, peeled, cored and chopped	1
1	large red onion, chopped	1
3	cloves garlic, minced	3
½ cup	each: chopped dried apricots, prunes and dates	125 mL
⅓ cup	chopped mixed glacéed fruit	75 mL
2 tbsp	chopped minced Candied Ginger (page 301) or crystallized ginger	25 mL
1 cup	cider vinegar	250 mL
½ cup	water	125 mL
½ tsp	each: cayenne, ground allspice, ground cardamom and salt	2 mL
1 cup	lightly packed dark brown sugar	250 mL

1. Combine banana, apple, onion, garlic, apricots, prunes, dates, glacéed fruit, ginger, vinegar and water in a large stainless steel or enamel saucepan. Bring to a boil over high heat, reduce heat and boil gently, uncovered, for 10 minutes, stirring occasionally. Add cayenne, allspice, cardamom, salt and sugar; boil gently, stirring occasionally, for 10 minutes or until thickened.

2. Remove hot jars from canner and ladle chutney into jars to within ½ inch (1 cm) of rim (head space). Process 10 minutes for half-pint (250 mL) jars and 15 minutes for pint (500 mL) jars as directed on page 133 (Longer Time Processing Procedure).

Makes 4 cups (1 L).

HELLFIRE CHUTNEY

Margaret's daughter Martha learned of this unusual chutney from someone who brought the recipe with her when she moved from India to Toronto. She generously shares it with us. You'll find it wonderful served with rice dishes and curries. But don't let the name frighten you. You control the amount of spicing and the resulting hellfire.

1 lb	pitted dates, cut up	500 g
1¼ cups	white vinegar, divided	425 mL
¾ cup	granulated sugar	175 mL
½–1 tsp	cayenne pepper *	2–5 mL
¾ tsp	each: ground cinnamon and ground ginger	4 mL
¼ tsp	each: ground cloves and salt	1 mL
3 tbsp	liquid honey	45 mL

1. Place dates in a large stainless steel or enamel saucepan with 1½ cups (375 mL) vinegar and allow to soak for 30 minutes. Bring to a boil over medium-high heat, reduce heat to low and cook, covered, for 10 minutes or until dates are tender. Remove from heat and cool. Place in a food processor and purée until smooth.

2. Return mixture to saucepan; add sugar, cayenne, cinnamon, ginger, cloves, salt, honey and remaining ¼ cup (50 mL) vinegar. Cook, uncovered, over low heat until hot, about 5 minutes, stirring constantly.

3. Remove hot jars from canner and ladle chutney into jars to within ½ inch (1 cm) of rim (head space). Process 10 minutes for half-pint (250 mL) jars and 15 minutes for pint (500 mL) jars as directed on page 133 (Longer Time Processing Procedure).

Makes 3½ cups (875 mL).

TIP *As everyone knows, cayenne pepper is very hot. Add at your own discretion to suit your own taste.*

SAVORY SAUCES

SAUCES add zest to foods. Tomato sauces, chili sauces, mustards as well as unusual piquant sauces such as Sun-Dried Tomato Tapenade (page 247), each give their own special nuance to the foods they accompany.

Consider how often in your day-to-day cooking you open a can of tomato, spaghetti or pizza sauce. Think how nice it would be, instead, to have a variety of homemade sauces lining your pantry shelves, ready to use in the quantities you require. Our Chunky Basil Pasta Sauce, Roasted Vegetable Pasta Sauce and Seasoned Tomato Sauce (pages 239, 240 and 237) are a start to a useful addition to your pantry shelf.

Chili sauces are ketchup-like spicy sauces but with a coarser consistency. They are made with tomatoes, onions, green peppers, chile peppers or chili powder, vinegar, sugar and spices. Asian cooking uses many appealing sauces to accompany a great variety of dishes. Enjoy our easily prepared Asian Plum Sauce (page 248) and Thai Chili Sauce (page 250).

The pungent flavor of mustard seed has been enhancing food since early Greek and Roman days. The Romans carried mustard north to England, and no English kitchen has since been without it. The French combined mustard seed with white wine and spices to create the classic Dijon blend, as in Dijon-Style Mustard (page 232).

You can influence the sharpness of the mustard you make by changing the liquid you use. Mixing mustard with water produces the hottest, sharpest taste by releasing an enzyme in the seed that frees the fiery compounds. Acids such as vinegar or wine give a much milder flavor. Vinegar is used in English-style mustard, Champagne or white wine in Dijon-style mustard, and flat beer is often used by the Chinese. Different kinds of seeds also have different flavors. The darker seeds have a more pungent aroma and flavor.

SERVING SUGGESTIONS:

Brush a sauce such as Summer Sizzle Barbecue Sauce (page 238) or Raspberry Mustard Sauce (page 233) on meat for broiling or outdoor grilling. Asian Whisky Sauce (page 249) is the best flavor marinade for salmon and swordfish, although we recently tried it on chicken with great results. And, of course, no self-respecting meat loaf would be content without some Mango Chile Sauce (page 244).

LIST OF RECIPES

MUSTARDS

Mustard has been used since Roman times and commercial makers offer us many varieties. The mustard seed is usually ground before being mixed with a liquid to mellow its natural bitterness. Then the mustard is cooked at length to decrease the pungency and aged to develop the flavors. Commercial makers jealously guard their secret recipes, but you can make a delectable alternative that will keep for months in your refrigerator.

BASIC COARSE MUSTARD

Using mustard seeds instead of mustard powder gives the interesting coarse texture to this condiment. This recipe can be used in its basic form or in its several variations.

⅓ cup	mustard seeds	75 mL
⅓ cup	cider vinegar	75 mL
1	clove garlic, halved	1
3 tbsp	water	45 mL
3 tbsp	liquid honey	45 mL
¼ tsp	salt	1 mL
⅛ tsp	ground cinnamon	0.5 mL

1. Combine mustard seeds, vinegar and garlic in a small bowl. Cover and refrigerate for 36 hours.

2. Discard garlic. Process mixture in a food processor with water until coarse consistency. Stir in honey, salt and cinnamon.

3. Divide mixture into 3 equal parts and proceed as below.

Horseradish Mustard: To one part, add 1 tsp (5 mL) horseradish.
Peppercorn Mustard: To one part, add 1 tsp (5 mL) green peppercorns, crushed.
Herb Mustard: To one part, add ¼ tsp (1 mL) or more as desired of any dried herb. (Try tarragon, dill, thyme, basil or oregano).

Refrigerate in tightly sealed containers.

Makes ¼ cup (50 mL) of each.

SERVING SUGGESTIONS:

Dijonnaise Mustard
Try this on sandwiches with cold cuts, ham or roast beef.
Add ⅓ cup (75 mL) mayonnaise to 2 tbsp (25 mL) Basic Coarse Mustard.
Makes about ½ cup (125 mL).

Creamy Mustard Sauce
Use on cooked vegetables, to top baked potatoes and to dress a cabbage or tossed green salad.
To ¼ cup (50 mL) Horseradish Mustard, add ½ cup (125 mL) light sour cream, 2 tbsp
(25 mL) lemon juice and 2 tbsp (25 mL) chopped fresh parsley.
Makes about ¾ cup (175 mL).

WINE MUSTARD

Legend has it that a vinegar and mustard maker in Dijon first added wine to his
mustard in the 1700s, and so began the resurgence of mustards in Europe.

½ cup	liquid honey	125 mL
⅓ cup	white wine	75 mL
¼ cup	dry mustard	50 mL
1	egg	1
1 tbsp	vegetable oil	15 mL
1 tsp	all-purpose flour	5 mL

1. Combine honey, wine and dry mustard in a small saucepan. Whisk in egg, oil and
   flour; cook over medium heat for 2 to 3 minutes or until bubbly, stirring constantly.
   Cook for 1 minute longer, stirring constantly. Remove from heat.

2. Cool to room temperature. Cover and refrigerate in a tightly sealed container for up
   to 2 weeks.

Makes 1 cup (250 mL).

DIJON-STYLE MUSTARD

This smooth, flavorful mustard compares well to fine commercial Dijon mustards. And it's easy and quick to make. Increase the amount of hot pepper sauce if you want your mustard to have more bite. Mix it with your favorite jam for a sweet and tangy sauce that is perfect for dipping or spreading on meat before broiling. Use it to make the specialty sauces described below. With little effort you can have a refrigerator full of fancy mustards.

¾ cup	dry white wine	175 mL
¼ cup	chopped onion	50 mL
1	small clove garlic, minced	1
½ cup	dry mustard	125 mL
1 tbsp	each: liquid honey and canola oil	15 mL
½ tsp	salt	2 mL
2–3 drops	hot pepper sauce	2–3 drops

1. Combine wine, onion and garlic in a small saucepan. Bring to a boil over high heat, reduce heat and boil gently, uncovered, for 5 minutes. Strain and discard solids.

2. Whisk wine into mustard in a small bowl until well blended. Return to saucepan; add honey, oil, salt and pepper sauce. Bring to a boil and boil gently for 10 minutes to blend flavors and thicken slightly, stirring frequently. Store in a tightly sealed container in the refrigerator for up to 1 month.

Makes ⅔ cup (150 mL).

SERVING SUGGESTION:

Honey Lemon Mustard Sauce
Turn Dijon-Style Mustard into a chic sauce to drizzle over steamed vegetables or fish.
Melt ¼ cup (50 mL) butter or margarine in a small saucepan. Stir in 2 tbsp (25 mL) liquid honey, 2 tbsp (25 mL) Dijon-Style Mustard, 1 tbsp (15 mL) lemon juice and 1 tsp (5 mL) grated lemon rind. Cook over low heat until thoroughly heated.
Makes about ½ cup (125 mL).

MORE SERVING SUGGESTIONS:

Raspberry Mustard Sauce
Use Dijon-Style Mustard to make this wonderful sauce full of the essence of raspberries. Serve it with ham, make Raspberry Mustard Coating for Chicken (page 324) and, of course, use it to complement the taste of roast pork.
Combine ½ cup (125 mL) Dijon-Style Mustard, 1 tbsp (15 mL) Red Wine Raspberry Vinegar (page 271), ¼ cup (50 mL) crushed raspberries and 2 tsp (10 mL) granulated sugar. Stir well to combine. Store in a tightly sealed container in the refrigerator for up to 1 week.
Makes ¾ cup (175 mL).

Savory Mustard Sauce
Parsley and oregano transform Dijon-Style Mustard into a superb sauce to spread on any kind of meat or cheese sandwich.
Combine ¼ cup (50 mL) Dijon-Style Mustard, 2 tsp (10 mL) chopped fresh parsley, 1 tsp (5 mL) chopped fresh oregano, ½ tsp (2 mL) each: lemon juice and grated lemon rind. Store in a tightly sealed container in the refrigerator for up to two weeks.
Makes ¼ cup (50 mL).

Mustard Fruit Dip
Wonderful as a dip for cooked shrimp or chicken cubes.
Combine 2 tbsp (25 mL) Dijon-Style Mustard, ¼ cup (50 mL) chutney (see Chapter 9, pages 210–227) and 2 tsp (10 mL) lemon juice.
Makes ⅓ cup (75 mL).

SUN-DRIED TOMATO MUSTARD

The subtle sun-dried tomato flavor and interesting coarse texture of this mustard gives a meal extra "zip."

¼ cup	mustard seeds	50 mL
½ cup	chopped sun-dried tomatoes (not oil-packed)	125 mL
¼ cup	balsamic vinegar	50 mL
2 tbsp	dry mustard	25 mL
2 tbsp	extra virgin olive oil	25 mL
1 tsp	salt	5 mL
½ tsp	granulated sugar	2 mL

Cover mustard seeds with warm water and refrigerate overnight. Drain and rinse seeds. Place mustard seeds, tomatoes, vinegar, dry mustard, oil, salt and sugar in a food processor. Process until almost smooth and thickened. Store in a tightly sealed container in the refrigerator for up to 1 month or freeze for longer storage.

Makes about 1 cup (250 mL).

OLD-STYLE WHOLE SEED MUSTARD

Yellow or brown mustard seeds may be used in this grainy home-style mustard. The brown seeds have a more pungent aroma and flavor than their yellow cousins.

¼ cup	yellow mustard seeds	50 mL
¼ cup	brown mustard seeds	50 mL
½ cup	white wine vinegar	125 mL
1	bay leaf	1
1 tbsp	each: liquid honey and canola oil	15 mL
¼ tsp	salt	1 mL

Combine mustard seeds, vinegar and bay leaf and refrigerate for 24 hours. Remove bay leaf and discard. Place seeds and their liquid, honey, oil and salt in a food processor. Process until seeds are broken and mustard is pasty. Store in a tightly sealed container in the refrigerator for up to 1 month or freeze for longer storage.

Makes about 1 cup (250 mL).

TIP *The liquid used to soak the seeds is important to the taste of the mustard. Vinegar gives a mustard with a mild flavor. For a sharper taste, use water to replace the vinegar. Water releases an enzyme that reacts with compounds in the seeds to produce the sharp mustard oils. You can also replace vinegar with your favorite wine for a spicier taste or with beer for an extremely hot bite.*

PIQUANT TOMATO SAUCE

A dash of this tangy sauce adds zip to other sauces or use it to top meat loaves and ground beef patties. We like to keep a bottle in the refrigerator ready to put on the table to add zing to egg dishes, soups and sandwich fillings.

3 cups	coarsely chopped peeled tomatoes (about 4 large)	750 mL
3	cloves garlic, minced	3
3	stalks celery, finely chopped	3
3	jalapeño peppers or 1 long hot yellow wax pepper, seeded and finely chopped	3
1	medium onion, finely chopped	1
1 cup	water	250 mL
½ cup	cider vinegar	125 mL
¼ cup	each: lightly packed brown sugar and tomato paste	50 mL
1 tsp	each: chili powder and cumin	5 mL
½ tsp	each: dry mustard and pickling salt	2 mL

1. Combine tomatoes, garlic, celery, jalapeño peppers, onion and water in a large stainless steel or enamel saucepan. Bring to a boil, reduce heat, cover and boil gently for 20 minutes or until mixture is thickened and vegetables are soft, stirring occasionally. Cool slightly. Purée in a blender or food processor until smooth.

2. Return tomato mixture to saucepan. Stir in vinegar, sugar, tomato paste, chili powder, cumin, mustard and salt; boil gently for 5 minutes to blend flavors, stirring continuously. (The sauce has a tendency to "jump" from the pot).

3. Remove hot jars from canner and ladle sauce into jars to within ½ inch (1 cm) of rim (head space). Process 15 minutes for half-pint (250 mL) jars and 20 minutes for pint (500 mL) jars as directed on page 133 (Longer Time Processing Procedure).

Makes about 4 cups (1L).

SERVING SUGGESTION:

Easy Seafood Sauce
Blend 1 cup Piquant Tomato Sauce, 1 tbsp (15 mL) horseradish and 1 tsp (5 mL) lemon juice. Makes 1 cup (250 mL).

YOUR BASIC MULTI-USE TOMATO SAUCE

This fabulous tomato-rich sauce is made with three kinds of tomatoes, sun-dried, plum and regular. We like to add it to soups and beef stews for a nice flavor boost.

10	plum tomatoes, peeled and chopped (about 2½ lb/1 kg)	10
10	large tomatoes, peeled and chopped (about 4 lb/2 kg)	10
4	large cloves garlic, minced	4
2	large stalks celery, chopped	2
2	medium carrots, chopped	2
1	large onion, chopped	1
1	large zucchini, chopped	1
1	large sweet green pepper, chopped	1
½ cup	sun-dried tomatoes	125 mL
⅔ cup	dry red wine	150 mL
½ cup	red wine vinegar	125 mL
2	bay leaves	2
1 tbsp	pickling salt	15 mL
2 tsp	each: dried oregano and basil	10 mL
1 tsp	granulated sugar	5 mL
¼ tsp	each: ground cinnamon and pepper	2 mL
¼ cup	chopped fresh parsley	50 mL

1. Combine tomatoes, garlic, celery, carrots, onion, zucchini and green pepper in a very large stainless steel or enamel saucepan. Add 1 cup (250 mL) water. Bring to a boil over high heat, reduce heat and boil gently, covered, for 25 minutes or until mixture begins to thicken, stirring occasionally.

2. Soak sun-dried tomatoes in boiling water until softened. Drain and dice. Add to sauce with wine, vinegar, bay leaves, salt, oregano, basil, sugar, cinnamon and pepper. Continue to boil gently until desired consistency, stirring frequently. Discard bay leaves and stir in parsley.

3. Remove hot jars from canner and ladle sauce into jars to within ½ inch (1 cm) of rim (head space). Process 35 minutes for pint (500 mL) jars and 40 minutes for quart (1 L) jars as directed on page 133 (Longer Time Processing Procedure).

Makes 12 cups (3 L).

SEASONED TOMATO SAUCE

Whenever there is an abundance of tomatoes, it's time to make this fresh-tasting basic sauce. Use it anytime a tomato sauce is called for—in pasta sauces, soups, stews, pizzas or casseroles. Plum tomatoes give the thickest consistency.

12 cups	chopped ripe tomatoes (about 6 lb/3 kg)	3 L
1 cup	chopped onion	250 mL
2	cloves garlic, minced	2
2 tbsp	chopped fresh oregano or 1 tsp (5 mL) dried	25 mL
2 tsp	granulated sugar	10 mL
½ tsp	freshly ground black pepper	2 mL
2	bay leaves	2
2 tbsp	lemon juice	25 mL
½ tsp	salt	2 mL

1. Combine tomatoes, onion, garlic, oregano, sugar, pepper and bay leaves in a large stainless steel or enamel saucepan. Bring to a boil over high heat, reduce heat and boil gently, uncovered, until very thick, about 1¼ hours; stir frequently. Press through a food mill or coarse sieve to remove seeds and skins. Add lemon juice and salt.

2. Remove hot jars from canner and ladle sauce into jars to within ½ inch (1 cm) of rim (head space). Process 35 minutes for half-pint (250 mL) or pint (500 mL) jars as directed on page 133 (Longer Time Processing Procedure).

Makes about 4 cups (1 L).

SERVING SUGGESTIONS:

No need to clutter your fridge with an assortment of commercial sauces when this basic sauce is so easily transformed as needed.

Savory Seafood Sauce
Stir together ½ cup (125 mL) Seasoned Tomato Sauce, 2 tbsp (25 mL) each: lemon juice and prepared horseradish.

Herbed Pizza Sauce
Combine 1 cup (250 mL) Seasoned Tomato Sauce, ½ tsp (2 mL) each: dried oregano, dried basil and dried parsley and 1 clove crushed garlic.

SUMMER SIZZLE BARBECUE SAUCE

Whether served with beef, chicken and pork, or humble burgers and hot dogs, this barbecue sauce gives meat a real sizzle. When grilling season arrives or in households where it's year round, this is a very valuable sauce to have on hand.

2 tbsp	canola oil	25 mL
2	medium onions, chopped	2
2	large cloves garlic, minced	2
4	large tomatoes, peeled and finely chopped (about 3 cups/750 mL)	4
½ cup	dry red wine or beef broth	125 mL
3 tbsp	liquid honey	45 mL
1 tbsp	each: Worcestershire sauce and cider vinegar	15 mL
1 tsp	each: dry mustard and green peppercorns	5 mL
½ tsp	each: chili powder and salt	2 mL
½ cup	tomato sauce	125 mL
1 tbsp	brown sugar	15 mL
¼ tsp	hot pepper sauce	1 mL

1. Heat oil in a medium stainless steel or enamel saucepan over medium-high heat. Add onions and garlic and sauté for 5 minutes or until tender, stirring frequently.

2. Add tomatoes, wine, honey, Worcestershire sauce, vinegar, mustard, peppercorns, chile powder and salt. Bring to a boil, reduce heat and boil gently, uncovered, for 30 minutes or until thickened. Remove from heat and purée in a food processor or blender until smooth. Stir in tomato sauce, sugar and pepper sauce, return to saucepan and bring to a boil.

3. Remove hot jars from canner and ladle sauce into jars to within ½ inch (1 cm) of rim. Process 15 minutes for half-pint (250 mL) and pint (500 mL) jars as directed on page 133 (Longer Time Processing Procedure).

Makes 3 cups (750 mL).

TIP *For an extra heat "hit," add more pepper sauce or cayenne pepper to taste.*

CHUNKY BASIL PASTA SAUCE

Fall is the time to turn the rich flavors of field-ripened tomatoes and fresh basil into a delicious sauce to have on hand during the winter months. We love it served on fresh pasta and topped with freshly grated Parmesan cheese.

8 cups	coarsely chopped peeled tomatoes (about 9–12 tomatoes or 4 lb/2 kg)	2 L
1 cup	chopped onion	250 mL
3	cloves garlic, minced	3
⅔ cup	red wine	150 mL
⅓ cup	red wine vinegar	75 mL
½ cup	chopped fresh basil	125 mL
1 tbsp	chopped fresh parsley	15 mL
1 tsp	pickling salt	5 mL
½ tsp	granulated sugar	2 mL
1	can (6 oz/156 mL) tomato paste	1

1. Combine tomatoes, onion, garlic, wine, vinegar, basil, parsley, salt, sugar and tomato paste in a very large stainless steel or enamel saucepan. Bring to a boil over high heat, reduce heat to low and simmer, uncovered, for 40 minutes or until mixture reaches desired consistency, stirring frequently.

2. Remove hot jars from canner and ladle sauce into jars to within ½ inch (1 cm) of rim (head space). Process 35 minutes for pint (500 mL) jars and 40 minutes for quart (1 L) jars as directed on page 133 (Longer Time Processing Procedure).

Makes 8 cups (2 L).

SERVING SUGGESTION:

Speedy Pizzas
We also find this sauce useful for making a quick pizza.
Spread Chunky Basil Pasta Sauce over individual or large pizza crusts. Top with your favorite toppings such as pepperoni, chopped green peppers and sliced mushrooms. Sprinkle with shredded mozzarella cheese. Bake in a 350°F (180°C) oven for about 10 minutes or until cheese is bubbly. Cut each pizza into wedges.

ROASTED VEGETABLE PASTA SAUCE

Roasting vegetables for this full-flavored tomato sauce changes a few simple ingredients into an epicurean treat. Serve with linguine or other pasta and a generous sprinkling of freshly grated Parmigiano-Reggiano cheese.

10	plum tomatoes (about 2½ lb/1 kg) unpeeled	10
4	cloves garlic, unpeeled	4
2	small onions, unpeeled	2
1	sweet red pepper	1
¼ cup	balsamic vinegar	50 mL
1 tbsp	chopped fresh oregano or 1 tsp (5 mL) dried	15 mL
1 tsp	granulated sugar	5 mL
1 tsp	salt	5 mL

1. Place tomatoes, garlic, onions and red pepper on a lightly greased baking sheet. Roast in a 450°F (230°C) oven for 45 minutes, removing the garlic after 12 to 15 minutes or when soft. Remove remaining vegetables when they are soft and the skins blistered. Let stand until cool enough to handle.

2. Peel tomatoes, being careful to catch all the juice. Squeeze garlic and onions to remove soft centers. Peel and seed pepper. Place all vegetables in a food processor; process until smooth.

3. Place vegetable purée in a large stainless steel or enamel saucepan. Add vinegar, oregano, sugar and salt. Bring to a boil over high heat, reduce heat, cover and boil for about 15 minutes, stirring frequently.

4. Remove hot jars from canner and ladle sauce into jars to within ½ inch (1 cm) of rim (head space). Process 35 minutes for pint (500 mL) jars and 40 minutes for quart (1 L) jars as directed on page 133 (Longer Time Processing Procedure).

Makes 3½ cups (875 mL).

PUTTANESCA FREEZER PASTA SAUCE

This spicy classic Italian sauce is spicy in more ways than one. First, it is well spiced. Second, the name of the sauce is derived from *puttana*, the Italian word for prostitute. According to one story, the intense aroma and robust flavor of the sauce were like a siren's call to the men who visited these "ladies of pleasure." Another has it that this quick and easy sauce allowed the girls to get on with their work without delay. Whatever the origin, the sauce is delicious served over fresh pasta. Keep some in your freezer for a fast dinner.

¼ cup	extra virgin olive oil	50 mL
1 cup	finely chopped onion	250 mL
4	cloves garlic, minced	4
1	pkg (50 g) anchovy fillets	1
24	plum tomatoes, peeled and chopped (about 6 lb/3 kg)	24
1 cup	chopped black olives	250 mL
¼ cup	drained capers, rinsed	50 mL
½ tsp	each: dried oregano and salt	2 mL
¼ tsp	freshly ground black pepper	1 mL

1. Heat oil over medium heat in a very large saucepan. Add onion and garlic and cook until soft, about 5 minutes.

2. Drain oil from anchovies into saucepan; finely chop anchovies. Add anchovies, tomatoes, olives, capers, oregano, salt and pepper. Bring to a boil over high heat, reduce heat and cook gently, uncovered, for ¾ hour or until thickened, stirring frequently.

3. Cool sauce, then spoon into freezer containers, cover tightly, label and store in the freezer. Sauce will keep for up to 4 days in the refrigerator.

Makes 6 cups (1.5 L).

 TIP   *Use two cans (28 oz/798 mL) plum tomatoes when fresh ones are unavailable.*

GRANDMA'S CHILI SAUCE

There are probably as many recipes for chili sauce as there are grandmothers. We especially like this recipe, shared with us by a home economist. It was her grandmother's specialty.

4 cups	diced peeled tomatoes (about 2 lb/1 kg)	1 L
5	stalks celery, finely diced	5
2	apples, peeled, cored and diced	2
1	small sweet green pepper, finely diced	1
1	small hot red pepper, seeded and finely chopped	1
1	small onion, finely chopped	1
½	sweet red pepper, finely diced	½
1 cup	white vinegar	250 mL
⅓ cup	granulated sugar	75 mL
½ tsp	pickling salt	2 mL
3	cinnamon sticks, each 3 inches (8 cm) long	3
1	1-inch (2.5 cm) piece dried whole ginger	1
1 tsp	whole allspice berries	5 mL

1. Place tomatoes, celery, apples, green pepper, hot pepper, onion, red pepper, vinegar, sugar and salt in a large stainless steel or enamel saucepan.

2. Tie cinnamon, ginger and allspice in a small square of cheesecloth. Add to vegetables. Bring to a boil over high heat, reduce heat and boil gently, uncovered, for about 1½ hours or until mixture is thick, stirring occasionally. Discard spice bag.

3. Remove hot jars from canner and ladle sauce into jars to within ½ inch (1 cm) of rim (head space). Process 15 minutes for half-pint (250 mL) and pint (500 mL) jars as directed on page 133 (Longer Time Processing Procedure).

Makes 4 cups (1 L).

FRUIT CHILI SAUCE

This traditional relish originates from the fruit-growing regions of Canada where peaches and pears are abundant in the fall.

6 cups	chopped peeled tomatoes (about 3lb/1.5 kg)	1.5 L
2 cups	finely chopped onions	500 mL
2 cups	each: chopped peeled peaches, pears and apples	500 mL
1 cup	finely chopped celery	250 mL
2	sweet green peppers, finely chopped	2
1	sweet or hot red pepper, seeded and finely chopped	1
1½ cups	white or cider vinegar	375 mL
1 tbsp	pickling spice	15 mL
2 tsp	pickling salt	10 mL
2 cups	granulated sugar	500 mL

1. Combine tomatoes, onions, peaches, pears, apples, celery, green and red peppers and vinegar in a very large stainless steel or enamel saucepan. Place pickling spice in a tea ball or tie in a piece of cheesecloth. Add spice and salt to saucepan. Bring to a boil over high heat, reduce heat and boil gently, uncovered, for 1 hour or until thick, stirring occasionally.

2. Stir in sugar. Return to a boil and boil gently for 30 minutes, stirring occasionally. Remove spice bag.

3. Remove hot jars from canner and ladle sauce into jars to within ½ inch (1 cm) of rim (head space). Process 15 minutes for half-pint (250 mL) and pint (500 mL) jars as directed on page 133 (Longer Time Processing Procedure).

Makes 8 cups (2 L).

VARIATION:

For a spicier version, double the pickling spice and add 1 tsp (5 mL) whole cloves and 1 broken cinnamon stick to the spice bag.

MANGO CHILE SAUCE

Mangoes, pineapple juice, rice vinegar and gingerroot blend with traditional ingredients in this flavorful sauce. Use it as you would use the traditional sauce. It does wonders to dress up a plain meat loaf.

3 cups	coarsely chopped peeled plum tomatoes (about 6–8 tomatoes or 1½ lb/750 g)	750 mL
2 cups	chopped mango (about 3 mangoes)	500 mL
1	small hot red chile, seeded and finely chopped	1
¾ cup	rice vinegar	175 mL
½ cup	pineapple juice	125 mL
½ cup	each: chopped onion and celery	125 mL
1 tbsp	minced gingerroot	15 mL
3	whole cloves	3
1	bay leaf	1
⅓ cup	granulated sugar	75 mL
½ tsp	pickling salt	2 mL

1. Combine tomatoes, mango, chile, vinegar, pineapple juice, onion, celery, gingerroot, cloves and bay leaf in a large stainless steel or enamel saucepan. Bring to a boil over high heat, reduce heat and boil gently, uncovered, for 1 hour or until thickened, stirring occasionally.

2. Add sugar and salt; return to a boil and boil gently for 10 minutes. Remove and discard bay leaf.

3. Remove hot jars from canner and ladle sauce into jars to within ½ inch (1 cm) of rim (head space). Process 15 minutes for half-pint (250 mL) and pint (500 mL) jars as directed on page 133 (Longer Time Processing Procedure).

Makes 4½ cups (1.125 L).

TIP *A mango is ripe when it's fragrant and plump around the stem area, and gives slightly*

BLENDER KETCHUP

If you thought ketchup was only for kids, try this adult version and you'll change your mind. Our Blender Ketchup is less sweet and has a fresher tomato flavor than commercial ketchups. It adds zest to casseroles, soups and meat loaves.

7 cups	chopped peeled plum tomatoes, about (4 lb/2 kg)	1.75 L
½ cup	chopped onion	125 mL
½ cup	chopped sweet red pepper	125 mL
⅔ cup	cider vinegar	150 mL
¼ cup	granulated sugar	50 mL
2 tsp	pickling salt	10 mL
1	cinnamon stick, 2 inches (5 cm) long	1
½ tsp	each: whole allspice, whole cloves, peppercorns	2 mL
1	bay leaf	1

1. Combine tomatoes, onion and red pepper in a blender or food processor and process until smooth. Remove to a large stainless steel or enamel saucepan. Bring to a boil over high heat, reduce heat and boil gently, uncovered, for 30 minutes.

2. Add vinegar, sugar and salt. Tie cinnamon, allspice, cloves, peppercorns and bay leaf in cheesecloth and add to saucepan. Return to a boil and boil gently, uncovered, stirring frequently, until volume is reduced by half or until mixture rounds up on a spoon without separation, about 1½ hours. Remove cheesecloth bag.

3. Remove hot jars from canner and ladle ketchup into jars to within ½ inch (1 cm) of rim (head space). Process 15 minutes for half-pint (250 mL) and pint (500 mL) jars as directed on page 133 (Longer Time Processing Procedure).

Makes about 3 cups (750 mL).

 Dip tomatoes in boiling water for 20–30 seconds so skins will peel easily.

MICROWAVE MANGO KETCHUP

Ketchup hasn't always been made from tomatoes. This popular condiment originated in seventeenth-century China, when it was made of spicy pickled fish. British
seamen took it home and later added tomatoes, making the blend we know today.
Try this interesting version on chicken or beef burgers or blackened fish.

2	mangoes, peeled and finely chopped	2
¼ cup	granulated sugar	50 mL
¼ cup	dry white wine	50 mL
¼ cup	cider vinegar	50 mL
1 tsp	ground ginger	5 mL
½ tsp	salt	2 mL
¼ tsp	each: ground allspice and cloves	1 mL

1. Combine mangoes, sugar, wine, vinegar, ginger, salt, allspice and cloves in a medium
   microwavable container. Microwave, uncovered, on High (100%) for 5 minutes. Stir.

2. Microwave on Low (30%) for 3 to 5 minutes or until mixture is very thick, stirring
   several times.

3. Remove hot jars from canner and ladle ketchup into jars to within ½ inch (1 cm)
   of rim. Process 15 minutes for half-pint (250 mL) jars and 20 minutes for pint (500
   mL) jars as directed on page 133 (Longer Time Processing Procedure).

Makes 2 cups (500 mL).

SUN-DRIED TOMATO TAPENADE

Replacing traditional olives with sun-dried tomatoes makes this a very different tapenade. Used as a pasta sauce, or on cream or chèvre cheese spread on crackers or crusty French bread, it is superlative.

2 cups	boiling water	500 mL
1 cup	sun-dried tomatoes chopped (not oil-packed)	250 mL
4	cloves garlic	4
⅓ cup	packed fresh basil leaves	75 mL
1 tbsp	olive oil	15 mL
1 tsp	coarse salt	5 mL

1. Pour boiling water over tomatoes in a small bowl; allow to stand for 30 minutes to soften. Drain, reserving ⅓ cup (75 mL) liquid.

2. Place tomatoes, garlic and reserved liquid in a food processor; chop with on/off motion until coarsely chopped. Add basil, oil and salt. Continue to chop until paste-like consistency.

3. Spoon into a tightly sealed container and refrigerate for up to 3 days or freeze for longer storage.

Makes 1 cup (250 mL).

SERVING SUGGESTIONS:

Tomato Tapenade Salad Dressing
Use this sparkling dressing with cabbage slaw, as a topping for sliced tomatoes with a fresh basil garnish, or make it into a dip by adding extra yogurt for raw veggies.
Combine 2 tbsp (25 mL) Sun-Dried Tomato Tapenade with ½ cup (125 mL) light mayonnaise or low-fat plain yogurt.

Melted Brie with Sun-Dried Tomato Tapenade
Place a small, round Brie cheese on a cookie sheet and spread with 2 tbsp (25 mL) Sun-Dried Tomato Tapenade. Bake in a 325° F (160° C) oven for about 8 minutes or until cheese just begins to melt.

ASIAN PLUM SAUCE

Sauces of this type are not only difficult to find but often expensive. The Asian flavors complement roast pork, meatballs and of course such Oriental foods as spring and egg rolls. Margaret's daughter Janice, who gave us this recipe, uses it as a dipping sauce for cheese bites and sausage rolls.

9	purple plums, washed and pitted (about 1½ lb/750 g)	9
1½ cups	firmly packed brown sugar	375 mL
1 cup	cider vinegar	250 mL
1½ tsp	salt	7 mL
1½ cups	finely chopped onion	375 mL
3	cloves garlic, crushed	3
¼ cup	raisins	50 mL
2 tsp	soy sauce	10 mL
¼ tsp	chili powder	1 mL
⅛ tsp	each: ground cloves, cinnamon, ginger and allspice	0.5 mL

1. Finely chop plums in a food processor or by hand. You should have about 1¾ cups (425 mL).

2. Combine plums, sugar, vinegar and salt in a large stainless steel or enamel saucepan. Bring to a boil over high heat and boil gently, uncovered, for 3 minutes, stirring occasionally.

3. Add onion, garlic, raisins, soy sauce, chili powder, cloves, cinnamon, ginger and allspice to saucepan. Return to a boil, reduce heat and boil gently, uncovered, for 45 minutes or until mixture is thickened, stirring occasionally.

4. Remove hot jars from canner and ladle sauce into jars to within ½ inch (1 cm) of rim (head space). Process 10 minutes for half-pint (250 mL) and pint (500 mL) jars as directed on page 133 (Longer Time Processing Procedure).

Makes 3½ cups (875 mL).

ASIAN WHISKY SAUCE

Margaret has been using this seafood sauce and marinade since time immemorial, or so it seems. And it never fails to please everyone who tastes it. She uses it for marinating fish fillets as well as whole fish, chicken and pork.

¼ cup	each: canola oil and soy sauce	50 mL
2	cloves garlic, minced	2
½ cup	rye whisky	125 mL
4 tsp	brown sugar	20 mL
¼ tsp	freshly ground pepper	1 mL
	Small piece gingerroot, chopped, optional	

Combine oil, soy sauce, garlic, rye whisky, sugar, pepper and gingerroot (if using) in a tightly sealed container, shake to blend well. Refrigerate until ready to use.

Makes 1 cup (250 mL).

TIP   *Use about ⅓ cup (75 mL) of Asian Whisky Sauce to marinate 4 chicken breasts or drumsticks or about 1 lb (500 g) fish or pork. Any unused sauce may be stored in the refrigerator for up to 1 month.*

SERVING SUGGESTIONS:

Asian Salmon
Place 4 salmon steaks or 2 fillets in a resealable plastic bag. Pour ½ cup (125 mL) Asian Whisky Sauce over salmon, seal the bag and turn to coat the food evenly. Refrigerate for 1 to 2 hours, turning bag occasionally. Remove salmon from the marinade and grill or broil. Bring the remaining marinade to a boil for 5 minutes, then use to brush on salmon during the cooking.
Makes 4 servings.

Asian Cabbage Slaw
Toss shredded cabbage, red or green or both, and chopped green onions with Asian Whisky Sauce. Sprinkle with toasted sesame seeds and refrigerate until ready to serve.

THAI CHILI SAUCE

Thai flavors of fish sauce, lime and garlic combine to make this amazing sauce to serve with fish or chicken. It gives an irresistible flavor to Thai Chicken Wings (page 315).

1	small tomato, chopped	1
½	small sweet red pepper, chopped	½
½ cup	chopped onion	125 mL
1	clove garlic, minced	1
3 tbsp	minced gingerroot	45 mL
½ cup	chicken stock	125 mL
⅓ cup	fish sauce	75 mL
3 tbsp	lime juice	45 mL
2 tbsp	each: brown sugar and rice vinegar	25 mL
2 tsp	hot pepper flakes	10 mL
¼ cup	chopped fresh cilantro	50 mL

1. Combine tomato, pepper, onion, garlic, gingerroot, chicken stock, fish sauce, lime juice, sugar, vinegar and hot pepper flakes in a medium saucepan. Bring to a boil over high heat, reduce heat and boil gently, uncovered, for 10 minutes. Remove from heat and stir in cilantro.

2. Remove hot jars from canner and ladle sauce into jars to within ½ inch (1 cm) of rim. Process 15 minutes for half-pint (250 mL) and pint (500 mL) jars as directed on page 133 (Longer Time Processing Procedure).

Makes 2 cups (500 mL).

SERVING SUGGESTION:

Thai Baked Fish
Spread several spoonfuls of Thai Chili Sauce over fish fillets such as orange roughy, halibut or salmon. Bake in a 400°F (200°C) oven for 12 minutes or until fish is opaque and flakes easily with a fork. Serve with additional sauce.

CRANBERRY SAUCE WITH SPIRIT

There will be no going back to traditional cranberry sauce once you have tried cranberries cooked with port wine.

1 cup	granulated sugar	250 mL
¼ cup	water	50 mL
1 tbsp	red wine vinegar	15 mL
2½ cups	fresh or frozen cranberries	625 mL
½ cup	port	125 mL
2	cinnamon sticks, each 3 inches (8 cm) long	2

1. Combine sugar, water and vinegar in a medium stainless steel or enamel saucepan. Bring to a boil over high heat, stirring to dissolve sugar. Add cranberries; return to a boil, reduce heat and boil gently, uncovered, for 5 minutes, stirring frequently. Stir in port.

2. Remove sterilized jars from canner and place a cinnamon stick in each jar. Ladle sauce into jars to within ½ inch (1 cm) of rim (head space). Process 15 minutes for half-pint (250 mL) and pint (500 mL) jars as directed on page 133 (Longer Time Processing Procedure).

Makes 2 cups (500 mL).

HERBED RASPBERRY AND RED CURRANT SAUCE

This great fruit combo provides lots of flavor interest to grilled or barbecued chicken breasts and pork chops. Stirred into plain yogurt, it makes an excellent fruit salad topping.

2 cups	fresh or frozen unsweetened raspberries	500 mL
2 cups	fresh or frozen red currants	500 mL
½ cup	water	125 mL
1½ cups	granulated sugar	375 mL
½ tsp	each: dried tarragon and thyme	2 mL

1. Combine raspberries, currants and water in a medium stainless steel or enamel saucepan. Bring to a boil over high heat, reduce heat and boil gently, covered, for 20 minutes. Strain mixture through a fine sieve or cloth; discard pulp.

2. Return sauce to pan, return to a boil and slowly add sugar, stirring constantly until sugar is dissolved. Stir in tarragon and thyme; boil gently for 5 minutes.

3. Remove hot jars from canner and ladle sauce into jars to within ½ inch (1 cm) of rim (head space). Process 10 minutes for half-pint (250 mL) and pint (500 mL) jars as directed on page 133 (Longer Time Processing Procedure).

Makes 3 cups (750 mL).

INDONESIAN SATAY SAUCE

Fabulous as a sauce for pork kabobs or satays, this sauce also makes a delightful dip for raw vegetables.

2 tsp	vegetable oil	10 mL
1 cup	finely chopped onion	250 mL
4	cloves garlic, minced	4
⅔ cup	cider vinegar	150 mL
½ cup	each: molasses and soy sauce	125 mL
2 tsp	hot pepper flakes	10 mL
2 tsp	minced peeled gingerroot	10 mL
½ cup	peanut butter	125 mL

1. Heat oil in a nonstick saucepan over medium-high heat and sauté onion and garlic for 3 minutes or until tender, stirring frequently.

2. Add vinegar, molasses, soy sauce, hot pepper flakes and gingerroot. Bring to a boil, reduce heat and boil gently for 5 minutes. Blend in peanut butter; boil gently for 1 minute.

3. Remove hot jars from canner and ladle sauce into jars to within ½ inch (1 cm) of rim. Process 20 minutes for half-pint (250 mL) and pint (500 mL) jars as directed on page 133 (Longer Time Processing Procedure).

Makes 2 cups (500 mL).

SERVING SUGGESTION:

Chicken Barbecued with Indonesian Satay Sauce
Indonesian Satay Sauce imparts a rich glaze to chicken. For faster barbecuing, microwave chicken on Medium (50%) until partially cooked before placing on hot grill.
Marinate chicken pieces in Indonesian Satay Sauce, covered, for 1 hour at room temperature or up to 6 hours in refrigerator. Remove chicken from marinade, reserving marinade. Boil marinade for 5 minutes. Place chicken on hot barbecue grill. Cook on low heat for 45 minutes, turning several times and basting with hot marinade. Alternatively, arrange chicken in a single layer on a foil-lined baking dish. Bake in a 375°F (190°C) oven for 30 to 35 minutes. Discard any leftover marinade.

SPINACH PESTO SAUCE

This recipe extends fresh basil with spinach. Whether you do it to economize, or because basil is in short supply, or because you enjoy its marvelous flavor and fresh bright green color, it's your choice.

3 cups	torn spinach leaves	750 mL
½ cup	coarsely chopped fresh basil	125 mL
2	cloves garlic, minced	2
3 tbsp	extra virgin olive oil	45 mL
⅓ cup	pine nuts	75 mL
⅓ cup	freshly grated Parmesan cheese	75 mL

1. Process spinach, basil and garlic in a food processor with on/off motion until finely chopped. Slowly add oil and pine nuts; process until blended. Stir in cheese.

2. Transfer to 3 small containers, cover tightly and refrigerate for up to 1 week or freeze for longer storage. One container will serve 2 or 3 people as a pasta sauce.

Makes about 1¼ cups (300 mL) concentrated pesto.

VARIATIONS:

Broccoli Pesto Sauce
This pesto extends basil with broccoli.
Replace spinach with 3 cups (750 mL) cut-up broccoli stems and florets and proceed as above.

Cilantro Pesto Sauce
Replace basil with fresh cilantro.

TIP   *The uses for pesto are many. As well as mixing some with hot pasta, try adding a spoonful to oil and vinegar for a vinaigrette, to mayonnaise for a potato or cabbage salad, or to your favorite casserole or stew. We also like it spread on pizza crusts for a quick appetizer or tucked under the skin of chicken before it is grilled. And sliced tomatoes benefit from a small spoonful. For an easy appetizer, see Pesto Torta Appetizer (page 316).*

ALL THOSE

EXTRAS

Introduction To
All Those Extras

THIS section contains three chapters, all with recipes that add "extra" interest to the art of preserving food and thereby "extra" interest and enjoyment to our taste experiences.

Chapter 11, Flavored Oils and Specialty Vinegars, reflects the growing interest in the many possibilities offered by these condiments. Little effort is needed to make these otherwise expensive items in your own kitchen. Using only small amounts in cooking or in marinades gives marvelous results.

Flavored oils get their flavors from added ingredients, often garlic and hot peppers. Safe preparation is of utmost importance, as there is a risk of botulism when making flavored oils if they are improperly processed. Health Canada has confirmed our method for making these flavored oils. Carefully follow our directions (page 257) to enjoy their wonderful flavors without concern about their safety.

Unlike the oils, there is no safety issue with the vinegars because their high acid level prevents the growth of the botulism organism. They are easy and economical to make and when added to salad dressings or marinades transform the ordinary into the extraordinary.

The Finishing Touch, Chapter 12, provides wonderful dessert ideas ranging from fresh fruit salsas to decadent and positively yummy sauces. Spoon Hazelnut Blueberry Mango Sauce (page 281) or Cherry Compote (page 280) over ice-cream or yogurt for a delicious "finishing touch" to any meal. Fruit liqueur recipes are wonderful to end a meal with finesse.

With our pantries full of sparkling jellies, tangy pickles, luscious dessert sauces and zesty savory sauces, we needed to look for ways to use them beyond just eating as is. Chapter 13, Let's Open the Lid and Use What's Inside, gives us a hint of the endless ways to use these preserved foods. Our suggestions include appetizers and spreads, some breakfast ideas, soups, main dishes, vegetables, marinades and sauces plus a number of desserts including cakes and squares.

FLAVORED OILS AND SPECIALITY VINEGARS

FLAVORED oils and specialty vinegars are currently riding a wave of popularity as a way to enhance the taste of many foods. And because they are so highly flavored, just a little goes a long way. We love to have them on hand for making a simple vinaigrette, for livening up a marinade or for drizzling over steamed vegetables.

FLAVORED OILS

Flavored oils are made by infusing the essence of such foods as garlic, herbs or chile peppers into an oil. We are excited about our new Nut-Infused Oils. You can make a variety of exotic nut oils at a fraction of the expense of the commercial ones.

Flavored oils pack a lot of flavor into just a few drops. They are an excellent way to lower the amount of fat in your diet. Little effort is needed to make these versatile condiments. But be sure to follow the instructions carefully and make note of the Food Safety Alert, for if these oils are not made and stored properly, there can be a risk of botulism. Then enjoy the wonderful flavors oils offer with no concern for their safety.

The problem with infusing oils with fresh foods is *Clostridium botulinum* spores. Although found widely on foods, the spores are seldom a concern because they find few conditions where they can grow. However, whenever a fresh food, such as garlic, is immersed in oil and kept at temperatures over 50°F (10°C), the food provides enough moisture to enable the spores to grow and produce a potentially fatal toxin. Any oil with a flavoring essence, such as herbs, garlic or fresh peppers, should be heated at a low oven temperature (300°F/150°C) for a specified time. This process, which has been confirmed by Health Canada, drives off the water that is in the food and has an additional advantage of speeding up the infusion of the flavor from the food into the oil.

The oil is then strained and put into bottles. After proper processing, flavored oils need to be kept refrigerated for safety and to prolong their flavor.

When making the oils, we use a 2-cup (500 mL) glass measuring cup or a clean 28-oz (796 mL) can with the lid removed. Follow the recipe instructions carefully and be sure not to increase the amount of foods you add to the oil, because the heating time is based on the amounts in the recipe. Check that the finished oil is clear and the vegetables blackened. After the oil is strained, if it is cloudy or if there is a separate layer at the bottom of the bottle, the oil was not heated long enough and must be heated until it becomes clear, or it can be refrigerated and used within a week.

Canola, a neutral-tasting oil, is perfect for letting the flavor of added foods come through. However, you may prefer to make the oils using extra virgin olive for the unique taste it provides. Olive oil becomes cloudy with refrigerator storage, but when the oil is slightly warmed, this cloudiness disappears. Just remember with any flavored oil not to leave it at room temperature for longer than 1 hour and to discard any oil that has sat out for a longer time.

SPECIALTY VINEGARS

Vinegars are a fundamental part of any good cook's pantry. Yet many are very expensive. Share our enjoyment of these economical, easy-to-prepare homemade vinegars to enliven a dressing for a tossed green salad, add sparkle to steamed vegetables and transform a meat or poultry marinade into something memorable.

Specialty vinegars are incredibly easy to make because the high acid level of vinegar prevents the growth of the botulism organism and eliminates any need to process them in a hot-water canner.

To make speciality vinegars, we steep fresh herbs and other flavorful produce in a variety of vinegars. Experiment with cider, wine or rice vinegars for the interesting flavors they offer.

It is most important to start with a good-quality vinegar especially when using wine vinegars. If herbs are used, bruise or crush them to increase their surface area for maximum flavor extraction during steeping. Most can be made within a week, but allow a little longer for further flavor development.

Variations on our Basic Fresh Herb Vinegar include the use of chive blossoms or rosemary (page 267) and the choice of either strawberries, raspberries, blueberries or cherries give a distinct flavor to our Fruit Vinegar (page 265). Garlic vinegars (page 268 and page 272) are especially good for salad dressings and for a very special occasion, Champagne Vinegar (page 272) is one of our favorites.

SERVING SUGGESTIONS:

To start a meal with pizzazz, garnish a small dish of flavored oil with fresh herbs and serve with pieces of crusty bread for dipping. Be sure to try the Five-Pepper Oil (page 262) on your next pizza. Specialty vinegars dress up tossed greens, pasta and rice salads. We hope you will enjoy one of our homemade vinaigrettes (page 273–275), using our oils and vinegars. Add one of our flavored vinegars to a marinade for less tender meat to get flavor as well as tenderness. A splash of a specialty vinegar or a flavored oil (or both) added to vegetables such as green beans, cauliflower or broccoli is a new eating adventure.

TIP   *Poured into a decorative bottle, Specialty Vinegars make a most attractive gift.*

FOOD SAFETY ALERT

Accurate measurement of the amounts called for in the recipe is essential to making an oil that will not support growth of harmful micro-organisms. If you want a larger quantity of oil than one recipe produces, put a second batch of ingredients (a second recipe) into a separate container. Two containers can be heated at the same time in the oven; just don't put more than 1 cup (250 mL) of oil into one or use a smaller container. When the oil has cooled, it is of the utmost importance to keep the oil refrigerated at all times when it's not in use, and to keep it no longer than 1 month. It is a good idea to check the temperature of your oven with an oven thermometer for accuracy.

LIST OF RECIPES

FLAVORED OILS

Impress your guests with these wonderful flavored oils. Remember to store in the refrigerator and use within a month.

BASIL OIL WITH LEMON AND BLACK PEPPERCORNS

Oil infused with fresh basil has extraordinary flavor, yet is so simple to make. Serve it in a small bowl with a sprinkling of chopped fresh basil and small pieces of crusty French bread for dipping.

1 cup	canola or extra virgin olive oil	250 mL
6	leaves fresh basil	6
2	strips lemon rind, about ½ x 3 inches (1 x 7.5 cm)	2
8	black peppercorns	8

1. Place oil, basil, lemon rind and peppercorns in a 2-cup (500 mL) glass measuring cup or a 28-oz (796 mL) can that has been washed and dried and had the label removed. Set container on a pie plate. Bake in a 300°F (150°C) oven for 90 minutes or until the basil is blackened and crisp. Remove to a rack to cool for 30 minutes.

2. Line a small strainer with a coffee filter or several layers of cheesecloth. Strain oil into a clean glass jar, cover and store in the refrigerator at all times. Use within a month.

Makes about 1 cup (250 mL).

VARIATIONS:

Chile Basil Oil: Replace lemon rind with 1 small red or green hot chile pepper, halved and omit peppercorns.
Basil Oil with Garlic: Replace lemon rind with 3 cloves garlic, halved and omit peppercorns
Thyme Oil with Lemon and Black Peppercorns: Replace basil with 4 sprigs fresh thyme
Rosemary Oil with Orange and Black Peppercorns: Replace basil with 2 sprigs fresh rosemary and replace lemon rind with orange rind.

FIVE-PEPPER OIL

Five peppers team to give amazing flavor to this powerful oil. Be sure to notice that the increased amount of peppers significantly increases the cooking time. The peppers should be blackened and crisp when the oil is finished.

1	small hot red chile pepper	1
1	habañero chile pepper	1
1	small jalapeño pepper	1
¼	sweet red or orange pepper	¼
8	whole black peppercorns	8
1 cup	canola or extra virgin olive oil	250 mL

1. Remove stems from peppers and cut each in half. Place peppers, peppercorns and oil in a 2-cup (500 mL) glass measuring cup or a 28-oz (796 mL) can that has been washed and dried and had the label removed. Set container on a pie plate. Bake in a 300°F (150°C) oven for 4 hours or until the peppers are blackened and crisp. Remove to a rack to cool for 30 minutes.

2. Line a small strainer with a coffee filter or several layers of cheesecloth. Strain oil into a clean glass jar, cover and store in the refrigerator at all times. Use within a month.

Makes about 1 cup (250 mL).

DRIED PORCINI MUSHROOM & ROSEMARY OIL

In Northern Italy, cooks use ingredients that are readily available. So porcini mushrooms and rosemary, which are kitchen basics, and the ever-available olive oil fit this description. A great oil to brush on pizza shells before adding the toppings.

1 cup	extra virgin olive oil	250 mL
¼ cup	dried porcini mushrooms	50 mL
2	sprigs fresh rosemary or 2 tsp (10 mL) dried	2

1. Place oil, mushrooms and rosemary in a 2-cup (500 mL) glass measuring cup or a 28-oz (796 mL) can that has been washed and dried and had the label removed. Set container on a pie plate. Bake in a 300°F (150°C) oven for 1 hour or until the mushrooms are golden brown. Remove to a rack to cool for 30 minutes.

2. Line a small strainer with a coffee filter or several layers of cheesecloth. Strain oil into a clean jar, cover and store in the refrigerator at all times. Use within a month.

Makes about 1 cup (250 mL).

OIL DE PROVENÇE

The flavors of Provençe inspired this excellent and versatile oil. Team it with a mild flavored vinegar when making a salad vinaigrette.

1 cup	canola or extra virgin olive oil	250 mL
2	strips fresh orange rind (about ½ x 3 inches/1 x 7.5 cm)	2
2	thinly sliced shallots	2
1	bay leaf	1
1 tbsp	chopped fresh thyme leaves or 1 tsp (5 mL) dried	15 mL
1 tsp	fennel seeds	5 mL

1. Place oil, orange rind, shallots, bay leaf, thyme and fennel seeds in a 2-cup (500 mL) glass measuring cup or a 28-oz (796 mL) can that has been washed and dried and had the label removed. Set container on a pie plate.

2. Bake in a 300°F (150°C) oven for 90 minutes or until the shallots are blackened and crisp. Remove to a rack to cool for 30 minutes.

3. Line a small strainer with a coffee filter or several layers of cheesecloth. Strain oil into a clean glass jar, cover and store in the refrigerator. Use within a month.

Makes about 1 cup (250 mL).

NUT-INFUSED OILS

Authentic nut oils are very expensive, but their ambrosial flavor can be reproduced by the following method. We recommend leaving the nuts in the oil after heating to develop a more intense nut flavor. Although oils made with other flavoring essences must always be strained before storing, nut-infused oils can be stored with the nuts and strained just before use, if desired. We love them in a salad dressing with the nuts providing a nice garnish, either in the mixture or sprinkled on top. No doubt you will find other uses for these exotic oils in your own recipes.

1 cup	canola oil	250 mL
¼ cup	chopped nuts, such as walnuts, pecans or hazelnuts or sliced almonds	50 mL

1. Place oil and nuts in a 2-cup (500 mL) glass measuring cup or a 28-oz (796 mL) can that has been washed and dried and had the label removed. Set container on a pie plate.

2. Bake in a 300°F (150°C) oven for 1 hour or until the nuts are dark brown. Remove to a rack to cool for 30 minutes.

3. Pour oil and nuts into a clean glass jar, cover and store in the refrigerator at all times. Use within a month.

Makes about 1 cup (250 mL).

SPECIALITY VINEGARS

Once they are made, it is best to use these specialty vinegars within six months since flavor declines during storage.

FRUIT VINEGAR

Vinegars made with fruit are the most versatile of all the flavored vinegars. Use either fresh or frozen fruit for an ambrosial vinegar.

2 cups	sliced hulled strawberries or 1 cup (250 mL) raspberries, cherries or blueberries	500 mL
½ cup	rice vinegar	125 mL
2 tsp	granulated sugar	10 mL

1. Place fruit in a clean jar. Heat vinegar to boiling, pour over fruit, cover and steep for several days at room temperature, out of direct sunlight.

2. Strain through a fine sieve, pressing to extract liquid; discard pulp. Heat vinegar with sugar until sugar dissolves; pour into a clean jar with a tight-fitting lid. Store in the refrigerator.

Makes 1 cup (250 mL).

VARIATION:

Mint leaves or tarragon may be added during steeping.

Citron Vinegar

The flavor of citrus adds a bright note to many foods such as fish, steamed vegetables and vinaigrettes.

1	lime	1
½	orange	½
1	lemon, thinly sliced	1
2 cups	white wine vinegar	500 mL
⅛ tsp	each: salt and paprika	0.5 mL
2 tsp	granulated sugar	10 mL
	Strips of lemon rind (optional)	

1. Finely grate rind of lime and orange; combine with lemon slices in a saucepan. Squeeze juice from lime and orange; set aside.

2. Add vinegar, salt and paprika to saucepan; bring to a boil over high heat, remove from heat and let cool. Stir in reserved juice; pour into a clean jar. Cover and steep in a sunny location for 1 week or longer.

3. Strain through a fine sieve and discard pulp. Heat vinegar with sugar until sugar dissolves; pour into a clean jar with a tight-fitting lid. Add lemon rind (if using). Store in the refrigerator.

Makes about 1½ cups (375 mL).

Serving Suggestion:

Creamy Citron Dressing
One of the neatest ways to use this vinegar is in an oil and vinegar dressing with crumbled feta cheese.
Place 2 tbsp (25 mL) crumbled feta cheese, 2 tbsp (25 mL) olive oil, 2 tbsp (25 mL) water, 1 tbsp (15 mL) Citron Vinegar and 1 tbsp (15 mL) mayonnaise in a blender or food processor; blend until smooth.
Makes ½ cup (125 mL).

BASIC FRESH HERB VINEGAR

Experiment with various herbs to make flavorful vinegars. Crush or bruise the herbs before adding them for best release of flavor.

2 cups	vinegar (white wine, red wine, rice, white or cider)	500 mL
½ cup	fresh herbs (rosemary, sage, tarragon, thyme, basil, parsley, chives and chive blossoms, mint, dill, oregano) or 3 tbsp (45 mL) dried	125 mL

1. Bring vinegar to a boil.

2. Crush or bruise fresh herbs. Place herbs in a clean jar and pour in vinegar. Cover and steep in a sunny location for 2 weeks or longer.

3. Taste vinegar occasionally and when flavor is satisfactory, strain vinegar and pour into a clean jar with a tight-fitting lid. Add a fresh sprig of herb to the jar if desired. Store in the refrigerator.

Makes 2 cups (500 mL).

SUGGESTED COMBINATIONS:

Red wine vinegar with sage, oregano or thyme
White wine vinegar with chive blossoms, basil or parsley
Rice vinegar with rosemary
Cider vinegar with tarragon, dill or mint
White wine vinegar with lemon herbs (lemon balm, lemon basil, lemon thyme or lemon verbena)

CIDER SAGE VINEGAR

Sage gives a special flavor to this vinegar; use only the tender stems, discarding the woody ones. Use this vinegar as a glaze for ham or pork. It is also interesting mixed with oil to make a vinaigrette.

2 cups	cider vinegar	500 mL
1	bunch fresh sage leaves	1
3	cinnamon sticks, each 3 inches (8 cm) long	3
½ tsp	whole allspice	2 mL
¼ tsp	whole cloves	1 mL

1. Bring vinegar to a boil. Crush or bruise sage. Half fill a clean pint (500 mL) jar with sage leaves. Add cinnamon sticks, allspice and cloves.

2. Pour vinegar into jar, cover and steep in a sunny location for up to 2 weeks, tasting occasionally.

3. When flavor is satisfactory, strain vinegar and pour into a clean jar with a tight-fitting lid. Add some of the sage leaves and spices, if desired. Store in the refrigerator.

Makes 2 cups (500 mL).

CHILE HERB GARLIC VINEGAR

Garlic vinegars are among our favorites to use for salad dressings and the many dishes where vinegar is added.

2 cups	white wine vinegar	500 mL
3-4	sprigs fresh herb such as basil or thyme	3-4
1	clove garlic, crushed	1
1	hot chile pepper	1

1. Bring vinegar to a boil. Crush or bruise herb. Place herb, garlic and chile in a clean jar.

2. Proceed as in steps 2 and 3 above.

Makes 2 cups (500 mL).

HERBED LEMON VINEGAR

We love the fresh flavor of this lemon vinegar. Splash it lightly on fish before baking or use it instead of butter with cooked vegetables. We also use it in a vinaigrette for a fruit salad. Garlic lovers will certainly want to include the garlic!

2	lemons	2
2 cups	white wine vinegar	500 mL
1 tbsp	dried dill weed, basil, rosemary or	15 mL
	tarragon or 4 small sprigs fresh herbs	
2	cloves garlic, sliced, optional	2
2 tsp	granulated sugar	10 mL

1. Finely grate outside rind of lemons and thinly slice lemons. Combine rind, lemon slices, vinegar, herbs and garlic (if using) in a medium stainless steel or enamel saucepan. Bring to a boil over high heat, remove from heat and let cool.

2. Pour into a clean jar. Cover and steep in a cool dark place for several weeks. Taste vinegar occasionally and when strength is satisfactory, strain vinegar and discard pulp. Heat vinegar with sugar until sugar is dissolved; pour into a clean jar with a tight-fitting lid. Store in the refrigerator.

Makes about 2 cups (500 mL).

HONEY HERB VINEGAR

The honey gives the vinegar much the same sweetness of balsamic vinegar.

2 cups	red wine vinegar	500 mL
2 tbsp	honey	25 mL
½ cup	fresh thyme or basil leaves	125 mL

1. Bring vinegar to a boil; stir in honey until dissolved.

2. Crush or bruise herbs. Place herbs in a clean jar and pour in vinegar. Cover and steep in a sunny location for 2 weeks or longer, tasting occasionally.

3. When flavor is satisfactory, strain vinegar and pour into a clean jar with a tight-fitting lid. Store in the refrigerator.

Makes 2 cups (500 mL).

PINK PEPPERCORN VINEGAR

The pink peppercorns give a beautiful color to this simple-to-make vinegar. Use both green and pink for a variation.

2 cups	white wine vinegar	500 mL
2 tbsp	pink peppercorns	25 mL

Bring vinegar and peppercorns to a boil, reduce heat and boil gently for 5 minutes. Pour into a clean jar with a tight-fitting lid. Steep in a cool, dark place for several weeks. Store in the refrigerator.

Makes 2 cups (500 mL).

VARIATIONS:

Pink and Green Peppercorn Vinegar
Use 1 tbsp (15 mL) green and 1 tbsp (15 mL) pink peppercorns.

Tarragon Green Peppercorn Vinegar
Add ½ cup (125 mL) fresh tarragon or 2 tbsp (25 mL) dried.

PROVENÇE-STYLE VINEGAR

This is one of our most popular vinegars. Its delicate flavor is a perfect partner for salads made from young greens. To retain the flavor after bottling, add 2 fresh strips of orange rind, 1 thyme sprig, a slice shallot, 1 bay leaf and a few fennel seeds.

2 cups	white wine vinegar	500 mL
½ cup	fresh thyme leaves	125 mL
5	wide strips orange rind	5
⅓ cup	thinly sliced dried shallots	75 mL
2	bay leaves	2
2 tsp	fennel seeds	10 mL

1. Bring vinegar to a boil. Wash and dry thyme, then crush or bruise. Place thyme, orange strips, shallots, bay leaves and fennel seeds in a clean jar. Pour vinegar into jar, cover and set in a cool, dark place for several weeks.

2. Taste vinegar and when strength is satisfactory, strain it and discard solids. Pour into a clean jar with a tight-fitting lid. Store in the refrigerator.

Makes 2 cups (500 mL).

RED WINE RASPBERRY VINEGAR

The technique used for this recipe produces a more intense fruit flavor than is found in other raspberry vinegars. As a result, you can use it more sparingly. Add a hint of mint by including several sprigs of fresh mint with the raspberries.

2 cups	fresh or frozen raspberries	500 mL
1¼ cups	red wine vinegar	300 mL
⅓ cup	granulated sugar	75 mL
¼ cup	water	50 mL

1. Place raspberries, vinegar, sugar and water in a medium stainless steel or enamel saucepan. Bring to a boil over high heat, reduce heat, cover and boil gently for 5 minutes. Cool before storing; store in the refrigerator overnight.

2. Strain through a fine sieve, pressing to extract liquid; discard pulp. Pour liquid into a clean jar with a tight-fitting lid. Store in the refrigerator.

Makes 2 cups (500 mL).

RED WINE AND ROSEMARY VINEGAR

A pungent, colorful vinegar to use for salad dressings or marinades.

2 cups	red wine vinegar	500 mL
1 tsp	granulated sugar	5 mL
½ cup	fresh rosemary leaves	125 mL
½	clove garlic, crushed	½

1. Bring vinegar and sugar to a boil. Crush or bruise rosemary. Place rosemary and garlic in a clean jar and pour in vinegar. Cover and steep in a sunny location for up to 2 weeks, tasting occasionally.

2. When flavor is satisfactory, strain vinegar and pour into a clean jar with a tight-fitting lid. Store in the refrigerator.

Makes 2 cups (500 mL).

VARIATION:

Cranberry and Rosemary Vinegar
Use white vinegar, omit garlic and add ¼ cup fresh cranberries to jar before pouring in vinegar.

RED WINE OREGANO GARLIC VINEGAR

2 cups	red wine vinegar	500 mL
1 cup	fresh oregano	250 mL
3	cloves garlic, crushed	3

Bring vinegar to a boil. Crush or bruise oregano. Place oregano and garlic in a clean jar. Pour vinegar into jar, cover and steep in a sunny location for up to 2 weeks, tasting occasionally. When flavor is satisfactory, strain vinegar and pour into a clean jar with a tight-fitting lid. Store in the refrigerator.

Makes 2 cups (500 mL).

SHERRY VINEGAR

Sherry vinegar is a superb source of flavor to enliven many foods. Try adding it to hot or cold soups or a simple vinaigrette.

1 cup	white wine vinegar	250 mL
1 cup	sherry	250 mL

Bring vinegar and sherry just to a boil, cool slightly and pour into a clean jar with a tight-fitting lid. Steep in a cool, dark place for several weeks. Store in the refrigerator.

Makes 2 cups (500 mL).

CHAMPAGNE VINEGAR

It is truly exciting to be able to use champagne, the most celebrated of sparkling wines to make a homemade vinegar. So why not celebrate with Champagne Vinegar in a vinaigrette on a salad or splashed over cooked vegetables.

1 cup	dry champagne	250 mL
1 cup	white wine vinegar	250 mL
1 tsp	granulated sugar	5 mL

Bring champagne, vinegar and sugar just to a boil. Remove from heat and cool slightly. Pour into a clean jar with a tight-fitting lid. Steep in a cool, dark place for several weeks. Store in the refrigerator.

Makes 2 cups (500 mL).

VINAIGRETTES AND DRESSINGS

Now that we have talked about specialty vinegars and flavored oils, here are some of our favorite ways to use them. See Chapter 13 for others.

LIGHT GARLIC BASIL VINAIGRETTE

Use this dressing on a salad of tossed greens or mesclun, to marinate meats or to sprinkle on steamed vegetables for a vegetable salad.

¼ cup	chicken broth	50 mL
3 tbsp	Basil Oil with Lemon and Black Peppercorns (page 261)	45 mL
1 tbsp	red wine vinegar	15 mL
2 tsp	lemon juice	10 mL
1 tsp	Dijon-Style Mustard (page 232)	5 mL
1	clove garlic, crushed	1
1 tbsp	chopped fresh basil or 1 tsp (5 mL) dried	15 mL

Combine all ingredients in a small container with a tight-fitting lid. Cover and shake well. Refrigerate until ready to use.

Makes ½ cup (125 mL).

OREGANO PEPPER VINAIGRETTE

This is a robust vinaigrette. It delivers zip to many an ordinary green salad. Drizzle some on sliced tomatoes. We like it with a pasta salad.

⅓ cup	Five-Pepper Oil (page 262)	75 mL
¼ cup	dry red wine	50 mL
1 tbsp	chopped fresh oregano or	15 mL
	1 tsp (5 mL) dried	
1 tbsp	red wine vinegar	15 mL
1	clove garlic, crushed	1
¼ tsp	salt	1 mL

Combine all ingredients in a small container with a tight-fitting lid. Cover and shake well. Refrigerate until ready to use.

Makes about ½ cup (125 mL).

SERVING SUGGESTION:

Greek Salad
Place 8 cups (2 L) torn romaine lettuce, ½ red onion and ½ English cucumber, thinly sliced, ¼ cup (50 mL) pitted kalamata olives, 2 medium tomatoes cut into wedges and ½ cup (125 mL) crumbled feta cheese in a large bowl. Pour Oregano Pepper Vinaigrette over salad; toss well.
Makes 8 servings.

RASPBERRY ORANGE VINAIGRETTE

This is the perfect vinaigrette to use with fruit salads and with cottage cheese salads. And use it as a marinade for chicken and pork before grilling.

⅓ cup	orange juice	75 mL
¼ cup	each: extra virgin olive oil and water	50 mL
2 tbsp	Red Wine Raspberry Vinegar (page 271)	25 mL
1	chopped green onion	1
⅛ tsp	each: salt and freshly ground pepper	0.5 mL

Combine all ingredients in a small container with a tight-fitting lid. Cover and shake well. Refrigerate until ready to use.

Makes ⅔ cup (150 mL).

CREAMY CHAMPAGNE DRESSING

You don't need to wait for a special day to make this flavorful dressing using our Champagne Vinegar. Use it for salads of shredded cabbage, chopped celery and diced apple, or for a light potato salad.

3 tbsp	light mayonnaise	45 mL
3 tbsp	Champagne Vinegar (page 272)	45 mL
2 tbsp	canola oil	25 mL
1 tbsp	chopped fresh parsley	15 mL
1 tbsp	water	15 mL
1 tsp	Old-Style Whole Seed Mustard (page 234) or coarse mustard	5 mL

Whisk together mayonnaise, vinegar, oil, parsley, water and mustard in a small bowl. Transfer to a container with a tight-fitting lid. Cover and refrigerate until ready to use.

Makes about ½ cup (125 mL).

TIP

Mesclun: Today there is much consumer interest in a variety of lettuces usually called mesclun or mixed young salad greens. They are available in almost every produce store and supermarket, sold by weight. Typically they are a combination of mild- and bitter-flavored tender young leaves of different colors. The combination usually includes oak leaf and red leaf lettuces, frisée (curly endive), mâche and radicchio, and may include spinach, red mustard, arugula and others. Store as you would other greens and use as soon as possible, ideally within a couple of days.

The Finishing Touch

THIS is a chapter of wonderful "finishing" ideas. Not all of them are completed desserts, but all are used in some way in the dessert part of the meal. For example, Raspberry Coulis and Hazelnut Fudge Sauce (pages 292 and 296) are luscious ideas for topping ice-cream, cake, fresh fruit or pudding. But you may still be tempted to eat them with a spoon directly from the jar. Our Pear and Sour Cherry Mincemeat and Traditional Rumtopf (pages 285 and 286) are other topping ideas.

Most of our finishing ideas, once prepared, are then available for fast dessert delivery at a moment's notice. Having dessert sauces and syrups on hand opens up endless possibilities for making more complex recipes easier. Think of using a dessert sauce or syrup as part of the liquid in a cake batter or using Cherry Compote (page 280) to make Cherries Jubilee. And a real favorite, so elegant yet very simple, is fresh pears and chèvre cheese in Rosemary Wine Syrup (page 299) served with a sweet wafer cookie.

And then there are the liqueurs. They are not really desserts, but are used to accompany after-dessert coffee. We offer you fresh-tasting fruit liqueurs which can be used as dessert toppings and creamy liqueurs which are best with coffee. We believe our finishing touch ideas are well worth your preparation time and will meet your needs for easy to make desserts.

SERVING SUGGESTIONS

Add Candied Fruits (page 300) to cakes, muffins and squares. Keep Brandied Butterscotch Sauce (page 295) on hand to serve as a tasty dip for apple slices. Fruit Liqueurs (pages 303–305) added to chilled soda water or white wine make wonderful spritzers.

List of Recipes

FRUITS WITH SPIRIT

Fruit can be magically transformed into an enchanting dessert with the addition of your favorite wine or liqueur.

Fruit and Preparation for 4 pint (500 mL) jars

Fruit	Preparation of Fruit	Spirit per Pint (500 mL) Jar	Processing Time
Apricots 7 cups (1.75 L) halved (about 2 lb/1 kg)	Dip in boiling water 30–60 seconds to blanch. Remove skins, cut in half and pit.	1 tbsp (15 mL) peach schnapps or Amaretto or 2 tbsp (25 mL) brandy or rum	20 minutes
Cherries (sweet) 7 cups (1.75 L) (about 2 lb/1 kg)	Pit.	1 tbsp (15 mL) kirsch or Amaretto or 2 tbsp (25 mL) port or sherry	15 minutes
Grapes, seedless 8 cups (2 L) whole or halved (about 2 lb/1 kg)	Remove stems. Leave whole or cut in half.	1 tbsp (15 mL) orange liqueur or kirsch or 2 tbsp (25 mL) port or sherry	15 minutes
Peaches or Nectarines 6 cups (1.5 L) sliced (about 2.5 lb/1.2 kg)	Dip peaches in boiling water 30–60 seconds to blanch. Slip off skins, cut in half, pit and slice.	1 tbsp (15 mL) orange liqueur or Chambord or 2 tbsp (25 mL) peach schnapps	20 minutes
Pears 6 cups (1.5 L) sliced (about 2.5 lb/1.2 kg)	Peel, core and slice.	2 tsp (10 mL) crème de menthe or 1 tbsp (15 mL) Frangelica or 2 tbsp (25 mL) brandy or rum	20 minutes
Pineapple 1 whole, cubed	Peel deep enough to remove eyes. Cut into quarters and remove core. Cut into cubes or spears.	2 tsp (10 mL) crème de menthe or kirsch or 2 tbsp (25 mL) brandy or rum	15 minutes
Plums 6 cups (1.5 L) sliced (about 2.5 lb/1.2 kg)	Pit and slice.	1 tbsp (15 mL) Amaretto or peach schnapps or 2 tbsp (25 mL) port or rum	15 minutes

SYRUP FOR 4 PINT (500 ML) JARS

1	lemon	1
2½ cups	water	625 mL
2 cups	granulated sugar	500 mL

Canning Procedure:

1. Partially fill a boiling-water canner with hot water. Place clean pint (500 mL) canning jars in canner, cover and begin to bring water to a boil over high heat.

2. Prepare fruit as directed. As you work, place all fruits except grapes, pineapple and sweet cherries in 4 cups (1 L) water mixed with ¼ cup (50 mL) lemon juice. Drain fruit before placing in jars.

3. Prepare syrup: grate rind of lemon; place in a medium saucepan. Squeeze 2 tbsp (25 mL) juice from lemon; add to rind. Stir in water and sugar. Bring to a boil over high heat and boil gently for 1 minute. Meanwhile, place lids in hot or boiling water according to manufacturer's directions.

4. Remove jars from canner. Add choice of liqueur as suggested in chart and pack fruit into jars. Ladle hot syrup over fruit to within ½ inch (1 cm) of rim (head space). Remove air bubbles by sliding a small clean wooden or plastic spatula between glass and food; readjust head space to ½ inch (1 cm). Wipe jar rim to remove any stickiness. Center lid on jar; apply screw band just until fingertip tight. Place jars in canner and adjust water level to cover jars by 1–2 inches (2.5–5 cm). Cover canner and return water to a boil. Process for times given in chart.

5. Remove jars from canner and cool for 24 hours. Check jar seals (sealed lids turn downward). Wipe jars, label and store in a cool, dark place.

TIP   *Sugar greatly enhances the flavor and texture of canned fruit, but it is not essential in the preserving process. Reduce the sugar if you choose.*

CHERRY COMPOTE

Compotes are fresh or dried fruits slowly cooked in a sugar syrup to retain their shape. Compotes frequently contain wine or liqueur. This one is delicious served over a slice of cheesecake or pound cake.

1 cup	dry red wine	250 mL
⅔ cup	granulated sugar	150 mL
2 tsp	lemon juice	10 mL
4 cups	fresh or frozen pitted sour cherries	1 L
1 tbsp	cornstarch	15 mL
1 tbsp	water	15 mL
1 tbsp	kirsch	15 mL

1. Place wine, sugar and lemon juice in a medium saucepan. Bring to a boil over high heat, stirring to dissolve sugar. Add cherries; return to a boil. Reduce heat and boil gently, uncovered, for 15 minutes, stirring occasionally.

2. Remove hot jars from canner. Remove cherries from liquid with a slotted spoon; pack into the jars. Continue simmering syrup until it is reduced to ⅔ cup (150 mL).

3. Stir together cornstarch and water; stir into syrup. Return to a boil and boil gently for 1 minute, stirring constantly. Remove from heat and stir in kirsch.

4. Pour syrup over cherries to within ½ inch (1 cm) of rim (head space). Process 15 minutes for half-pint (250 mL) jars and 20 minutes for pint (500 mL) jars as directed on page 133 (Longer Time Processing Procedure).

Makes 3 cups (750 mL).

HAZELNUT BLUEBERRY MANGO SAUCE

Enjoy this blending of the tropical flavor of mango with down-home blueberry. Serve it over pancakes, waffles or angel food cake. If mangoes are unavailable, substitute nectarines or peeled peaches.

2	mangoes, peeled and diced	2
2 cups	fresh or frozen unsweetened blueberries	500 mL
1 cup	granulated sugar	250 mL
1 cup	apple juice or water	250 mL
2 tbsp	lemon juice	25 mL
1 tsp	grated lemon rind	5 mL
2 tbsp	hazelnut liqueur or 1½ tsp (7 mL) almond extract	25 mL

1. Combine mangoes, blueberries, sugar, apple juice, lemon juice and lemon rind in a large stainless steel or enamel saucepan. Bring to a boil, reduce heat and simmer, uncovered, for 25 minutes or until fruit is softened and liquid has thickened. Stir in liqueur and cook for 5 minutes.

2. Remove hot jars from canner and ladle compote into jars to within ½ inch (1 cm) of rim (head space). Process 10 minutes for half-pint (250 mL) jars and 15 minutes for pint (500 mL) jars as directed on page 133 (Longer Time Processing Procedure).

Makes 4 cups (1 L).

VARIATION:

8 nectarines or peeled peaches may be substituted for the mangoes.

BRANDIED DRIED FRUIT PRESERVES

Elegant desserts are easy and fast with this spirited preserve on hand. Serve over ice-cream, frozen yogurt, fresh fruits and cake. You will probably find other uses as well.

1½ cups	dried mixed fruits	375 mL
1	1-inch (2.5 cm) piece Candied Ginger (page 301) or thinly sliced piece crystallized ginger	1
⅓ cup	lightly packed brown sugar	75 mL
2	thin strips orange rind, chopped	2
½ cup	brandy or cognac	125 mL

1. Place dried fruits and ginger in a saucepan. Cover with cold water, bring to a boil, remove from heat and let cool. Refrigerate for 8 hours or overnight.

2. Drain fruit, reserving liquid. Add enough water to liquid to make ¾ cup (175 mL). In a medium stainless steel or enamel saucepan, combine liquid, sugar and orange rind. Bring to a boil, stirring, until sugar has dissolved. Add drained fruit; warm. Remove from heat and stir in brandy.

3. Remove hot jars from canner. Pack fruit into jars. Ladle liquid over fruit in jars to within ½ inch (1 cm) of rim (head space). Process 10 minutes for half-pint (250 mL) jars and 15 minutes for pint (500 mL) jars as directed on page 133 (Longer Time Processing Procedure).

Makes 2 cups (500 mL).

SPICED CRANBERRY PRESERVES

Add making this preserve to your "must do" list. Kept on hand, it provides a fast way to brighten up ice-cream, frozen yogurt, cake or rice pudding.

4 cups	fresh or frozen cranberries	1 L
1	large apple, peeled, cored and diced	1
1	large pear, peeled, cored and diced	1
½ cup	golden raisins	125 mL
1 cup	granulated sugar	250 mL
1 tbsp	grated orange rind	15 mL
½ cup	orange juice	125 mL
1 tsp	ground cinnamon	5 mL
¼ tsp	ground nutmeg	1 mL
⅓ cup	orange liqueur	75 mL

1. Combine cranberries, apple, pear, raisins, sugar, orange rind, orange juice, cinnamon and nutmeg in a large stainless steel or enamel saucepan. Bring to a boil over high heat, reduce heat and boil gently, uncovered, for 20 minutes or until thickened, stirring frequently. Remove from heat and stir in liqueur.

2. Remove hot jars from canner and ladle preserves into jars to within ½ inch (1 cm) of rim (head space). Process 10 minutes for half-pint (250 mL) jars and 15 minutes for pint (500 mL) jars as directed on page 133 (Longer Time Processing Procedure).

Makes 4 cups (1 L).

VARIATION:

Raspberry Cranberry Dessert Preserves
Replace pear and apple with 1½ cups (375 mL) fresh or frozen unsweetened raspberries.

APPLE CRANBERRY MINCEMEAT

Our favorite mincemeat because of its fruitiness and freshness, this one is positively addictive. In fact, it is good enough to eat right out of the jar. Use it in pies and squares or warm it as an ice-cream topping.

6 cups	finely chopped tart apples (about 2 lb/1 kg)	1.5 L
1 cup	sultana raisins	250 mL
1 cup	dark raisins	250 mL
1 cup	currants	250 mL
⅔ cup	lightly packed brown sugar	150 mL
½ cup	dried cranberries	125 mL
⅓ cup	water	75 mL
	Grated rind and juice of 2 lemons	
2 tsp	ground cinnamon	10 mL
½ tsp	ground cloves	2 mL
¼ cup	brandy	50 mL

1. Combine apples, sultana raisins, dark raisins, currants, sugar, cranberries, water, lemon rind, lemon juice, cinnamon and cloves in a large stainless steel or enamel saucepan. Bring to a boil over high heat, reduce heat, cover and simmer for 20 minutes, stirring frequently. Stir in brandy and return to a boil.

2. Remove hot jars from canner and ladle preserves into jars to within ½ inch (1 cm) of rim (head space). Process 20 minutes for half-pint (250 mL) and pint (500 mL) jars as directed on page 133 (Longer Time Processing Procedure).

Makes 6 cups (1.5 L).

TIP   *Be sure to try Apple Cranberry Mincemeat Squares (page 340) the next time you need an accompaniment for coffee or tea.*

PEAR AND SOUR CHERRY MINCEMEAT

For many years making mincemeat has been a tradition in our families. Lighter in color and flavor than traditional mincemeat, this pear version has wider uses than just for pies and tarts. Try it as a topping for pound cake, ice-cream, and waffles or pancakes. Or use it in place of date filling in your favorite date square recipe. Sour cherries or cranberries add color and just a hint of tartness.

4	Bartlett pears, peeled, cored and finely chopped	4
1 cup	golden raisins	250 mL
½	orange, chopped (include rind as well as pulp)	½
½ cup	chopped sour cherries or cranberries	125 mL
¾ cup	lightly packed brown sugar	175 mL
¼ cup	water	50 mL
	Grated rind and juice of 1 lemon	
½ tsp	each: ground cinnamon and allspice	2 mL
¼ tsp	ground nutmeg	1 mL
2 tbsp	brandy	25 mL

1. Combine pears, raisins, orange, cherries, sugar, water, lemon rind and juice, cinnamon, allspice and nutmeg in a medium stainless steel or enamel saucepan. Bring to a boil over high heat, reduce heat, cover and boil gently for 20 minutes or until thickened, stirring frequently. Stir in brandy and return to a boil.

2. Remove hot jars from canner and ladle mincemeat into jars to within ½ inch (1 cm) of rim (head space). Process 20 minutes for half-pint (250 mL) and pint (500 mL) jars as directed on page 133 (Longer Time Processing Procedure).

Makes 2¾ cups (675 mL).

TRADITIONAL RUMTOPF

Rumtopf comes from the German word *Topf*, meaning "pot." The traditional version is made in a large crock, different fruits added as they ripen during the growing season. If you don't have a crock, simply layer the fruit in either a very large glass jar or a large non-reactive container.

1½ cups	strawberries, whole or halved if large	375 mL
½ cup	granulated sugar	125 mL
¾ cup	light rum	175 mL

Add ¾ cup (175 mL) of any or all of the following: red currants, pitted sweet cherries, raspberries, blueberries, sliced peaches, sliced nectarines, quartered apricots, quartered blue or yellow plums

Granulated sugar
Rum

1. Place strawberries into an 8-cup (2 L) container and layer with sugar. Allow to stand for 30 minutes. Slowly pour rum down inside of jar so it measures about 2 inches (5 cm) over fruit. Cover loosely with plastic film. Store in a cool location (basement or a cool room) for about 2 weeks.

2. Combine next choice of fruit and ¼ cup (50 mL) sugar; add to contents of jar. Top up with rum, if required, so fruit is covered with liquid. Since the fruit has a tendency to float, place a small plate or other non-reactive item on top of the fruit to keep it submerged. Otherwise stir every few days.

3. Repeat with other fruits as they are available. With each addition, add ¼ cup (50 mL) sugar and top up with rum if required.

4. When fermentation is complete, fruit is no longer bubbling; transfer fruit to clean jars with tight-fitting lids. Store in the refrigerator.

Makes 6 to 12 cups (1.5 to 3 L) depending on how many fruits you use.

SWEET FRUIT SAUCES

These exceptional fruit sauces turn plain cake, waffles, French toast, ice-cream and frozen yogurt into elegant desserts at a moment's notice. Tucked in your refrigerator or freezer, they are great to have on hand.

SLOW-BAKED APPLE WEDGES

Slow baking transforms apples into rich golden wedges. Wonderful with crepes or a spice cake!

¾ cup	liquid honey	175 mL
½ cup	water	125 mL
3 tbsp	lemon juice	45 mL
⅛ tsp	ground nutmeg	0.5 mL
8	large tart apples, peeled and cut into thick wedges	8

1. Combine honey, water, lemon juice and nutmeg in a large bowl. Add apple wedges, stirring to coat well.

2. Spread apples in a 10 x 15-inch (24 x 40 cm) jelly roll pan, pouring any remaining liquid over top. Cover with foil and bake at 300°F (150°C) for 45 minutes or until apples are soft. Remove foil and bake until apples are golden and most of liquid has evaporated, about 75 minutes (50 minutes in a convection oven). Using a flat lifter, gently turn apples once or twice during baking.

3. Pack into clean jars or plastic containers to within ½ inch (1 cm) of rim. Cover with tight-fitting lids. Store in refrigerator for up to 1 week or freeze for longer storage.

Makes 3 cups (750 mL).

PEACH SLICES WITH MAPLE SYRUP

This is a wonderful topping to make when peaches are at their most flavorful.

½ cup	pure maple syrup	125 mL
¼ cup	granulated sugar	50 mL
2 tbsp	sherry, optional	25 mL
6	large peaches, peeled and sliced	6

1. Combine syrup and sugar in a 4-cup (1 L) microwavable container. Microwave at High (100%) for 1½ minutes or until sugar is dissolved. Stir in sherry, if using.

2. Add peach slices, cover and microwave for 5 minutes or just until mixture begins to boil. Cool, stirring occasionally.

3. Pack into clean jars or plastic containers to within ½ inch (1 cm) of rim. Cover with tight-fitting lids. Store in refrigerator for up to 1 week or freeze for longer storage.

Makes about 3 cups (750 mL).

Chile Basil Oil (page 261), Basic Fresh Herb Vinegar (page 267)

Preserving the Harvest

PIQUANT SOUR CHERRY SAUCE

This bright flavorful sauce always brings requests for the recipe. If you prefer it less piquant, add a bit of extra sugar.

4½ cups	fresh or frozen pitted sour cherries	1.125 L
1½ cups	water	375 mL
¾ cup	pineapple juice	175 mL
1	cinnamon stick, 4 inches (10 cm) long	1
¾ cup	granulated sugar	175 mL
3 tbsp	cornstarch	45 mL
⅓ cup	cold water	75 mL
2 tbsp	lemon juice	25 mL

1. Combine cherries, water, pineapple juice and cinnamon stick in a medium stainless steel or enamel saucepan. Bring to a boil over high heat, reduce heat, cover and boil gently for 10 minutes. Remove cinnamon and discard.

2. Add sugar to cherries. Blend together cornstarch and water and stir into cherries. Return to a boil, reduce heat and boil gently, uncovered, for 5 minutes or until clear and thickened. Stir in lemon juice.

3. Pack into clean jars or plastic containers to within ½ inch (1 cm) of rim. Cover with tight-fitting lids. Store in refrigerator for up to 3 weeks or freeze for longer storage.

Makes about 2¼ cups (550 mL).

WINE-BERRY SAUCE

A bright-hued sauce that is perfect for spooning over angel cake, pudding or ice-cream.

2 cups	strawberries, sliced	500 mL
¼ cup	granulated sugar	50 mL
⅓ cup	dry red wine	75 mL
2 tsp	Amaretto or ¼ tsp (1 mL) almond extract	10 mL

1. Place strawberries in a bowl and toss with sugar. Let stand for 12 hours.

2. Drain liquid from berries into a small saucepan; add wine. Bring to a boil over high heat, reduce heat and boil gently for 1 minute.

3. Pour wine and liqueur over berries and mix well. Refrigerate for 1 week or freeze for longer storage.

Makes 2 cups (500 mL).

VARIATION:

Raspberries with Port
Raspberries, port and 1 tbsp (15 mL) brandy in place of strawberries, red wine and liqueur are also delicious served over ice-cream.

BRANDIED FRUIT SAUCE

Looking for the perfect hostess gift? Here's a sensational and simple recipe to fold into whipped cream, serve over ice-cream or fresh fruit or use as a pudding topping. The recipe is so easy, why not double it and have some yourself!

1 cup	each: golden raisins and mixed candied peel	250 mL
½ cup	candied pineapple cubes, diced	125 mL
⅓ cup	each: candied red and green cherries	75 mL
⅓ cup	diced Candied Ginger (page 301)or crystallized ginger	75 mL
¼ cup	dried cranberries	50 mL
½ tsp	ground cinnamon	2 mL
⅛ tsp	each: ground cloves and allspice	0.5 mL
1 cup	dark rum or brandy	250 mL

1. Place raisins, peel, pineapple, cherries, ginger and cranberries in a sterilized quart (1 L) jar.

2. Stir together cinnamon, cloves, allspice and rum in a small saucepan. Heat until just warm. Pour over fruit. Seal jar securely and rotate each day for 6 days.

3. Spoon into smaller attractive jars for gift giving. Keeps in a cool, dark place almost indefinitely.

Makes 2 cups (500 mL).

RASPBERRY COULIS

Raspberry coulis has a myriad of uses, both as a topping for crêpes or pancakes and with an elegant dessert such as a frozen cream mousse or over waffles.

4 cups	fresh or frozen raspberries	1 L
½ cup	icing sugar	125 mL
1 tbsp	orange liqueur, optional	15 mL

1. Purée raspberries in a food processor or blender. Stir in sugar and liqueur and press through a medium sieve to remove seeds.

2. Pack into clean jars or plastic containers to within ½ inch (1 cm) of rim. Cover with tight-fitting lids. Store in refrigerator for up to 3 weeks or freeze for longer storage.

Makes 1¾ cups (425 mL).

WARM APPLE CIDER SAUCE

Enjoy this sauce strained and added to hot tea for a warming experience after a winter outing.

2 tbsp	butter or margarine	25 mL
1 cup	apple cider	250 mL
¾ cup	lightly packed brown sugar	175 mL
2 tbsp	cornstarch	25 mL
1–2 tbsp	rum, brandy or Calvados (optional)	15–25 mL

1. Melt butter in a microwavable 2-cup (500 mL) container on High (100%) for 30 seconds.

2. Stir together cider, sugar and cornstarch. Whisk into butter. Microwave, uncovered, on High for 3 minutes or until smooth and thickened.

3. Stir in rum (if using). Serve warm.

Makes 1½ cups (375 mL).

BLUEBERRY MAPLE SAUCE

A spoonful of this sauce is a scrumptious topping for sliced fresh peaches or other fruit. Of course, serve it on pancakes and waffles as well.

2 cups	fresh or frozen unsweetened blueberries	500 mL
¼ cup	water	50 mL
1 tbsp	lemon juice	15 mL
1	cinnamon stick, 4 inches (10 cm) long	1
½ cup	granulated sugar	125 mL
½ cup	maple syrup	125 mL

1. Combine blueberries, water, lemon juice and cinnamon stick in a 4-cup (1 L) microwavable bowl. Microwave, uncovered, on High (100%) for 5 minutes, stirring once. Stir in sugar and maple syrup. Microwave, uncovered, on High for 3 minutes or until sugar is dissolved and mixture comes to a boil. Let cool.

2. Discard cinnamon stick and store sauce in a tightly sealed container in refrigerator for up to 1 month.

Makes 2 cups (500 mL).

CRANBERRY RASPBERRY SAUCE

Try this bright sauce the next time you serve pancakes. It is one of our favorites to spoon over vanilla pudding.

2½ cups	fresh or frozen cranberries	625 mL
3 cups	fresh or frozen unsweetened raspberries (10 oz/300 g)	750 mL
¾ cup	cranberry fruit cocktail	175 mL
½ cup	lightly packed brown sugar	125 mL
½ cup	corn syrup	125 mL
½ tsp	almond extract	2 mL

1. Combine cranberries, raspberries, cranberry cocktail, sugar and corn syrup in a medium saucepan.

2. Bring to a boil, reduce heat and boil gently for 15 minutes or until fruit is softened.

3. Remove from heat, purée in a food processor or blender until smooth. Stir in almond extract and cool.

Makes 3½ cups (875 mL).

RICH DESSERT SAUCES

We like to keep several of these sauces in the refrigerator. They make wonderful quick toppings for puddings, fresh fruit, crêpes, pound cake, angel food cake or ice-cream. You can also serve them under cream puffs or as a dessert fondue sauce.

BRANDIED BUTTERSCOTCH SAUCE

This sauce's authentic butterscotch flavor and hint of brandy make it a wonderful dip for apple slices.

⅔ cup	lightly packed brown sugar	150 mL
⅓ cup	butter	75 mL
¼ cup	corn syrup	50 mL
½ cup	18% cream	125 mL
2 tbsp	brandy	25 mL
1 tsp	vanilla extract	5 mL

1. Combine sugar, butter and corn syrup in a small saucepan. Bring to a boil, over high heat, stirring frequently; reduce heat to medium and boil gently for 3 minutes. Remove from heat.

2. Cool for 5 minutes; stir in cream, brandy and vanilla. Pour into a clean jar with a tight-fitting lid. Store in refrigerator for up to 3 weeks. Stir before serving.

Makes 1½ cups (375 mL).

HAZELNUT FUDGE SAUCE

This rich chocolate sauce brims with the taste of toasted hazelnuts.

¼ cup	butter	50 mL
½ cup	coarsely chopped hazelnuts	125 mL
1 cup	granulated sugar	250 mL
½ cup	cocoa	125 mL
⅛ tsp	salt	0.5 mL
⅓ cup	corn syrup	75 mL
¾ cup	10% cream	175 mL
½ tsp	vanilla extract	2 mL

1. Melt butter in a medium saucepan over medium heat. Add nuts and sauté for 5 minutes or until lightly browned. Remove from heat.

2. Stir in sugar, cocoa and salt. Blend in corn syrup, mixing well; stir in cream. Return to medium heat and boil gently for 1 minute, stirring constantly. Remove from heat and stir in vanilla.

3. Pour into a clean jar with a tight-fitting lid. Store in refrigerator for up to 3 weeks.

Makes 2 cups (500 mL).

MOCHA CARAMEL SAUCE

This is an exquisite chocolate sauce graced with a hint of caramel and coffee.

½ cup	granulated sugar	125 mL
3 tbsp	water	45 mL
¼ cup	espresso or very strong coffee	50 mL
2 tbsp	corn syrup	25 mL
2 tbsp	butter	25 mL
½ cup	10% cream	125 mL
3	squares semi-sweet chocolate	3
½ tsp	vanilla extract	2 mL

1. Combine sugar and water in a heavy medium saucepan. Bring to a boil over medium-high heat, stirring just until sugar is dissolved. Swirl pan slightly to dissolve any sugar crystals on sides. Continue to boil gently without stirring until sugar turns a rich golden caramel color, about 7 minutes. Watch carefully toward the end of the cooking time as it will burn very quickly.

2. Remove from heat and carefully pour in coffee, stirring well until all the caramel is dissolved. Stir in corn syrup and butter; return to heat and bring just to a boil, stirring constantly. Remove from heat.

3. Pour hot mixture slowly into cream; blend in chocolate and vanilla. Pour into a clean jar with a tight-fitting lid. Store in refrigerator for up to 1 month. Serve slightly warmed.

Makes 1¼ cups (325 mL).

DESSERT SYRUPS

The Rosemary Wine Syrup (page 299) is a knockout with fresh fruit and chèvre cheese. Drizzle with the syrup and garnish with fresh mint. Mint Lime Syrup (page 299) is marvelous over fresh fruit. We love Cinnamon Rum Syrup over cooked rhubarb sauce, ice-cream and especially on fruit pancakes.

BLUEBERRY SYRUP

2 cups	fresh or frozen blueberries	500 mL
1 cup	granulated sugar	250 mL
⅓ cup	water	75 mL
1 tbsp	lemon juice	15 mL
½ tsp	ground cinnamon	2 mL

Combine blueberries, sugar, water, lemon juice and cinnamon in a medium saucepan. Bring to a boil over high heat, reduce heat, cover and boil gently for 10 minutes or until fruit is tender. Strain through a lined sieve; discard solids. Pour syrup into a clean jar with a tight-fitting lid and store in the refrigerator.

Makes 1 cup (250 mL).

CINNAMON RUM SYRUP

¾ cup	granulated sugar	175 mL
½ cup	water	125 mL
1 tsp	ground cinnamon	5 mL
1 tbsp	dark rum	15 mL
1 tsp	lemon juice	5 mL

1. Combine sugar, water and cinnamon in a small saucepan. Bring to a boil over high heat and boil until sugar is dissolved. Remove from heat; stir in rum and lemon juice. Let cool.

2. Pour syrup into a clean jar with a tight-fitting lid and store in the refrigerator.

Makes 1 cup (250 mL).

MINT LIME SYRUP

1	lime	1
½ cup	granulated sugar	125 mL
½ cup	white wine	125 mL
¼ cup	chopped fresh mint or 1 tbsp (15 mL) dried	50 mL

1. Remove 2 strips rind from lime. Squeeze 2 tbsp (25 mL) juice from lime; set aside.

2. Combine rind, sugar, wine and mint in a small saucepan. Bring to a boil over high heat, cover, reduce heat and boil gently for 5 minutes. Remove from heat and let cool. Strain mixture through a fine sieve; discard solids.

3. Stir in lime juice. Pour syrup into a clean jar with a tight-fitting lid and store in the refrigerator.

Makes 1 cup (250 mL).

ROSEMARY WINE SYRUP

½ cup	granulated sugar	125 mL
½ cup	dry white wine	125 mL
¼ cup	fresh rosemary leaves	50 mL
¼ cup	water	50 mL
2 tbsp	balsamic vinegar	25 mL
½ tsp	peppercorns	2 mL
2	strips lemon rind	2
2	bay leaves	2

1. Combine sugar, wine, rosemary, water, vinegar, peppercorns, lemon rind and bay leaves in a small saucepan. Bring to a boil over high heat, cover, reduce heat and boil gently for 5 minutes. Remove from heat and let cool. Strain mixture through a fine sieve; discard solids.

2. Pour syrup into a clean jar with a tight-fitting lid and store in the refrigerator.

Makes about 1¼ cups (300 mL).

CANDIED FRUITS

Dried fruits have many uses. Serve them as a sweet treat for nibbling, add them to baking or stir them into frozen desserts.

CANDIED CITRUS PEEL

A zesty treat on its own, candied peel is also a nice addition to many desserts and baked products. For special occasions, dip candied peel in chocolate.

	Rind from 2 grapefruit, or 3 sweet or blood oranges, or 3 lemons, or a mixture of all three	
	Cold water	
¾ cup	**granulated sugar**	**175 mL**
¾ cup	**water**	**175 mL**
½ tbsp	**corn syrup**	**7 mL**
	Extra granulated sugar	

1. Cut fruit in quarters lengthwise. Remove the rind from pulp; save pulp for another use. Slice rinds into ½-inch (1 cm) slices. You should have about 2 cups (500 mL).

2. Place rinds in a medium saucepan and cover with cold water. Bring to a boil over high heat, reduce heat and boil gently for 2 minutes or longer if you do not like the strong citrus flavor (see Tip). Drain well.

3. Combine sugar, ¾ cup (175 mL) water and corn syrup in pan and bring to a boil over high heat. Add rinds, return to boil, cover and boil gently for 15 minutes. Remove cover and continue to boil gently for about 30 minutes or until liquid is reduced to about 2 tablespoons (25 mL). Remove rinds to a cooling rack to drain.

4. When rinds are well drained, roll a few at a time in extra sugar, being careful to coat well. Place on a baking sheet or wax paper. Repeat until all are done. Let sit at room temperature to air-dry for 24 hours.

5. Pack in airtight containers and store in the refrigerator.

Makes 2 cups (500 mL).

TIP *If you are using lemon rinds, cook them first for 15 minutes before adding remaining rinds; cook 2 minutes longer.*

CANDIED GINGER

Candied ginger, often called crystallized ginger, is a spirited addition to a candy tray and a pleasant compliment to chocolate. Its lively flavor is a nice addition to a variety of baked products. Remember to make extra for gifts during the holidays. We have used it in many of our other recipes throughout the book.

1 cup	thinly sliced peeled gingerroot	250 mL
	Cold water	
¾ cup	water	175 mL
½ cup	granulated sugar	125 mL
	Extra granulated sugar	

1. Place ginger in a small saucepan and cover with cold water. Bring to a boil over high heat, reduce heat, cover and boil gently for 15 minutes. Drain and repeat process with fresh cold water.

2. Combine ginger, ¾ cup (175 mL) water and sugar in a saucepan. Bring to a boil over high heat, reduce heat and boil gently, uncovered, for about 30 minutes or until liquid is evaporated completely. Watch carefully during last 10 minutes to prevent scorching.

3. Put extra sugar in a flat dish about ¼ inch (1 cm) thick. Remove a few pieces of ginger with a fork and toss them in sugar to coat both sides; place on a cooling rack set on a baking pan. Repeat until all slices are done. Dry in a 200°F (93°C) oven for 1 hour or until ginger feels soft and no longer sticky. Let stand at room temperature for 1 day to finish drying.

4. Place slices in an airtight container and store in the refrigerator.

Makes 1 cup (250 mL).

DRIED CRANBERRIES

Commercial dried cranberries are expensive and their availability is unreliable. However, fresh cranberries can be dried at home using our simple method. Keep them on hand to add flavor and color to muffins, squares and holiday baking. They turn plain cooked oatmeal into a breakfast treat.

2 cups	fresh cranberries	500 mL
¼ cup	granulated sugar	50 mL

1. Cut cranberries in half and place in a medium bowl; mix in sugar. Cover and let stand for 24 hours, stirring occasionally. Drain off liquid.

2. Place cranberries on a baking sheet and place in a 100°F (38°C) oven for 4 hours or until berries are almost dry. Remove from oven and leave on baking sheet at room temperature to air-dry for 24 hours.

3. Pack in an airtight container and store in the refrigerator up to 1 month or freeze for longer storage.

Makes ¾ cup (175 mL).

LIQUEURS

Making liqueurs is within the reach of the home cook. As well as being economical, the liqueurs are typically lighter and less sweet than the commercial ones. All of these liqueurs may be stored in the refrigerator for several months to enjoy at your leisure.

BASIC FRUIT LIQUEUR

Try a variety of fruits such as raspberries, strawberries, sour cherries, nectarines, peaches and plums. A splash of a fruit liqueur does wonders for fresh fruit to add elegance to a simple dessert. Added to soda water, it makes a refreshing summer spritzer. And of course pour some over ice-cream or frozen yogurt. Either vodka or 40% alcohol may be used for these liqueurs.

2 cups	fruit cut in halves or slices if larger	500 mL
1 cup	alcohol or vodka	250 mL
2 tbsp	brandy	25 mL
½ cup	granulated sugar	125 mL

1. Place fruit in a clean 1-quart (1 L) jar. Stir in alcohol and brandy. Marinate, covered, for several weeks in a cool, dark place.

2. Strain though a fine sieve lined with cheesecloth; reserve fruits for another use. Stir in sugar.

3. Pour into sterilized bottles, cork, label and store in a cool place for at least 4 weeks.

Makes about 2 cups (500 mL).

CRANBERRY ORANGE LIQUEUR

Ruby-red cranberry and orange liqueur has a smooth and pleasingly tart taste. It is wonderful "on the rocks" or served as a spritzer with chilled soda water.

3 cups	cranberry juice	750 mL
½ cup	orange juice concentrate, thawed	125 mL
½ cup	granulated sugar	125 mL
1 cup	vodka	250 mL
½ tsp	vanilla extract	2 mL

1. Combine cranberry cocktail, orange juice and sugar in a medium saucepan. Bring to a boil over medium-high heat, stirring until sugar is dissolved. Reduce heat and boil gently, uncovered, for about 10 minutes or until reduced by half. Remove from heat.

2. Cool to room temperature, stir in vodka and vanilla. Pour into a clean jar with a tight-fitting lid. Store in the refrigerator.

Makes about 3 cups (750 mL).

Tipsy Fruit Topping
A simple elegant topping for pound or angel food cake, ice-cream or fresh seasonal fruit.
Combine 1 cup (250 mL) each: orange and pineapple juice, ½ cup (125 mL) granulated sugar and a cinnamon stick in a large shallow skillet. Bring to a boil, reduce heat and boil gently for 5 minutes. Add sliced peeled pears, peaches or nectarines, and boil gently 5 minutes or until fruit is tender. Remove from heat and add ¼ cup (50 mL) of your choice of fruit liqueur. Serve warm or chilled.

FRAMBOISE

More commonly known as a raspberry liqueur, our Framboise is quickly made using frozen raspberry concentrate, orange juice and some brandy or vodka. It is delicious served over ice with sparkling mineral water.

1	can (12 oz/355 mL) frozen undiluted raspberry cocktail, thawed	1
1 cup	vodka or brandy	250 mL
½ cup	granulated sugar	125 mL
3 tbsp	orange juice concentrate	45 mL

1. Place raspberry cocktail, vodka, sugar and orange juice in a clean jar with a tight-fitting lid. Seal tightly and shake until sugar is blended.

2. Let stand at room temperature for at least 2 weeks for flavors to blend. Shake jar occasionally. When ready to use, store in the refrigerator.

Makes 2½ cups (625 mL).

COFFEE LIQUEUR

Try it in milk or over crushed ice.

½ cup	freshly brewed espresso	125 mL
½ cup	lightly packed brown sugar	125 mL
1 cup	alcohol or vodka	250 mL
⅓ cup	brandy or rum	75 mL
1 tsp	vanilla extract	5 mL

1. Place hot coffee in a 2-cup (500 mL) measure and stir in sugar until dissolved.

2. Stir in alcohol, brandy and vanilla. Pour into a clean bottle. Store 4 weeks before using.

Makes 2 cups (500 mL).

 TIP   *If you wish, ½ cup (125 mL) water and 1 tbsp (15 mL) instant coffee powder may be substituted for the espresso.*

LIQUEURS FOR COFFEE

Pair one of these easily made liqueurs with freshly brewed coffee for a luxurious finish to a good meal. Both have an alcohol content of approximately 15% so they will keep in the refrigerator for up to 2 months. Use one half of the base for each liqueur recipe.

LIQUEUR BASE

| 2 cups | 18% cream | 500 mL |
| 1 | can (14 oz/300 mL) sweetened condensed milk | 1 |

Whisk cream and milk together until well blended. Divide into 2 equal parts of 1⅔ cups (400 mL) each. Use 1 part to make each recipe below or make a double recipe of your favorite.

Makes 3½ cups (825 mL).

SERVING SUGGESTIONS:

Irish Isles Cream
Irish Isles Cream is an affordable simulation of the famous Irish Cream. Use rye whisky for a Canadian version. Miniature bottles of coconut rum are available in most liquor stores.
Combine one-half recipe Liqueur Base, 1 cup (250 mL) Irish whisky, ¼ cup (50 mL) coconut rum or ½ tsp (2 mL) coconut extract, 1 tbsp (15 mL) chocolate drink syrup and 1 tsp (5 mL) vanilla extract. Pour into a clean bottle with a tight-fitting lid. Store in refrigerator for up to 2 months.
Makes 3 cups (750 mL).

Spanish Cream
Spanish Cream combines the requisite liqueurs for Spanish Coffee in a convenient ready-to-use form.
Combine one-half recipe Liqueur Base, ¾ cup (175 mL) brandy, ½ cup (125 mL) Coffee Liqueur (page 305) and ¼ cup (50 mL) Triple Sec. Pour into a clean bottle with a tight-fitting lid. Store in refrigerator for up to 2 months.
Makes 3 cups (750 mL).

LET'S OPEN THE LID AND USE WHAT'S INSIDE

WITH our pantries full of sparkling jellies, tangy pickles, luscious dessert sauces and zesty savory sauces, we needed to find ways to use their contents beyond just eating them as is. This sent us back into our kitchens with creative juices at full throttle. The results are in the following pages. We know you will think of many more uses for your preserves, but these will be a start.

We have divided the chapter into recipes and ideas for breakfasts, appetizers, soups and sandwiches, sauces and marinades, vegetables, salads and dressings and, naturally, a few favorite sweets, mainly baked items.

We believe that canning and preserving is one of the most creative areas of culinary endeavor. We hope this chapter, along with the rest of the book will pique your interest and help you turn another meal into a creative dining experience. *Bon appétit*!

LIST OF RECIPES

BREAKFAST

SHAKES AND SMOOTHIES

How often are you too rushed to make, let alone eat, a sit-down breakfast? One of these breakfast drinks fits the bill on those mornings. But don't limit yourself—these shakes are delicious and refreshing any time of the day.

PEACH AND BANANA SHAKE

⅓ cup	**Spiced Wine Peach Jam (page 42)**	75 mL
1	**peeled and frozen banana, cut into chunks**	1
⅓ cup	**vanilla yogurt**	75 mL
½ tsp	**vanilla extract**	2 mL

Place jam, banana, yogurt and extract in a blender or food processor. Process until smooth. Pour into a glass and enjoy.

Makes about 1 cup (250 mL).

 TIP   *Replace banana with ¾ cup (175 mL) sliced strawberries, peaches or nectarines.*

TRI-FRUIT SMOOTHIE

½ cup	**sliced mango**	125 mL
½ cup	**sliced peaches, fresh or frozen**	125 mL
⅓ cup	**Elegant Oven Strawberry Jam (page 25)**	75 mL
⅓ cup	**orange juice**	75 mL
¼ tsp	**almond extract**	1 mL

Place mango, peaches, jam, orange juice and extract in a blender or food processor. Process until smooth. Pour into a glass.

Makes about 1 cup (250 mL).

BREAKFAST ORANGE SHAKE

¼ cup	marmalade (preferably an	50 mL
	orange-flavored one from Chapter 3)	
¼ cup	grapefruit juice	50 mL
¾ cup	milk	175 mL

Place marmalade, juice and milk in a blender or food processor. Process until smooth. Pour into a glass.

Makes 1¼ cups (300 mL).

APRICOT PAPAYA SMOOTHIE

¼ cup	Fresh Apricot Jam (page 43)	50 mL
½	papaya, peeled and cut into chunks	½
½ cup	pineapple juice	125 mL
1 tbsp	lime juice	15 mL

Place jam, papaya, pineapple and lime juice in a blender or food processor. Process until smooth. Pour into a glass.

Makes 1 cup (250 mL).

PANCAKE AND WAFFLE SAUCES

Use one of the flavorful jams or marmalades in Chapters 1 and 3 for an easy-to-make sauce for pouring over waffles, pancakes, French toast or pound cake. We show recipes for two but any of the other sweet spreads matched with your choice of fruit juice can be used. Serve them warm for best flavor.

MARMALADE SAUCE

3 cups	orange juice	750 mL
⅔ cup	marmalade (from Chapter 3)	150 mL
2 tbsp	light brown sugar	25 mL
1 tbsp	each: cornstarch and water	15 mL
1 tsp	butter or margarine	5 mL
1 tsp	rum or vanilla extract	5 mL

Bring orange juice to a boil on high heat in a medium saucepan. Reduce heat to medium and boil gently for 15 minutes or until reduced by half. Whisk in marmalade and brown sugar until smooth. Mix cornstarch and water, stir into orange juice mixture. Cook until smooth and slightly thickened. Remove from heat and stir in butter and extract.

Makes about 2½ cups (625 mL).

MANGO BLUEBERRY SAUCE

1¼ cups	cranberry juice	300 mL
½ cup	orange juice	125 mL
½ cup	Mango Blueberry Freezer Jam (page 58)	125 mL
2 tbsp	granulated sugar	25 mL
1 tbsp	each: cornstarch and water	15 mL
2 tsp	butter or margarine	10 mL
¼ tsp	each: ground cinnamon, nutmeg and ginger	1 mL

1. Bring cranberry juice and orange juice to a boil on high heat in a medium saucepan. Reduce heat to medium and boil gently, uncovered, for 15 minutes or until reduced by half. Whisk in jam and sugar.

2. Mix cornstarch and water, stir into cranberry juice mixture. Cook until smooth and slightly thickened. Remove from heat and stir in spices.

Makes about 1½ cups (375 mL).

MUFFINS

A batch of muffins in the freezer is always ready to defrost for a quick breakfast or when a friend drops in for coffee or tea.

BRAN GINGER MUFFINS

There is plenty of fiber and flavor in these muffins with their hint of ginger. Using one of the fruit butters (pages 110–114) makes them much lower in fat.

1¼ cups	natural wheat bran or oat bran	300 mL
1 cup	all-purpose flour	250 mL
1 cup	whole wheat flour	250 mL
⅔ cup	lightly packed brown sugar	150 mL
1 tsp	each: baking powder and baking soda	5 mL
¼ tsp	salt	1 mL
1½ cups	buttermilk	375 mL
½ cup	fruit butter (pages 110–114)	125 mL
2 tbsp	vegetable oil	25 mL
1	egg	1
3 tbsp	finely chopped Candied Ginger (page 301) or crystallized ginger	45 mL

1. Combine bran, flours, sugar, baking powder, baking soda and salt in a large mixing bowl.

2. Stir together buttermilk, fruit butter, oil and egg in a second bowl. Pour into dry ingredients; stir just until moistened. Stir in ginger.

3. Fill 18 medium non-stick or paper-lined muffin cups with batter, using half-cup (125 mL) measure. Bake in a 400°F (200°C) oven for 15 minutes or until muffins are lightly browned and firm to the touch.

Makes 18 medium muffins.

VARIATIONS:

Apple Ginger Bran Muffin
Add 1 large apple, peeled and chopped.

Raspberry Bran Muffin
Add ¼ cup (50 mL) fresh or frozen raspberries.

SPICED PLUM BUTTER BRAN MUFFINS

Spiced Plum Butter gives moisture and a very pleasing plum flavor to these hearty and nutritious muffins. The batter for this large-batch recipe will keep for up to 6 days in the refrigerator.

3 cups	all-purpose flour	750 mL
2 cups	natural bran	500 mL
⅔ cup	lightly packed brown sugar	150 mL
1½ tsp	each: baking powder, baking soda and ground cinnamon	7 mL
½ tsp	salt	2 mL
⅛ tsp	ground nutmeg	0.5 mL
½ cup	canola oil	125 mL
2	eggs, lightly beaten	2
1 cup	Spiced Plum Butter (page 113)	250 mL
1 cup	buttermilk	250 mL
¾ cup	raisins	175 mL
⅓ cup	molasses	75 mL
1	medium apple, peeled, cored and chopped	1

1. Stir together flour, bran, sugar, baking powder, baking soda, cinnamon, salt and nutmeg in a medium bowl.

2. Stir together oil, eggs, Spiced Plum Butter, buttermilk, raisins, molasses and chopped apple in a second bowl.

3. Stir liquid into dry ingredients just until moistened; do not over-mix.

4. Pour batter into a sealed container and refrigerator up to 6 days, until ready to use. To bake muffins: Spoon batter into lightly greased non-stick or paper-lined medium muffin tins. Bake in 375°F (190°C) oven for 18 minutes or until muffins are lightly browned and firm to the touch. Cool on a wire rack.

Makes 30 medium muffins.

VARIATION:

Sweet and Chunky Apple Butter (page 110) may replace Spiced Plum Butter.

MARMALADE FRUIT MUFFINS

Marmalade adds moisture and lively flavor to these elegant muffins. Any marmalade can be used, but we like the more intense flavor of those made with Seville oranges.

2 cups	all-purpose flour	500 mL
2 tsp	baking powder	10 mL
½ tsp	salt	2 mL
¼ tsp	baking soda	1 mL
¾ cup	granulated sugar	175 mL
¼ cup	soft butter or margarine	50 mL
2	eggs	2
1 cup	Traditional English Seville Marmalade (page 80)	250 mL
¼ cup	orange juice	50 mL
½ cup	dried cranberries, raisins or nuts	125 mL

1. Combine flour, baking powder, salt and baking soda in a medium bowl. Set aside.

2. Cream sugar and butter with an electric mixer or by hand; beat in eggs. Stir in marmalade until blended. Fold in half of flour mixture. Add orange juice, mixing just until combined, and then fold in remaining flour and cranberries.

3. Spoon into greased or paper-lined medium muffin pans, using half-cup (125 mL) measure. Bake in a 375°F (190°C) oven for 20 minutes or until lightly browned and firm to the touch.

Makes 18 medium muffins.

APPETIZERS

When you open the lid of the condiment jar, much of the work is already done for these great appetizers.

SHORTCUT APPETIZERS

Hot Melted Brie with Chutney

Remove rind from whole Brie (approximately 4 inches/10 cm in diameter) and place in a shallow heatproof dish. Top with ½ cup (125 mL) chutney (chapter 9) and ¼ cup (50 mL) chopped almonds. Bake in 425°F (220°C) oven for 7 minutes or until cheese softens and starts to melt. Serve warm with apple or pear slices and crackers.

Jalapeño Cheddar Canapés

Stir together 1 cup (250 mL) shredded old Cheddar cheese, 1 large egg and 2–3 tsp (10–15 mL) chopped drained Pickled Jalapeño Peppers (page 157). Mound a small spoonful onto sixteen 2 inch (5 cm) toast rounds. Place on a baking sheet and broil until puffed and golden. Makes 16 canapés.

Meatballs with Hot and Spicy Sauce

Prepare your favorite meatball recipe or, to keep this appetizer really simple, buy frozen ones. Place frozen meatballs on a baking sheet. Bake in 400°F (200°C) oven for 20 minutes or until browned and cooked through. Serve with Piquant Tomato Sauce (page 235) for dipping. A dollop of horseradish adds extra zip!

Meatballs with Oriental Chutney Sauce

Place ⅓ cup (75 mL) chutney (Chapter 9), ½ cup (125 mL) orange juice, 2 tbsp (25 mL) each: cornstarch and soy sauce, and 1 tsp (5 mL) mustard in a small saucepan. Simmer about 5 minutes or until smooth and thickened, stirring occasionally. Use as a meatball dipping sauce.

Thai Chicken Wings

Pour ½ cup (125 mL) Thai Chili Sauce (page 250) over 1 lb (500 g) chicken wings or cubed chicken in a baking dish. Bake in 400°F (200°C) oven for 25 minutes, stirring occasionally.

Curried Mango Chutney Dip

Blend ½ cup (125 mL) light mayonnaise, 2 tbsp (25 mL) Mango Chutney (page 218), 1 tbsp (15 mL) lemon juice, 1 chopped green onion and 1 tsp (5 ml) curry powder. Makes ¾ cup (175 mL). This is a must with raw vegetables.

Piquant Cream Cheese Dip

Process 1 pkg (250 g) light cream cheese, ½ cup (125 mL) drained Pickled Jalapeño Peppers (page 157), ½ sweet red pepper, chopped, and 1 clove garlic in a food processor until coarsely chopped. Transfer to a bowl and stir in 2 tbsp (25 mL) chopped fresh cilantro. Makes about 1½ cups (375 mL) dip. Extra may be frozen.

Pesto Torta Appetizer

Blend 1 pkg (250 g) softened cream cheese with ½ cup (125 mL) softened butter or margarine. Line a small bowl with plastic wrap. Layer one-third cheese mixture, ¼ cup (50 mL) Spinach Pesto Sauce (page 254), one-third cheese, ¼ cup (50 mL) pesto and one-third cheese. Cover and chill until firm. Unmold and serve at room temperature with assorted crackers or thinly sliced baguette. Makes 1½ cups (375 mL). This torta can be frozen.

Cranberry Port Conserve Cheese Spread

Blend 1 pkg (250 g) softened light cream cheese, ½ cup (125 mL) Cranberry Port Conserve (page 101) or Fresh and Dried Cranberry Salsa (page 198) and 2 tsp (10 mL) grated orange rind. Makes 1 cup (250 mL).

Pesto Pita Pizzas

Cut 2 whole wheat pitas in half. Split each half and spread with 1 tsp (5 mL) Spinach Pesto Sauce (page 254). Sprinkle each with some chopped sweet red pepper and shredded mozzarella cheese. Bake in 400°F (200°C) oven for 5 minutes or until cheese melts. Cut each pita quarter in half for appetizers or leave uncut for lunch. Makes 16 appetizers or 2–4 lunch servings.

CARAMELIZED RED ONION AND TOMATO PIZZA

This tasty appetizer is easily prepared using our Caramelized Red Onion Relish.

½ cup	**Caramelized Red Onion Relish** **(page 178)**	125 mL
4	**individual pizza crusts**	4
1	**medium tomato, diced**	1
2 cups	**shredded mozzarella cheese**	500 mL

Divide onion mixture among pizza crusts, spreading evenly. Combine tomato and cheese; sprinkle over onion. Bake in a 350°F (180°C) oven for about 10 minutes or until hot and cheese is melted. Cut each pizza into 6 wedges.

Makes 24 appetizers.

ITALIAN CHEESE AND RED PEPPER PIZZA

Buy an Italian-style flatbread, shred lots of cheese, chop an assortment of vegetables, open a jar of Puttanesca Freezer Pasta Sauce and in minutes you have an appetizer to serve to friends.

1	**round Italian-style gourmet flatbread** **(14 oz/400 g)**	1
1½ cups	**Puttanesca Freezer Pasta Sauce (page 241)**	375 mL
2 cups	**shredded Italian cheese ***	500 mL
1 cup	**chopped sweet red peppers**	250 mL
½ cup	**each: chopped onion and sliced mushrooms**	125 mL
¼ cup	**grated Parmesan cheese**	50 mL
3 tbsp	**slivered almonds**	45 mL
1 tbsp	**chopped fresh oregano or 1 tsp (5 mL) dried**	15 mL
2 tsp	**chopped fresh basil or 1 tsp (5 mL) dried**	10 mL

Place flatbread on a large baking pan. Spoon sauce over flatbread, spreading almost to edge. Top with Italian cheese, red pepper, onion, mushrooms, Parmesan cheese, almonds and seasonings. Bake in a 400°F (200°C) oven for about 15 minutes or until cheese is melted and vegetables are hot. Cut pizza into thin wedges.

Makes 16 servings.

 TIP   *Provolone, fontina or mozzarella are good cheeses to use.*

SALSA SAVVY APPETIZERS

Fiesta Nacho Appetizer

An attractive molded appetizer sure to be a highlight at your party.

Blend 1 cup (250 mL) cottage cheese, 1 pkg (250 g) light cream cheese and ½ cup (125 mL) salsa (chapter 8) in a food processor until smooth. Line a 2-cup (500 mL) bowl with plastic wrap. Pack mixture into bowl, cover and chill for 2 hours or overnight. Unmold cheese onto large serving plate and garnish with shredded lettuce and Cheddar cheese, chopped tomato and green onion. Serve with corn chips for dipping.

Makes 2 cups (500 mL).

Salsa with Mozzarella Toasts

Keep this easy appetizer in the freezer to bring out at a moment's notice.

Place 36 thin slices baguette on a baking sheet. Broil bread until lightly toasted on both sides. Spread one side lightly with softened butter and sprinkle with 1 cup (250 mL) shredded mozzarella cheese divided evenly over toasts. Store in freezer if desired. To serve: Bake toasts in 375°F (190°C) oven for 5 minutes or just until cheese melts. Serve warm with salsa (Chapter 8).

Makes 36 appetizers.

Warm Salsa Cheese Dip

Serve warm with tortilla chips, raw vegetables or crackers.

Combine 1 cup (250 mL) mild or medium salsa (Chapter 8), 2 pkgs (250 g) cream cheese and 1 cup (250 mL) shredded Monterey Jack cheese in a microwavable bowl. Microwave, uncovered, on Medium (50%) for 4 minutes or until cheese is melted, stirring once. Stir in 1 cup (250 mL) beer.

Makes 1½ cups (375 mL).

SOUPS AND SANDWICHES

JALAPEÑO QUESADILLAS

Pickled Jalapeño Peppers are the start of this Mexican version of a grilled cheese sandwich. This is a great lunch with a small salad. And we use the microwave for it.

4	9-inch (23 cm) flour tortillas	4
¾ cup	shredded Monterey Jack cheese	175 mL
¼ cup	Pickled Jalapeño Peppers (page 157), drained	50 mL
⅓ cup	plain yogurt	75 mL
⅓ cup	salsa (Chapter 8) or commercial salsa	75 mL
1 tbsp	chopped fresh cilantro	15 mL

1. Place 1 tortilla on a microwavable plate lined with a double thickness of paper towel. Sprinkle with half of cheese; top with several slices of jalapeños. Press second tortilla over top. Microwave at Medium-High (70%) for 2 minutes or until tortillas are warm and cheese has melted. Cut into quarters with a sharp knife. Repeat with remaining tortillas.

2. Stir together yogurt, salsa and cilantro. Serve warm quesadillas with yogurt-salsa sauce.

Makes 8 pieces, or 2–3 servings.

VARIATIONS:

What you fold into the tortilla is up to your imagination, although the recipe above is fairly traditional. Other ideas are:

Vegetarian:
Stir together 1 cup (250 mL) mashed kidney beans, 1 chopped green onion and 2 tbsp (25 mL) each salsa and plain yogurt. Spread evenly on tortilla and proceed as above.

French-Style
Spread goat cheese (chèvre) on tortilla. Sprinkle with several sliced Pickled Jalapeño Peppers (page 157), finely chopped red onion and chopped black olives. Proceed as above.

Open-Face Pizza
Spread homemade salsa on 1 tortilla, sprinkle with chopped onions, chopped sweet green peppers, sliced olives and shredded Cheddar cheese. Broil until cheese melts.

Pesto
Spread Spinach Pesto Sauce (page 254) on tortilla. Sprinkle with chopped sweet yellow peppers, diced tomato and sliced green onions. Proceed as above.

CRAB SANDWICH SPREAD WITH CHUTNEY

Ideal for canapes or sandwiches this interesting spread makes use of the intense flavors found in our fruit chutneys.

1	can (6 oz/170 g) crab meat	1
3	marinated artichoke pieces, chopped	3
1 cup	tightly packed spinach leaves, chopped	250 mL
1	green onion, chopped	1
2 tbsp	chopped almonds	25 mL
⅓ cup	fruit chutney *	75 mL
2 tbsp	light mayonnaise	25 mL
1 tbsp	lemon juice	15 mL
⅛ tsp	each: salt, pepper and curry powder, optional	0.5 mL

1. Flake crab meat and combine with artichoke, spinach, onion and almonds.

2. Stir together chutney, mayonnaise and lemon juice. Stir into crab mixture. Refrigerate for several hours for flavors to blend. Taste and adjust seasonings with a pinch of salt, pepper and curry powder, if desired.

Makes 2 cups (500 mL).

TIP   *We like Mango Papaya Chutney (page 219) or Red Pepper Apricot Chutney (page 223).*

Cinnamon Rum Syrup (page 298), Pink Peppercorn Vinegar (page 270)
Juniper Berry Chutney (page 217), Mango Papaya Chutney (page 219)

Pear Raspberry Jam (page 38)

NIPPY APPLE CHEDDAR SOUP

Cheddar cheese and apples are as much of a go-together as any food we know. Here's a new twist: put them in a steaming bowl of soup with a hint of curry. Bound to hit the spot on a cold day.

1 tbsp	butter or margarine	15 mL
2	medium carrots, thinly sliced	2
1	onion, chopped	1
1	clove garlic, minced	1
2 tsp	each: dry mustard and curry powder	10 mL
2 cups	chicken broth	500 mL
1 cup	apple juice or cider	250 mL
1 cup	Sweet and Chunky Apple Butter (page 110)	250 mL
	Salt and cayenne pepper	
1 cup	shredded old Cheddar cheese	250 mL

1. Melt butter in a medium saucepan over medium heat. Cook carrots, onion, garlic, mustard and curry powder for 5 minutes or until onion softens, stirring occasionally.

2. Add broth, apple juice and Apple Butter. Bring to a boil, reduce heat and boil gently for about 15 minutes or until vegetables are very tender; cool slightly. Process in a food processor or blender until smooth. Return to saucepan to reheat. Season to taste with salt and cayenne pepper. Spoon into bowls; sprinkle with cheese and serve.

Makes four 1-cup (250 mL) servings.

COUNTRY CORN CHOWDER

Taking the lid off Fiesta Corn Relish helps you make this simple but delicious soup in a hurry. Its robust corn taste is ideal for casual meals.

3	slices bacon, diced	3
1	medium onion, chopped	1
2 tbsp	all-purpose flour	25 mL
2 cups	milk	500 mL
1	large potato, peeled and cubed	1
1	large carrot, thinly sliced	1
1 cup	Fiesta Country Corn Relish (page 176)	250 mL
	Salt and pepper to taste	
2 tbsp	chopped fresh parsley	25 mL

1. Combine bacon and onion in a nonstick saucepan; cook on medium heat for 5 minutes or until onion is tender, stirring frequently. Stir in flour and cook for 30 seconds, stirring constantly. Gradually whisk in milk until smooth and thickened.

2. Add potato, carrot and Corn Relish. Cook on low heat for 20 minutes or until vegetables are tender, stirring often to prevent sticking.

3. Season to taste with salt and pepper; sprinkle each serving with parsley.

Makes four 1-cup (250 mL) servings.

SAUCES AND MARINADES FOR MEAT FISH AND POULTRY

SAUCES

Many of the condiments in Chapters 6 through 10 can be transformed into wonderful sauces for meats, poultry and fish just by adding a few ingredients.

Raspberry Mint Sauce

Serve this colorful and flavorful sauce with roast lamb.
Combine ½ cup (125 mL) Red Wine Raspberry Vinegar (page 271), ¼ cup (50 mL) granulated sugar, 1 tbsp (15 mL) finely chopped fresh mint and freshly ground pepper, to taste. Makes about ⅔ cup (150 mL).

Citrus Dijonnais Sauce

Spread this fruity mustard on fish fillets before cooking in the microwave. It also makes a lively topping for fresh asparagus or green beans.
Combine ¼ cup (50 mL) Dijon-Style Mustard (page 232), 1 tbsp (15 mL) mayonnaise, 1 tsp (5 mL) lemon, orange or lime juice, ½ tsp (2 mL) honey, ¼ tsp (1 mL) each: chopped fresh thyme and grated lemon or orange rind.
Makes ⅓ cup (75 mL).

Fruit Coulis

A marvelous sauce to accompany grilled or roasted chicken, veal or pork.
In a blender or food processor, place 6 peeled and chopped fresh apricots or small peaches, ½ cup (125 mL) champagne and ¼ cup (50 mL) Champagne Vinegar (page 272). Process until smooth. Pour purée into a small saucepan and boil gently, uncovered, until reduced to a sauce-like consistency. Stir in 2 tbsp (25 mL) chopped fresh basil or 2 tsp (10 mL) dried. Remove from heat, cool slightly before pouring into a tightly sealed container. Store in the refrigerator for up to 2 weeks.
Makes 1 cup (250 mL).

Dijon Cream Sauce for Salmon

A dollop of this sauce also enlivens baked potatoes.
Stir together ½ cup (125 mL) sour cream, 2 tsp (10 mL) Dijon-Style Mustard (page 232) and 1 tbsp (15 mL) chopped fresh dill. Place 4 salmon fillets, skin side down, on a baking tray lined with foil. Lightly brush the top of the fillets with oil. Bake in a 450°F (230°C) oven for 10 minutes or until done. (The skin should stick to the foil). Spoon a dollop of sauce on salmon and garnish with a sprig of fresh dill.
Makes 4 servings.

Raspberry Mustard Coating for Chicken

Raspberry Mustard transforms chicken breasts into an easy festive meal.

Wipe 6 large boneless, skinless chicken breasts with paper towel. Coat with ½ cup (125 mL) Raspberry Mustard Sauce (page 233). Combine ¾ cup (175 mL) dried bread crumbs, 1 tbsp (15 mL) chopped fresh rosemary or 1 tsp (5 mL) dried, a pinch of garlic powder and freshly ground pepper in a shallow bowl. Dredge chicken in bread mixture to coat thoroughly. Bake in a 350°F (180°C) oven for 25 minutes or until juices run clear and chicken is no longer pink inside.

Makes 6 servings.

Southwest Corn Sauce

The flavors of southwest cuisine predominate in this unusual sauce. Use it for firm fish such as tuna or swordfish, or for chicken breasts.

Combine 1 cup (250 mL) Fiesta Corn Relish (page 176), ¼ cup (50 mL) canola oil, 2 tbsp (25 mL) each: tomato sauce and finely chopped cilantro in a blender or food processor. Process until smooth.

Makes 1½ cups (375 mL).

Apricot Sauce for Chicken

Apricot Grand Marnier Conserve turns chicken breasts into elegant fare.

Combine ½ cup (125 mL) Apricot Grand Marnier Conserve (page 98), 1 peeled and chopped orange and 3 tbsp (45 mL) each: brandy and chicken broth in a medium saucepan. Bring to a boil and boil gently for 10 minutes or until slightly thickened. Serve with grilled chicken.

Makes ¾ cup (175 mL).

MARINADES FOR GRILLING

Marinades are a great way to add flavor and interest to grilled meats, poultry and fish. Made ahead, they will keep in the refrigerator up to 2 days. When ready to use, place meat or fish in a resealable plastic bag. Pour marinade over, seal bag, turn to coat and refrigerate for 2 hours or overnight (depending on the meat being used and the depth of flavor desired). All foods must be refrigerated while they are marinating. When you remove them from the marinade, pour it into a small saucepan. Bring to a boil, reduce heat and boil gently for 5 minutes; keep warm. Use to baste meat either on the grill or in the oven. Be sure to discard any leftover marinade that has been used.

Citrus Mustard Marinade
Marinate chicken breasts for up to 4 hours in the refrigerator before grilling. This marinade is also great to brush on pork chops as they grill.
Combine ½ cup (125 mL) orange juice, ¼ cup (50 mL) each: lemon juice and vegetable oil, 1 tsp (5 mL) each: Dijon-Style Mustard (page 232), dried oregano and Worcestershire sauce, 2 cloves garlic, minced, and a small amount of freshly ground black pepper.
Makes 1 cup (250 mL).

Szechwan Marinade
Use this spicy marinade when grilling chicken or shrimp, or when cooking them in a wok or skillet.
Combine ¼ cup (50 mL) tahini (sesame) paste, ¼ cup (50 mL) Five-Pepper Oil (page 262), 3 cloves garlic, minced, and 1 tbsp (15 mL) sherry.
Makes ½ cup (125 mL).

Herbes de Provençe Marinade
A light marinade, it is perfect for fillets of fish such as orange roughy, white fish or tuna.
Combine ¼ cup (50 mL) each: white wine and olive oil, 2 tbsp (25 mL) each: Provençe-Style Vinegar (page 270) and fresh lemon juice, 1 clove garlic, minced, and 1 sprig fresh rosemary, minced.
Makes ¾ cup (175 mL).

Asian Whisky Marinade
Use this marinade on lean lamb, chicken or fish.
Whisk together ½ cup (125 mL) Asian Whisky Sauce (page 249), 2 tbsp (25 mL) each: lemon juice, ketchup and 1 clove garlic, minced.
Makes ¾ cup (175 mL).

Oriental Plum Sauce Marinade

Brush Asian Plum Sauce directly on meat or poultry as it grills. These few additions make it even better.
Combine 1 cup (250 mL) Asian Plum Sauce (page 248), ¼ cup (50 mL) finely chopped fresh cilantro, 2 tbsp (25 mL) dry sherry, 1 tsp (5 mL) sesame oil and 2 cloves garlic, minced.
Makes 1 cup (250 mL).

Apricot Marinade

This is a wonderful glaze for spare ribs, as well as a good marinade for Cornish hens, pork chops or whole pork tenderloin. Marinate pork for 8 hours or longer and chicken for 3 to 4 hours.
Combine ½ cup (125 mL) dry white wine, ¼ cup (50 mL) each: Fresh Apricot Jam (page 43), vegetable oil and white wine vinegar, 1 tbsp (15 mL) Dijon-Style Mustard (page 232) and 1 tsp (5 mL) soy sauce.
Makes about 1¼ cups (300 mL).

Basil Lemon Marinade

Brush on chicken pieces as they cook on the barbecue.
Combine ¼ cup (50 mL) Basil Oil with Lemon and Black Peppercorns (page 261), 2 tbsp (25 mL) each: lemon juice, balsamic vinegar and finely chopped onion, 1 tsp (5 mL) freshly ground black pepper, ½ tsp (2 mL) dried thyme and 1 garlic clove, minced.
Makes ½ cup (125 mL).

Oriental Marinade

Marinate beef and pork in Oriental Marinade, then brush it on during grilling to add interesting flavors. Refrigerate any leftovers to cube and toss with salad greens or mesclun.
Combine ¼ cup (50 mL) rice wine vinegar, 3 tbsp (45 mL) Nut-Infused Oil (page 264), 2 tbsp (25 mL) pineapple juice, 1 tbsp (15 mL) soy sauce, ½ tsp (2 mL) each: granulated sugar and minced gingerroot and ⅛ tsp (0.5 mL) each: salt and freshly ground pepper.
Makes about ½ cup (125 mL).

Raspberry Orange Marinade

Raspberry Orange Vinaigrette (page 275) is a perfect marinade for grilled chicken and pork.

VEGETABLES

MUSTARD BUTTERS FOR VEGETABLES

Keep these versatile butters on hand in the refrigerator to serve with such vegetables as asparagus, green beans, cauliflower and broccoli. We also like them with grilled chicken and fish.

Dijon Mustard Butter

Combine 1 large clove garlic, minced, 1 tsp (5 mL) drained capers, rinsed, and ⅛ tsp (0.5 mL) each: salt and freshly ground pepper in a small bowl. Stir in ½ cup (125 mL) softened butter, ¼ cup (50 mL) Dijon-Style Mustard (page 232) and 3 tbsp (45 mL) chopped fresh basil or 1 tbsp (15 mL) dried. Place in a small covered container and refrigerate until needed.
Makes about ¾ cup (175 mL).

Marmalade Mustard Butter

Combine ⅓ cup (75 mL) marmalade (Chapter 3) with 2 tbsp (25 mL) Dijon-Style Mustard (page 232) and 1 tbsp (15 mL) each: butter and lemon or orange juice in a small saucepan. Heat until marmalade is melted and mixture hot. Drizzle over cooked vegetables.
Makes about ½ cup (125 mL).

Sun-Dried Tomato Mustard Butter

Combine ¼ cup (50 mL) Sun-Dried Tomato Mustard (page 234), 1 tbsp (15 mL) each: butter, orange juice and honey.
Makes ⅓ cup (75 mL).

POTATO BAKE WITH RELISH

Relish transforms an ordinary potato into an out-of-the-ordinary supper dish. Made quickly in the microwave, it can be ready in short order. And for an entrée, layer slices of cooked chicken, ham or salami with the vegetables.

1 tbsp	olive oil	15 mL
1	onion, thinly sliced	1
1	small green pepper, chopped	1
2	cloves garlic, minced	2
½ cup	relish (Chapter 7)	125 mL
5 cups	thinly sliced potatoes (about 2 lb/1 kg)	1.25 L
1 cup	grated Parmesan cheese	250 mL

1. Heat oil in a large non-stick skillet; cook onion, green pepper and garlic on medium high until tender, about 3 minutes. Remove from heat and stir in relish.

2. Arrange ⅓ of potatoes in an 8-cup (2 L) casserole. Cover with half the vegetables. Sprinkle with ⅓ of cheese. Repeat layers and top with remaining potatoes. Cover and microwave at High (100%) for 10 minutes. Sprinkle with remaining cheese, reduce power to Medium (70%) and microwave for 5 minutes. Let stand for 5 minutes before serving.

Makes 4 servings.

PROVENÇE-STYLE GRILLED VEGETABLES

An example of how very easy it is to make a zippy marinade from one of our specialty vinegars.

¼ cup	Provençe-Style Vinegar (page 270)	50 mL
2 tbsp	liquid honey	25 mL
1 tbsp	canola oil	15 mL
½ tsp	each: freshly ground pepper and salt	2 mL
4	cloves garlic, minced	4
4	plum tomatoes, halved	4
2	zucchini, cut lengthwise into ¼-inch (6 mm) slices	2
1	medium eggplant, cut crosswise into 1-inch (2.5 cm) thick slices	1
1	sweet red pepper, seeded and cut into 8 wedges	1
1	Vidalia or Spanish onion, cut into 2-inch (5 cm) thick wedges	1
1	small bunch kale, coarsely chopped	1

1. Combine vinegar, honey, oil, pepper, salt and garlic in a small bowl.

2. Combine tomatoes, zucchini, eggplant, red pepper, onion and kale. Divide vegetables and vinegar mixture between 2 large resealable plastic bags. Seal bags and refrigerate for up to 1 hour; turn bags occasionally.

3. Preheat grill to medium high and spray rack with non-stick coating. Place vegetables on rack; reserve marinade. Grill about 7 minutes on each side or until onion is tender, basting with reserved marinade.

Makes 8 servings.

TIP   *Kale becomes quite crisp during grilling, and is very tasty.*

VEGETABLE STIR-FRY WITH OREGANO PEPPER VINAIGRETTE

Using one of the recipes for vinaigrettes is a great way to add that extra-special flavor boost to any stir-fry.

1 tbsp	canola oil	15 mL
¾ cup	chopped green onions	175 mL
1 cup	diagonally sliced carrot	250 mL
1 cup	sliced yellow sweet pepper	250 mL
1 cup	sliced green or red sweet pepper	250 mL
3 cups	broccoli florets	750 mL
1 cup	fresh bean sprouts	250 mL
¼ cup	Oregano Pepper Vinaigrette (page 274)	50 mL

1. Heat oil in a large non-stick skillet or wok over medium-high heat. Add onions and stir-fry for 1 minute. Add carrot and peppers; stir-fry for 1 minute. Add broccoli; cover and cook for 2 minutes. Add sprouts and vinaigrette.

2. Bring to a boil, uncovered, and cook for about 30 seconds, stirring constantly.

Makes 4 to 6 servings.

SALADS AND DRESSINGS

Open the lid on some of your preserves to use in these delectable salads. Salsas, relishes and chutneys add marvelous taste and eye-appeal for an exceptional salad. And a dollop of one of the mustard sauces or a spoonful of chutney transforms a dressing to toss with a mixture of greens. The following salads can be made ahead of time and refrigerated until you are ready to serve them.

POTATO SALSA SALAD

4	large potatoes, halved	4
½ cup	each: chopped seedless cucumber and green pepper	125 mL
1	green onion, sliced	1
½ cup	Gazpacho Salsa (page 192)	125 mL
1 tbsp	each: olive oil and red wine vinegar	15 mL
2 tbsp	chopped fresh cilantro	25 mL
	Red leaf lettuce	

1. Boil potatoes until tender; drain and cool until easy to handle. Peel, cube and place in a large bowl. When potatoes are cool, stir in cucumber, green pepper and onion.

2. Combine salsa, oil, vinegar and cilantro. Pour over potatoes and stir. Cover and chill until serving time. Serve in a lettuce-lined bowl.

Makes 4–6 servings.

GARDEN PASTA SALAD

12 oz	fusilli, small shell or other pasta	375 g
1½ cups	relish *	375 mL
½ cup	each: plain yogurt and mayonnaise	125 mL
1 tsp	each: garlic powder and basil leaves	5 mL
1	sweet red or green pepper, chopped	1
1 cup	frozen green peas, thawed	250 mL
½ cup	chopped green onion	125 mL
	Freshly ground pepper	

1. Cook pasta in a large amount of boiling salted water according to manufacturer's directions or until *al dente*. Drain, rinse in cold water and drain thoroughly. Set aside.

2. Combine relish, yogurt, mayonnaise, garlic powder and basil in a large bowl. Stir in pasta, red pepper, peas and onion. Sprinkle with black pepper, cover and refrigerate for several hours.

Makes 8 generous servings.

 TIP *We like to use Fiesta Corn Relish or Easy Oven Relish (pages 176 and 175).*

Zucchini Corn Salad

This tasty summer salad needs little preparation time.

Combine 2 tbsp (25 mL) oil, 1 tbsp (15 mL) wine or other vinegar, ½ tsp (2 mL) granulated sugar, ¼ tsp (1 mL) salt and ½ cup (125 mL) Fiesta Corn Relish in a medium bowl. Stir in 1½ cups (375 mL) diced zucchini and 1 small chopped tomato. Cover and refrigerate for 2 hours or more before serving.
Makes 2 cups (500 mL).

SPICED ORANGE-SLICE SALAD

1½ cups	shredded romaine lettuce	375 mL
¼ cup	finely chopped red onion	50 mL
1 cup	frozen peas	250 mL
1	jar (½ pint/250 mL) Spiced Orange Slices (page 164)	1
½ cup	sliced water chestnuts	125 mL
⅓ cup	light mayonnaise	75 mL
½ –1 tsp	curry powder	2–5 mL
½ cup	shredded mozzarella cheese Paprika to taste	125 mL

1. Arrange lettuce in a medium glass salad bowl. Top with onion and peas.

2. Drain liquid from oranges, reserving ⅓ cup (75 mL). Layer orange slices and water chestnuts over peas.

3. Combine reserved orange liquid with mayonnaise and curry powder; stir well. Spoon over salad; sprinkle with mozzarella and paprika. Cover tightly and refrigerate for several hours before serving.

Makes 6 servings.

Southwest Black Bean and Rice Salad

Combine 1 cup (250 mL) Southwest Black Bean and Corn Salsa (page 204), 1 cup (250 mL) cooked rice and ½ cup (125 mL) chopped sweet green pepper in a salad bowl. Whisk together 2 tbsp (25 mL) oil, 1 tbsp (15 mL) red wine vinegar and a pinch of salt; pour over salad. Chill until serving time.
Makes 2 cups (500 mL).

DRESSINGS FOR SALADS

FAVORITE VINAIGRETTE DRESSING

Perfect vinaigrettes can be made from any combination of oil and vinegar. It's the proportions that are important. In addition to serving with assorted greens, drizzle over chilled cooked asparagus, carrots or long green beans.

¼ cup	flavored oil (pages 261–264)	50 mL
2 tbsp	specialty vinegar (pages 265–272)	25 mL
2 tbsp	water	25 mL
1 tsp	Dijon mustard	5 mL
⅛ tsp	each: granulated sugar, salt and freshly ground pepper	0.5 mL

Combine all ingredients in a small container with a tight-fitting lid. Cover and shake well. Refrigerate until ready to use.

Makes ½ cup (125 mL) vinaigrette.

MANGO CHUTNEY VINAIGRETTE

Mango Chutney's marvelous mango flavor makes a vinaigrette that is a natural with fruit salad and as a marinade for barbecued chicken, pork and ham.

½ cup	canola oil	125 mL
¼ cup	Mango Chutney (page 218)	50 mL
2 tbsp	rice vinegar	25 mL
2 tbsp	soy sauce	25 mL
2 tbsp	liquid honey	25 mL
1 tbsp	minced Candied Ginger (page 301) or crystallized ginger Grated rind and juice of 1 lime	15 mL

Whisk together oil, chutney, vinegar, soy sauce, honey, ginger, lime rind and lime juice. Refrigerate in a tightly sealed container.

Makes about 1 cup (250 mL).

HONEY MUSTARD DRESSING

An excellent use for this dressing is to marinate chicken pieces before baking or barbecuing.

⅓ cup	olive oil	75 mL
¼ cup	red wine vinegar	50 mL
2 tbsp	Honey Lemon Mustard Sauce (page 232)	25 mL
1 tbsp	lemon juice	15 mL
	Freshly ground pepper	

1. Whisk together oil, vinegar, mustard sauce and lemon juice. Add pepper to taste.

2. Refrigerate in a tightly sealed container until ready to serve over crisp salad greens.

Makes about ¾ cup (175 mL).

CREAMY MUSTARD DRESSING

Similar to the vinaigrette above, but a mayonnaise version for those times when you need a creamy dressing.

⅓ cup	Honey Lemon Mustard Sauce (page 232)	75 mL
⅓ cup	light mayonnaise	75 mL
2 tbsp	minced green onion	25 mL
1 tbsp	minced fresh parsley	15 mL
½ cup	canola oil	125 mL
¼ cup	cider vinegar	50 mL

1. Stir together mustard, mayonnaise, onion and parsley. Whisk in oil and vinegar.

2. Refrigerate in a tightly sealed container until ready to use with cabbage, potato or pasta salads.

Makes about 1¼ cups (300 mL).

SWEET TREATS

COFFEE CAKE WITH CRANBERRY CONSERVE

Brandied Cranberry Conserve (page 100) adds a festive note and bright flavor to coffee cake. Try other jams and marmalades with coffee cake, too.

Streusel Topping

½ cup	lightly packed brown sugar	125 mL
¼ cup	all-purpose flour	50 mL
¼ cup	soft butter or margarine	50 mL

Cake

¾ cup	granulated sugar	175 mL
¼ cup	soft shortening	50 mL
1	egg	1
½ cup	milk	125 mL
1⅓ cups	all-purpose flour	325 mL
2 tsp	baking powder	10 mL
½ tsp	salt	2 mL
1 cup	Brandied Cranberry Conserve (page 100)	250 mL

To Make Topping:

1. Combine sugar, flour and butter in a food processor.

2. Process with on/off turns until fine crumbs occur. Set aside.

To Make Cake:

1. Cream sugar, shortening and egg until smooth with an electric mixer or by hand; beat in milk.

2. Combine flour, baking powder and salt; stir into egg mixture. Spread batter into a greased 8-inch (2 L) square baking dish. Top with spoonfuls of conserve and sprinkle with topping. Bake in a 375°F (190°C) oven for 35 minutes or until a tooth pick inserted in center comes out clean. Serve warm.

Makes 9 servings.

LIGHT CHOCOLATE BROWNIES

These fat-free chocolate brownies taste like the real thing. They use Baker's Prune Butter (page 114) as a fat substitute. Its density and moisture give a taste and mouth-feel very much like brownies made with butter or margarine. The dark color of the prune butter makes it especially appropriate for making dark-colored cakes like brownies.

1 cup	cake and pastry flour	250 mL
¾ cup	granulated sugar	175 mL
½ cup	unsweetened cocoa	125 mL
1 tsp	baking powder	5 mL
½ tsp	salt	2 mL
⅓ cup	corn syrup	75 mL
⅓ cup	Baker's Prune Butter (page 114)	75 mL
2	beaten egg whites	2
	Confectioners' sugar, optional	

1. Stir together flour, sugar, cocoa, baking powder and salt in a large bowl.

2. Stir in syrup, prune butter and egg whites. Spoon batter into a lightly greased 8-inch (2 L) square baking pan.

3. Bake in a 350°F (180°C) oven for 30 minutes or until top springs back when lightly touched. Cool completely on a wire rack before cutting into 16 squares. Sprinkle lightly with icing sugar, if desired.

Makes 16 squares.

TIP *After the squares are cool, they keep fresh longer by being frozen in a tightly sealed container.*

SPICED FIG JAM BARS

Australian Spiced Dried Fig Jam (page 51) makes a marvelous rich cookie filling. Try it in these quick-to-make bars. Other fruity jams such as Sour Cherry Gooseberry and Spiced Wine Peach (pages 32 and 42) are delicious variations.

¾ cup	granulated sugar	175 mL
½ cup	butter or margarine	125 mL
2	eggs	2
1 tsp	vanilla extract	5 mL
2½ cups	all-purpose flour	625 mL
½ tsp	salt	2 mL
¼ tsp	baking soda	1 mL
1½ cups	Australian Spiced Dried Fig Jam (page 51)	375 mL

1. Cream sugar, butter, eggs and vanilla with an electric mixer or by hand in a large mixing bowl until smooth.

2. Combine flour, salt and baking soda; stir into butter mixture, forming a soft dough.

3. Divide dough into 2 parts. Roll half of dough on a floured surface into an 8 x 12-inch (20 x 30 cm) rectangle. Spread half of jam along the center of dough, leaving approximately a 2-inch (5 cm) strip on each side. Using a flat lifter, fold sides of dough to cover jam. Cut into 4 crosswise sections and place on a baking sheet. Repeat with second half of dough.

4. Bake in a 400°F (200°C) oven for 12 minutes or until slightly browned on edges. Transfer to a cooling rack. When cool, cut each into 2 lengthwise pieces, then cut each piece into 3 bars.

Makes 48 bars.

TIP *For special occasions, cut dough into 2-inch (5 cm) diameter rounds, spread half with a bit of jam, fold other half over to cover filling and seal edges with a fork.*

MARMALADE SQUARES

Any of our marmalades in Chapter 3 can be successfully used in this fruitcake, although one with lots of citrus is probably best.

½ cup	each: chopped dates, slivered dried apricots and diced candied pineapple	125 mL
½ cup	each: dried cranberries, raisins and coarsely chopped walnuts	125 mL
1 cup	marmalade (Chapter 3)	250 mL
½ cup	orange juice	125 mL
½ cup	mashed bananas	125 mL
1 cup	softened butter or margarine	250 mL
1 cup	lightly packed brown sugar	250 mL
3	eggs	3
2½ cups	all-purpose flour	625 mL
2 tsp	each: baking powder and cinnamon	10 mL
½ tsp	ground ginger	2 mL
¼ tsp	salt	1 mL
	Confectioners' sugar	

1. Combine dates, apricots, pineapple, cranberries, raisins and walnuts in a large bowl. Stir in marmalade and orange juice. Cover and let stand overnight. Stir in banana.

2. Cream butter and sugar. Beat in eggs. Stir into fruit mixture.

3. Blend flour, baking powder, cinnamon, ginger and salt; stir into fruit mixture. Spoon into lightly greased 9 x 13-inch (3.5 L) baking dish. Bake in 325°F (160°C) oven for 45 minutes or until a cake tester inserted in center comes out clean.

4. Cool completely; sprinkle with icing sugar.

Makes 16–24 pieces.

APPLE CRANBERRY MINCEMEAT SQUARES

Just as tasty as mincemeat pie without the bother of making pastry. They freeze really well.

1¼ cups	all-purpose flour	300 mL
½ cup	cold butter or margarine, cut in pieces	125 mL
¼ cup	lightly packed brown sugar	50 mL
1 tsp	baking powder	5 mL
2	eggs	2
1 cup	granulated sugar	250 mL
⅓ cup	finely chopped walnuts	75 mL
2 tbsp	melted butter or margarine	25 mL
1 tbsp	milk	15 mL
1 tsp	vanilla extract	5 mL
1½ cups	Apple Cranberry Mincemeat (page 284)	375 mL

1. Place flour, butter, brown sugar and baking powder in a food processor. Process until butter is finely chopped. Separate 1 egg, reserving white. Add egg yolk to food processor and process until blended.

2. Pat mixture into bottom of an 8-inch (2 L) square baking dish. Bake in 350°F (180°C) oven for 10 minutes. Remove from oven.

3. Beat together egg and reserved egg white until frothy. Stir in sugar, nuts, melted butter, milk and vanilla.

4. Spread mincemeat over crust. Pour egg mixture over mincemeat. Bake for 25 minutes or until lightly browned. Cool and cut into squares.

Makes 16 squares.

PEACH 'N' JAM SPICE UPSIDE-DOWN CAKE

Old favorites never really go out of style, and this simple cake proves it. Use any fruit jam or conserve. Replace the peaches with apples for an equally delicious cake.

¼ cup	melted butter or margarine	50 mL
½ cup	fruit jam or conserve (Chapter 1 & 4)	125 mL
¼ cup	firmly packed brown sugar	50 mL
1 tbsp	minced fresh peeled gingerroot	15 mL
12	slices peeled fresh peaches (3 peaches)	12

Cake:

⅓ cup	melted butter or margarine	75 mL
¼ cup	molasses	50 mL
1	egg, beaten	1
¾ cup	firmly packed brown sugar	175 mL
2 cups	all-purpose flour	500 mL
1½ tsp	baking powder	7 mL
½ tsp	each: baking soda and ground cloves	2 mL
¼ tsp	ground allspice	1 mL
¾ cup	buttermilk	175 mL

Stir together ¼ cup (50 mL) melted butter, jam, brown sugar and gingerroot. Spoon into a lightly greased 9-inch (2.5 L) springform pan. Arrange peach slices over jam.

Cake:

1. Beat melted butter, molasses, egg and brown sugar in a medium bowl until light and creamy.

2. Blend flour, baking powder, baking soda, cloves and allspice in second bowl.

3. Add flour mixture alternately with buttermilk to creamed mixture, ending with flour, and beating well after each addition. Spoon batter over peaches. Bake in 350°F (180°C) oven for 40 minutes or until a tester inserted in center comes out clean. Let cool for 10 minutes on a rack before inverting onto cake plate. Serve warm or at room temperature.

Makes 8 servings.

SWEET AND CHUNKY APPLE BUTTER SPICE CAKE

This easy one-bowl cake is full of fresh apple and spice flavors. Sweet and Chunky Apple Butter provides the moistness necessary to lower the fat yet maintain excellent texture and taste.

1 tbsp	butter or margarine	15 mL
1 cup	Sweet and Chunky Apple Butter (page 110)	250 mL
¾ cup	lightly packed brown sugar	175 mL
3 tbsp	canola oil	45 mL
½ cup	raisins	125 mL
½ cup	buttermilk	125 mL
1	egg, beaten	1
2 tsp	vanilla extract	10 mL
2¼ cups	all-purpose flour	550 mL
2 tsp	each: ground cinnamon and ginger	10 mL
1 tsp	each: baking soda, baking powder and ground allspice	5 mL
¼ tsp	salt	1 mL

1. Lightly spray a 9 x 13-inch (3.5 L) baking dish with vegetable spray.

2. Heat butter on medium-high heat in a small saucepan until it turns a nutty brown. Pour into a large mixing bowl. Add Apple Butter, sugar and oil. Stir until smooth.

3. Add raisins, buttermilk, egg and vanilla; mix well.

4. Combine flour, cinnamon, ginger, baking soda, baking powder, allspice and salt. Stir into wet ingredients just until combined. Pour into prepared pan.

5. Bake in 350°F (180°C) oven for 35 minutes or until cake tester inserted in center comes out clean. Let cool for 10 minutes before cutting.

Makes 12 servings.

MICROWAVE JAM APPLE CRISP

Your favorite jam gives a wonderful flavor to this easy dessert. We especially like to use Blueberry Freezer Jam with Cointreau (page 56). Cooking the topping separately makes for a nicely browned topping without heating a conventional oven.

⅓ cup	all-purpose flour	75 mL
⅓ cup	lightly packed brown sugar	75 mL
⅓ cup	quick-cooking rolled oats	75 mL
2 tbsp	butter or margarine	25 mL
½ cup	brown sugar	125 mL
3 tbsp	cornstarch	45 mL
½ cup	blueberry or other jam or marmalade	125 mL
4 cups	chopped, cored, peeled apples (4 to 5 apples)	1 L

1. Combine flour, ⅓ cup (75 mL) brown sugar, oats and butter in a bowl. Spread into an 8-inch (2 L) square microwavable baking dish; microwave on High (100%) for 4 minutes or until topping is browned and crumbly, stirring twice. Remove from dish and set aside.

2. Combine ½ cup (125 mL) brown sugar and cornstarch in a large microwavable container. Blend in jam and half the apples. Microwave, uncovered, on High (100%) for 3 minutes or until mixture is bubbly. Stir in remaining apples; spread in the baking dish.

3. Sprinkle reserved topping over apples and microwave, uncovered, on High for 5 minutes or until bubbly around edges. Cool and cut into pieces.

Makes 9 servings.

VARIATION:

Microwave Marmalade Rhubarb Crisp
Replace apples with chopped rhubarb and use English Seville, Five Fruit, or Ruby-Red Grapefruit Marmalade from Chapter 3.

TIP   *For a fast dessert, keep the topping made in step 1 on hand in a tightly closed jar. To make a single serving, slice 1 apple into a small microwavable bowl, mix with a bit of cinnamon and sugar and sprinkle with topping, Microwave at High (100%) for 2 minutes. Serve warm.*

LADY FINGERS WITH LEMON MOUSSE

Our Microwave Lemon Curd folded into whipped cream and layered with lady fingers produces this delicate and frothy dessert.

1 cup	Microwave Lemon Curd (page 115)	250 mL
¾ cup	whipping cream	175 mL
2 tbsp	confectioners' sugar	25 mL
1	pkg (12 oz/85 g) soft lady fingers	1
2 tbsp	sweet sherry, divided	25 mL

1. Place curd in a bowl. In a separate bowl whip cream and sugar until soft peaks form. Fold into curd.

2. Cut each lady finger in half, lengthwise. Place half of lady fingers in a shallow bowl or pie plate and drizzle with 1 tbsp (15 mL) sherry. Top with half of curd mixture. Repeat layers with remaining lady fingers, sherry and curd mixture.

3. Cover and refrigerate for several hours.

Makes 4 to 6 servings.

THAT SPECIAL GIFT

How often do you ask yourself, "What makes a good hostess gift other than the usual bottle of wine?" We suggest many of the sweet spreads and condiments in our book. Often, the most treasured gifts are something somebody took the time and trouble to make.

Naturally, gifts from the kitchen should suit the interests of the person receiving them. For instance, during the holiday season what could be more appropriate than something to help a busy host—a jar of mincemeat (page 284) or one of the special fruit curds (pages 115–116). Or consider one of our fruit liqueurs (pages 303–305). Dieters should appreciate a flavored vinegar for flavor without calories (pages 265–272). Any host who enjoys breakfast will be delighted with one of your cranberry treasures—try Cranberry Orange Marmalade (page 83). Those with an active life are bound to appreciate a jar of Tapenade-Style Salsa (page 205) or Green and Red Pepper Relish (page 170) to serve at cocktail time.

Packaging the Treasures

Attractive packaging certainly enhances the thoughtfulness of your gift. Creative is the key word when it comes to decorating. Here are a few ideas:

- line wicker baskets with leftover scraps of fabric;
- tie raffia to bottle necks;
- use seasonal fabrics with pine cones and holly for Christmas giving;
- decorate lids with freehand paintings or "add-ons" such as scrap fabric, wallpaper burlap, beads or silk flowers;
- cover lids with an appropriate fabric tied on with matching ribbon;
- decorate jars with decals, paint or découpage;
- sew reusable drawstring gift bags from leftover fabric;
- spruce up wooden baskets, berry baskets or grocery store and wine boxes with decorations and paint;
- personalize labels with handwriting or the graphics package on your home computer;
- wrap your gift in colored cellophane or other interesting wrapping material;
- place your gift in a container that has a practical use such as a bamboo steamer, a colander, a sieve, a pottery mug or cup and saucer, or a barbecue fish basket.

These ideas, and the many more you will think of, will make your gifts doubly appreciated—and memorable. And if your gift is to another cook, enclose a copy of the recipe.

INDEX